Will This Be on the Test?

Will This Be on the Test?

Reflections from a History Teacher

by Jim Gregory

ISBN 9781795608367

For Elizabeth

Table of Contents

Introduction: A Cautionary Note

I grew up in rural Arroyo Grande, California, with values shaped by my parents and by the Arroyo Grande Valley. I took what I'd learned from them to teach history to high-school students in San Luis Obispo County—first at the Catholic Mission Prep and then at my Alma Mater, Arroyo Grande High School.

These are essays and stories about my home, my family, and, of course, history. Many of them are journal or blog entries, inspired by an event and so in the moment. They are not intended to be scholarly, systematic or particularly profound, unless by accident.

I'm afraid, instead, that these essays are reflections of how I feel, and I feel history pretty deeply.

Even when I was a little boy, I could walk into an abandoned house and I could smell the meals that had been cooked there, flinch, even momentarily, at the family arguments that had buried themselves beneath peeling wallpaper and feel inchoate grief at the lives that had ended in bedrooms where the floorboards were now exposed.

I had a similar experience years later, when I chaperoned a Mission Prep prom at the Camp San Luis Obispo Officers' Club, I could almost smell the cigarette smoke and the perfume embedded in the woodwork from the dances there in 1944, when some young soldiers danced with their young wives for the last time.

When my students visited Anne Frank's home in Amsterdam nine years ago, what we *all* could feel there was the palpable and powerful presence of the Frank family and the terror they felt at their betrayal, at the moment of their arrest. That place struck us into a silence that lasted a long time afterward.

I could never, ever understand why some find history so boring.

Looking at old Arroyo Grande Union High School yearbooks reminds me of teenaged girls whose petticoats rustle as they walk the hallway of a high school that was demolished in 1961. There's a P.E. coach full of masculine bluster, a trait that will serve him well as a football coach and as a leader of Marines, at least until the bluster bleeds out on the beach at Guam in 1944.

In reading yellowing newspapers, I can almost see the haunted look in the face of a mother whose toddler fell into the fireplace in 1904 while she was preparing pie crusts in the kitchen. Not even Arroyo Grande's venerable Doctor Clark could save her little girl. I can visualize, in another newspaper story, the incomparable moment in 1940 when a bride and groom turn proudly toward the congregation and walk down the nave of Mission San Luis Obispo with the bell-ringer at work above them.

The problem is---and it's a blessing, too, I guess---is that I can still hear the discordance of those bells, cast in Mexico in 1769. What I tried to do in the classroom over thirty years—what I'll try to do in this book, as well—was to bring these sounds, these smells, these sights, and these people, to life again.

Some of these essays have appeared, in slightly different form, in *SLO Journal Plus,* the San Luis Obispo *Tribune, Coast News* and in the books *World War II Arroyo Grande, Patriot Graves* and *Central Coast Aviators in World War II.*

Prologue. Home

A ten-mile corridor of land between Valley Road in Arroyo Grande and Mary Hall Road in the Huasna Valley was the most formative influence of my life. I grew up in between, on Huasna Road in the Upper Arroyo Grande Valley, and I knew instantly the day we moved there, when I was five, that this was home. It had just rained, and the air smelled of ozone and the soil of a nearby field, just turned by a tractor. I never forgot that smell from the first day.

We never lacked for guests. There were mule deer, a weasel, red-tailed hawks, an unexplained peacock, and two barn owls that slept together on a ledge beneath the Harris Bridge. Coyotes yipped in the hills and a colony of beavers built a dam in the Arroyo Grande Creek filled with rainbow trout I did catch. In a another spot, in a rapids, there was one I didn't catch but will always remember: It was a furious and powerful steelhead. Once a mountain lion sniffed around our Branch School softball field.

Future history teacher in the front yard for the first day of school at Branch Elementary, 1958, Huasna Road, Arroyo Grande.

Just over the hill from the two-room school was the Branch family burying ground. I used to visit to wonder what Arroyo Grande Valley must have been like when Francis and Manuela Branch arrived in 1837, wonder at the heartbreak represented by the small tombstones of three daughters taken by smallpox in 1862. It was that school, built in the 1880s, and that family that would lead me to teach history.

Chapter 1. Growing Up

Dinner

Shannons and Gregorys share a meal, about 1959. Clockwise, from top left: Patricia Gregory, Michael Shannon, Jim Gregory, Roberta Gregory, Jerry Shannon, Bruce Gregory, Cayce Shannon.

This may be my one of my favorite photos from growing up in Arroyo Grande. You can see that I have just said something pithy and my sister is debating whether to pinch me. We used to play Confederates and Yankees with the Shannon boys, in this photo seated with us as guests.

My mother loved the Shannon boys, and the proof positive in this photograph is the Irish lace tablecloth she's laid out. That was normally reserved for Thanksgiving and Christmas.

It's dusk, and you can see the outline of the Santa Lucias beyond the glass doors. The view then was unencumbered by houses, and you could see Branch School in its corner of the Valley, a constant and comforting presence.

In the same direction, Doña Manuela Branch's home burned down about the same time as this photo was taken—1958 or 1959. This was the house that her sons had built for her after Francis Branch died in 1874. The fire happened in the early morning hours and the California Department of Forestry trucks and their sirens woke us up; we looked out that door as the house burned, giving off a white-hot light that was as bright as a star, and then it was gone. A neighbor gave me a ride on his homemade motor scooter to the site, today marked by palm trees, and Mrs. Branch's house was just a grey-black outline, with a few wisps of smoke, marking the foundation. It was tragic.

Out the side windows of the dining room in the photo were my mother's rose bushes and beyond that the little pasture where my sister's horses grazed. Mrs. Harris lived across the street, the Coehlos a little beyond, and then the Shannons across the fields, near the junction of Branch Mill and Huasna Roads.

Farm fields lay beyond the pasture. They were planted in peppers or sometimes in beans that climbed on their wooden stakes. On summer mornings, the ocean fog brushed the bean-stake tips until the sun burned it away. Sunrises were spectacular looking out those windows, and once snow dusted the line of foothills in the distance. A place like this is a wonderful place to grow up.

Glory Days at Branch School

The two-room Branch schoolhouse.

I wish I had more photos of my days at Branch Elementary School in the Upper Arroyo Grande Valley, which I attended between 1958 and 1966.

I started at the 1880s schoolhouse, shown in the photograph, but in 1962, we moved into one of those Sputnik School of Architecture schools that was twice as big as the old school. It had four rooms.

I remember seeing one photo of me, Dennis Gularte and Melvin Cecchetti, all decked out like cowboys, down to chaps and Mattel Fanner '50s ("If it's Mattel, it's swell!") on our hips.

A "Fanner '50" is a replica double-action Old West six-shooter that allows your shorter Old West gunfighter to get off approximately 1,200 shots without reloading. It was a marvel.

That was back in the days when gunfights on the playground were still permissible, although they were limited to Fridays, which remains my favorite day of the week.

There was even a glorious, if very brief, time when the television show *The Untouchables* was popular, so we re-enacted the St. Valentine's Day Massacre with Mattel-It's-Swell Tommy Guns. We died spectacular deaths after we had lined up, hands up, against one wall of the school. We took turns pretending to be the Moran Gang victims and Capone's button men. We were a democratic bunch.

The girls on the swings just thought we were gross. But they were girls, mind you, and they liked to pretend they were horses, which we found damned peculiar.

We liked to pretend we were '62 Corvettes.

So us Branch School kids–all 70-odd of us, first through eighth grades– were both rootin' and tootin'. But we also could be very good.

The entire third and fourth grades once went on a field trip to Morro Bay in our little yellow bus. We all walked through the crew quarters of the Coast Guard cutter *Alert* without awakening the young man busy contradicting the cutter's name, snoring softly in his bunk. We were impressed with how white his underwear was. The Coast Guard is a well-laundered service branch.

During that tour, we requested, but were denied, authorization to fire off a few rounds from the 40-mm Bofors gun on the forward deck, which put quite a damper on an otherwise fine outing. Firing that gun would've lifted our spirits and sustained us when, later in the day, we had to visit the extremely boring abalone processing plant. Abalone, we discovered, have little stage presence, so we watched, stifling yawns, as they lay lifeless and inert, pounded with wooden hammers by sad, unfulfilled men until they had achieved abalonability.

Years later, with a shock of recognition, I saw the same abalone factory ennui when I took some of my Arroyo Grande High School European history students to Munich. We ate schnitzel in a massive auditorium while an oompah band performed and two girls, in traditional costume, more or less danced. It must've been about their eighth performance of the day, in front of masses of greasy-cheeked, ungrateful American teenagers–except for our kids, of course– and they danced without enthusiasm.

By the time the disconsolate abalone pounders had finished with their victims, they looked disgusting, like Neptune's cow patties. By the time we were old enough to realize that they were tasty, they had all been eaten. Sea otters were the alleged culprits, but my money was always on the Morro Bay Elks Club.

(Clams are no more stimulating than abalone, by the way. The second-best show-and-tell ever, other than Tukie Cechetti's fingertip in a vial of alcohol, lost in a saber-saw accident, was the Pismo clam Dennis Gularte and Melvin Cecchetti attempted to keep alive in the classroom sink in the new school. Clams have all the entitlement and ingratitude of the Kardashian sisters and are only marginally smarter. Our clam said little during the school day, showed little interest when we tried to push a length of kelp, which we know had to be yummy, through its shell's opening, and then did nothing at all for about another day. It was deceased.)

We didn't always, by the way, have the luxury of a school bus driven by Elsie Cecchetti, whose job title should've included "Surrogate Mom." We first had a pickup painted school bus yellow, with two benches bolted to the truck bed and a tarp over the top, and when we crossed the creek, we all bounced like a bagful of marbles and squealed with delight.

Not everybody enjoyed the pickup. One morning, one of us got sick, and we decided he'd had scrambled eggs for breakfast.

We also used to go to Poly Royal, the local college's open house, before that event deteriorated into the kind of Roman Bacchanalia that would've made Caligula blush. We loved the jet engine when it was fired off in Aeronautical Engineering. We most of all loved the biology department, because its centerpiece was the genuine stuffed two-headed calf. We spent some time pondering another of their exhibits, an aquarium tank full of bullfrog tadpoles that was labeled soberly, "Elephant Sperm."

In our day, Branch no longer had the steeple and bell that originally was standard equipment for rural schoolhouses, but it did have the first multi-purpose room in San Luis Obispo County.

The hallway in between the two classrooms was used for both hanging up your coat and for the occasional beating of miscreant students with yardsticks. This encouraged us to learn harder and accounts for why, to this day, I still know all my state capitals, down to the fact that Pierre, South Dakota, is pronounced, "Peer," of which our teachers had none.

Yes, in that hallway, Mrs. Brown and Mrs. Fahey had perfected a technique called "Bad Cop, Other Bad Cop."

The powdered soap dispensers out back were incorporated into language lessons, which is why there are only two documented instances of That Word being uttered with impunity at Branch Elementary between 1888 and 1962, and I believe one of those involved a carpenter and the other a school board member.

It's a home today, and painted yellow, but in our day it was pink, sheathed in what I think what former classmate Michael Shannon has said were asbestos shingles, which serve as wonderful insulation, but, by the time you're in your fifties, your school days suddenly begin to produce clouds of what look like chalk dust every time you sneeze.

For the health-conscious reader, not to worry. On summer mornings, when school wasn't in session, my favorite thing to do was to wave at the biplane that crop-dusted the fields next to our house and then go frolic and gambol in the clouds of herbicide.

Of course, in those days, everybody smoked soon after they'd taken their first steps ("JIMMY'S WALKING! Here, son, light one up on Pop!")

We were a hardy breed, us Baby Boomers. Hack. Wheeze.

There were good things, too, mind you, like actual Pismo clams--all from the extended family of our classroom clam--at Pismo Beach. You didn't even need a clam fork. They'd just walk up to you and surrender, as if it were North Africa, not Pismo, and they were the Italian Army. But I digress. Since I'm in my late sixties now, that's permitted.

Somehow, We Survived

We need a new wireless router at our house. I know less about wireless routers than I do about Thomistic theology, but I'll just ask one of my Arroyo Grande High School students for help.

Oddly, "routers" and "signal strengths" reminded me of growing up in Arroyo Grande. In those days—the 1950s and 1960s—we got a grand total of two TV stations with an antenna that fetched signals magically out of the air, just what my sophomores' cell phones do today.

Turn it off. You're in class, Bub.

When KCOY, the Santa Maria CBS affiliate, arrived, having *three* television stations seemed prodigal. It might be like having *two* In 'n' Out Burgers in Arroyo Grande.

Our third-grade teacher, Leona Kaiser—teachers in my time seemed to have names like "Leona," "Edith," "Beulah," and "Medusa"—brought her TV to Branch School for JKF's Inauguration in January 1961. She, like the young president, came from Massachusetts, a place she remembered fondly except for the Great War years, when her last name became inconvenient. I remember the big boys carrying Mrs. Kaiser's Zenith black and white TV set carefully up the stairs, as solemn as Irish pallbearers.

A television at school was a technological event that to us was so staggering that I found the moon landing, the decade's other bookend, anticlimactic. But I had German measles in July 1969, and few illnesses will make you more cynical. I wanted to give my measles to Neil Armstrong.

Bruce, Jim and Roberta Gregory and their television, 1956,
Sunset Drive, Arroyo Grande.

At home, our television reception could be erratic, so when Shari Lewis and Lamb Chop (ask your grandparents) started to look like fuzzy cotton balls, Dad would climb to the roof, with no evident enthusiasm, to twist the antenna in different directions. We would all yell at each other:

"HOWZAT?" "WORSE!" "A LITTLE BETTER!" "BACK TO WHERE YOU HAD IT BEFORE!" "*WORSE!*"

During Antenna Time, every spectacular word Dad had learned from the World War II United States Army would come flooding out like GI's exiting Higgins boats. But the antenna *had* to be fixed: Television was so central to our lives that I would get Walter Cronkite withdrawals. I thought of him as my TV Dad.

So those were tough times for real dads, lonely on their windswept rooftops with just the antenna for company. But they were tough for kids, too. Our fingers became deeply callused from activities like changing the channel—you had to get UP to do this—or dialing rotary phones. Today, high-school students use *their* phones to photograph the homework assignment on the board. It's amazing.

I once tried to explain to my students the concept of long distance and the operator—Dad worked in San Luis Obispo for Madonna Construction and my parents called every day at lunch—and the sophomores whom I love so much looked at me blankly.

I can teach them with ease the cause of high 18th-century illegitimacy rates or explain the philosophical impact of relativity theory, but long distance is no clearer to them than Ramses III's family tree.

During my time as a student at Arroyo Grande High School, the benighted pre-driver's license underclassmen made do with *one* pay phone—another concept that eludes modern students—on the entire campus. After dances or basketball games there was a long, long line. We'd pass the time pretending that it was the Great Depression and we were waiting for soup. Eventually, we'd get to the head of the line to call our parents to come pick us up, which they frequently did.

"Bob, *how* many kids do we have?" Mom would ask absently, and Dad would come get me on the condition that he got to grumble about it all the way home.

So we were a hardy bunch. We lived life close to the edge. There was, for example, no such thing as "pizza" in Arroyo Grande. You want pizza? Go to San Francisco for your pizza.

What sustained us then were drive-ins with creamy root-beer freezes, two-handed cheeseburgers brought to us by car hops on roller skates. The roller skates qualified the cheeseburger as "fast food." If we were lucky, the car hop might look a little like the Mousketeer and Frankie Avalon beach date Annette Funicello.

Ask your grandfather.

A Haircut at Buzz's

A still from a home movie shows Carl "Buzz" Langenbeck in front of his shop in 1937. Bennett-Loomis Archives.

I made a friend, Gene Mintz, from the Kiwanis Club, today. He invited me to talk about the book *Central Coast Aviators in World War II*, but I got a lot more out of making a new friend than I did talking about my books.

Gene also grew up in Arroyo Grande. Like me, he got his hair cut at Buzz's Barbershop on Branch Street—today, it's the Heritage Salon—but, unlike me, had the good sense to go to the second chair, Kelly's chair. He also had the good sense, one day, to make Kelly his father-in-law.

Buzz was in the first chair. Buzz was a demon with the clippers, a master of the rapid haircut, and no extra charge for the divots. Buzz could've cut the entire First Infantry Division before they hit Omaha Beach in about two hours.

You went to Buzz less for a decent haircut and more for the chance that he might have an extra paper bag of avocados, because his were the best in Arroyo Grande. I might've gone more often than my usual every two weeks if I'd known about guacamole then.

Kelly, in the second chair, on the other hand, was kind of an artist. He had longish hair, a little scandalous in the late 50s and early 60s, and extravagantly waxed mustaches. Kelly could custom-cut almost any style you wanted, including the apotheosis of the age, the D.A., or Duck's Ass.

Mrs. Buzz had a ladies' shop in the back. It was vaguely pink, like the inside of a polished conch shell. Sometimes, but mostly not, her clients, who normally used the back door on Olohan Alley, would walk through the men's shop on their way to their hair appointments. Going through the front meant a struggle past cranky old men, slack-mouthed teenaged boys staring intently at every detail of every death photo in *California Highway Patrolman* magazine, and, most of all, dozens of deceased animals—heads of deer, elk, antelope, mountain goats, impalas—who stared accusingly at you with their glass eyes. The air, too, was thick with testosterone and witch hazel.

Sometimes we would hear uproarious laughter from Mrs. Buzz's. They were having fun in there. We were deadly serious. Haircuts were serious. They were, in the late 50s and early 60s, a civic responsibility, like voting, jury duty, and regular oil changes.

Gene. Remember Gene? This story's about Gene.

Gene was in high school, and Mrs. Gladys Loomis, Vard's wife, was his English teacher. She had assigned a Steinbeck novel. I have a hunch it was *Grapes of Wrath*, because Mrs. Loomis, given her devotion to her Japanese-

American friends—*our* friends--and her resentment of their wartime ordeal, would've been keen on a novel about social injustice.

No wonder I love the Loomises. Anyway, let's suppose that *Grapes* was, indeed, Gene's assignment.

Gene needed a haircut, and he needed to finish *Grapes of Wrath* for Mrs. Loomis, and I'm not sure the Joads had gotten to Needles yet. He was engrossed in the novel and not paying much attention. Gene was waiting for Kelly, in the second chair, to finish the customer he was with.

There was another customer, this one with a goatee, in Buzz's number-one chair. At that time, a goatee was pretty much an admission that you were an unrepentant communist or, worse, a beatnik.

We tolerated Kelly's goatee because, well, he was Kelly. You don't trifle with a man who's mastered Tukie Cecchetti's D.A. Also, Kelly was Kelly. He was kind of charismatic: Gruff as hell but soft as butterscotch underneath.

Buzz was chatting softly with the customer in his chair, did his usual five-minute job, and the guy left Buzz his buck-seventy-five and a quarter tip and went to get something to eat.

Now it was Gene's turn for Kelly. Kelly was wrapping the plastic apron around him and about to apply that paper collar tight as a tourniquet when he paused for a moment. Kelly noticed things. He noticed what Gene was reading for Mrs. Loomis's class.

"Gene, you know who that was in Buzz's chair just now?"

No, Gene didn't.

"That was John Steinbeck."

Gene probably was a little flustered, as I would've been in I'd been sitting in the same barber chair after the same comment. You had to be careful with 100% believing Kelly. He was Irish, after all.

Gene got his haircut, paid Kelly his buck-seventy-five and a quarter tip, and walked back out into the bright sunlight.

He noticed a big GMC pickup with a camper shell parked along Branch Street. On the passenger's side of the cab, drooling happily out the rolled-down window, there was a big handsome poodle.

It was Charley.

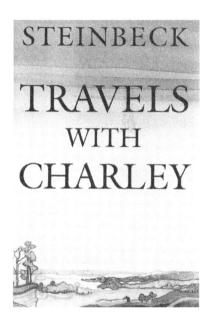

Nathan Hughes Hamilton, flickr.com

Hallowe'en in the Branch District

We did not trick or treat on Huasna Road in the 1950s and early 1960s. The problem was that the houses were so far apart.

The other problem, I was sure, occurred whenever there was a full moon on Hallowe'en. If you know the Arroyo Grande area at all, then you know that in moonlight the gnarled, twisted oak trees assume human shapes. Some of them have gaping knotholes in their trunks, just big enough to swallow unwary third-graders. These carnivorous oak trees lurked at the edges of Branch Mill Road. They were menacing, silent, sometimes sibilant in the wind, and occasionally they belched.

So, to avoid the potential loss of Branch School children and the tax dollars they represented, we had, by the 1950s, a relatively safe Hallowe'en Carnival at the schoolhouse.

The students' fathers would gather cornstalks for a properly decorative motif at school. I don't know where they got them. Branch fathers grew Brussels sprouts and cabbage, neither with strong Hallowe'en associations. Stiff, dead, dry cornstalks, vaguely resembling skeletons, were very nearly as scary as the oak trees. Moms would put out carved pumpkins, too, relatively harmless until you, at age seven, got around to watching Disney's terrifying "Legend of Sleepy Hollow," narrated by Bing Crosby, whom you never trusted again.

Damn you, Bing Crosby.

We had "fishing booths" at the carnival, where little kids tossed fishing lines--strings attached to willow branches-- over the top of a newsprint-paper enclosed booth to reel in a small toy or bite-sized Tootsie Rolls. We loved that--chocolate is the third-grade equivalent of catnip or, for the typical college student, grain alcohol mildly diluted by Hawaiian Punch.

The fishing booths were for minor-leaguers. The climax of the night, after the costume parade, was the eighth grade's Haunted House. The eighth graders were monstrous and mature people to us. They all seemed to be in their mid-thirties and so with enough life experience to reduce the smaller children to gelatinous puddles of terror in their dark, spooky, cavernous Haunted House, also known as a "classroom." They laid in plenty of dry ice for dramatic vapors.

They had discovered, when third-graders are blindfolded, that cold spaghetti is a splendid facsimile for human brains and that Jell-O does a passable job of resembling the squishy regions in the human digestive system that we had just finished studying for Mrs. Kaiser. The third-grade girls loved the Haunted House, which allowed them to emit high-pitched screams of many decibels. This put most of us off girls altogether until the sixth grade, when they were suddenly taller than us and vastly mysterious.

Those who survived the Haunted House were allowed to partake of the Hallowe'en climactic meal, which consisted of tens of dozens of heavenly cupcakes, in every flavor and color imaginable, baked by mothers driven by a still-persistent, albeit rural, late Victorian maternal superstition: The more cupcakes you baked, the better the harvest would be for your husband's farm.

So we ate them.

We ate the chocolate ones, of course, most of all.

We did not sleep for three days. We bounced off the walls of our school, with Mrs. Kaiser using a steel-shod yardstick to herd us back to our wooden desks with their vestigial inkwells, until we were quiet again, studying our state capitals, our times tables, and our American history dates. And so we learned: Communism was evil. Chocolate cupcakes were sublime.

I still know my state capitals, my times tables and my American history dates. I am a little weak on my measures--how many pecks in a bushel?--but that might have been a lesson that came the day after Hallowe'en.

A Very Short Story About Beavers

TO THE EDITOR, SAN LUIS OBISPO TRIBUNE:

Mr. Phil Christie of Cambria, in an April 9 Letter to the Editor on the Pismo Beach beaver situation, wanted to know if there were other beavers in San Luis Obispo County. The scientific answer is: Yup.

At least there were when I was a teenager, which was about the same time my close friend Sir Francis Drake was bumping around the coast on the *Golden Hinde.*

Actually, it was only the mid-1960s. But there was a beaver dam on the Arroyo Grande Creek, adjacent to Kaz Ikeda's cabbage fields in the Upper

Valley. I know because I fished in their pond. When I first found them, they were Angry Beavers (a popular cartoon show I used to enjoy with my sons when they were younger), but they soon became, if not mellow, at least tolerant of my presence. They do slap their tails on the water, by the way.

I wore out my welcome one day when a late-afternoon shaft of sunlight hit the pond at just the right angle, making the water translucent. There, meticulously aligned like a trout armada—I must be thinking of Drake again— were dozens of rainbows, noses upstream, waiting for me to catch them. I was ecstatic!

So, as a crack fisherman, my first move was to fall into the water with rod, tackle and some happily liberated night crawlers.

I think I hear the beavers trying to suppress hysterical laughter. My dignity was crushed, so I never went back to the pond. I'm sure, however—if there are still beavers in the county—that this anecdote has been passed down from generation to generations around whatever is the beaver equivalent of a campfire. Stupid humans.

Jim Gregory
Arroyo Grande

They're Layin' Eggs Now, Just Like They Used To…

When we lived on Huasna Road east of Arroyo Grande, the elder siblings got the hooved mammals. For Roberta, that meant Quarter horses, Morgans and Welsh Ponies. Bruce superintended heifers and lambs.

I got to feed the lamb her milk once, from a metal bucket with a big plastic nipple, but it was during the night we had a lightning storm. When a swatch of sheet lightning lit up the yard in front of me and my bucket, I amazed myself with newfound speed. I dropped the bucket and its contents and fled for the safety of our house.

By the way, my siblings didn't get custody of *all* the local mammals. There were the wild ones, after all, including one weasel, one fox, a Rotary Club of beavers, a mountain lion, the occasional dissolute coyote, bushy-tailed ground squirrels and mule deer does and fawns---heart-breakingly beautiful, especially if you'd seen *Bambi* at the Fremont Theater with Mom

But when it came to Animal Husbandry 101, I got the chickens.

One rooster, forty hens. One happy rooster.

Half of the hens were Leghorns, which laid white eggs and were no more interesting than Wonder Bread. They were a dim bunch.

The Plymouth Rocks were charming. Some of them were a barred grey. Others were more of a russet hue. They laid brown eggs, and one out of five or so was a double-yolker, which, in the chicken business, is the equivalent of an extra-base hit in baseball.

I would reach under them for the eggs every morning and they would look back at me, somewhat irate, as they had every right to be. But the hens were so soft and warm underneath, and their eggs were warm, too, so I kind of got attached to my Plymouth Rocks.

The Leghorns, meanwhile, seemed to think it was their duty to escape and poop on the sidewalk in the back yard where I would discover the evidence while barefoot.

The author encounters one of the roosters that inhabits downtown Arroyo Grande. Photo by Elizabeth Gregory.

28

We got their mash from E.C. Loomis and Son and kept it in a big wood barrel, and it was the sweetest smell when it came time to feed them. The hens, of course, appreciated it too.

We did have one homicidal Banty rooster who seemed to be constantly re-living the Charge of the Light Brigade. I was his Russians. He used to chase me mercilessly until Dad, the High Executioner, ended the little rooster's reign of terror. I was not sorry.

I *was* sorry when an equally homicidal black Lab named Shadow moved in behind us with his family. Shadow began to kill my hens and kept at it until the family, finally, moved away.

I miss my chickens. We can't have them where we live now, and they're not a good match with Irish Setters, who mistake them for ducks. But I miss them still, soft and warm in their roosts, the smell of sweet mash and fresh straw, clucking a little when I talked to them while they went about the business of motherhood.

Redheads Again: Remembering Joe Loomis

This Renoir, the exquisite 1880 portrait of eight-year-old Irene Caher d'Anvers, was part of today's lesson. Irene would live to be 91. Born in horse-

and-buggy Paris, she would die with humans hurtling through space at unimaginable speeds.

Irene reminded me of a something I'd mentioned in class a few days before. In 29 years of teaching, I told them, I have never taught so many red-haired girls, in particular, and hair in so many *shades* of red, from strawberry blonde to deep copper. Having this many redheads is extraordinary.

This anomaly led to intense meditation on redheads, an extended monologue in front of 31 slightly befuddled sophomores waiting for the rest of the lecture on the Agricultural Revolution--all of this was me processing information–and it led to one logical, unavoidable conclusion about them: They are beautiful.

My mother, by the way, had deep auburn hair.

One of the dearest friends of my life, Joe Loomis, died last fall. Joe was the kind of guy–you hear stories about this in him over and over again–who would drop anything and everything to help a friend who needed it.

Here's an example. My Mom died when I was 17. Nobody knew how to handle this terrible tragedy in my life. Joe did. He simply drove up to our front door in a jeep, invited me to jump in, and drove me—rapidly–up the Huasna to his family's Tar Springs Ranch. The Loomises gave me a place, their home, where I could feel safe again.

Years later, Joe and I had lost touch, but it didn't matter because I knew this great friend was around nearby and we would have the luxury of time to renew our friendship.

And now he isn't, and now we don't.

I made a color copy of a photograph of Joe– it radiates his kindness and good humor–and put it on the corner of my classroom desk. This is his year. I will be the best teacher I can be, and it's for him.

After school today, Kaylee and Maggie, two basketball players, were studying in my room. I work late, and I hate working alone, so having students do their homework with me is a comfort. The girls do their homework. They boys more or less do their homework: Boy study groups mean a snappy dialogue, slightly barbed, that makes me laugh out loud.

We were talking, I think, about Irene again—Irene with the red hair, because Maggie has red hair, too. I was talking to Maggie and suddenly I thought of Joe.

"One of my best friends died this year," I started.

The girls' faces fell. They started to stammer their "sorries." These are good kids.

"No, you don't understand. Maggie, go look at the photo of my friend on the corner of my desk."

She did. The girls thought he looked nice. I asked Maggie what color hair Joe had. Red, she said.

I don't think they completely got the point because I didn't completely make it, and coherence is in short supply when you need it most. They had to go to their game, and I think they believed they'd said or done something wrong, when in fact they'd given me a wonderful gift. I'd suddenly unwrapped it with them while they were studying in my classroom.

When you're in your sixties, you begin to understand that life isn't as accidental and random as you think it is. The fact that I have more redheads this year than I've ever had in 29 years of teaching might mean that Joe hasn't left me at all.

My little brace of red-haired girls lights me up inside every day they're in my classroom, because they are themselves beautiful and, as I now understand, because they connect me to the kind of friend you're lucky to have once in a lifetime.

Joe Loomis, 1952-2013.

32

Chapter 2. Valley Stories

Arroyo Grande, circa 1905. South County Historical Society.

The Branch Family Cemetery

Arroyo Grande's founding father led a life that was one part Charles Dickens novel and one part John Ford Western. Orphaned early in life, New Yorker Francis Ziba Branch would build a cattle empire on his Santa Manuela Ranch to become one of San Luis Obispo County's wealthiest citizens.

In his lifetime, Branch was a Great Lakes sailor, a mule-packer, trapper, grocer, bear-hunter, Indian fighter, frontier lawman, *ranchero* and elder statesman.

By the time of his death in 1874, the 72-year-old patriarch, father of 11 children, had lived enough to fill three ordinary lives.

It's fitting that Branch's final resting place, a family cemetery in a copse of oaks tucked into a fold in the hills above the Upper Arroyo Grande Valley, is so marked by its stillness.

In 1837, Branch, his 22-year-old wife and two-year-old daughter arrived on horseback from Santa Barbara to lay claim to nearly 17,000 acres granted him by the Mexican government.

The Branch family cemetery, Upper Arroyo Grande Valley.

The young family had traded the comfort of small-town frontier life to domesticate a valley frequented by grizzly bears and occasional raiding parties of Tulare Indians from the San Joaquin Valley.

By mid-century, Branch directly or in partnership ran thousands of cattle on nearly 40,000 acres of San Luis Obispo county land. Devastated by drought between 1862 and 1864, Branch lost $400,000—over $8 million in today's dollars. True to his nature—contemporaries described him as a slight but well-built man of terrific energy—he was well on the way to rebuilding his fortune when he died.

35

The hardships of 19th century frontier life are graphically demonstrated by the little cluster of graves that surround Branch's.

With the exception of Branch, his wife, Manuela Carlon Branch, who died in 1909 at 94, and a longtime ranch foreman, the occupants of the little cemetery are infants, children or young adults.

Guests in the family cemetery attest to the violence of frontier life.

A marker a short distance from the cluster of family members identifies the graves of Peter and Julius Hemmi, the father and son who, in 1886, were hanged by a lynch mob from the Pacific Coast Railway Bridge over Arroyo Grande Creek.

The 15-year-old Julius, described by some as possessing a "cruel disposition," had murdered a neighbor couple, the climax of a long-standing dispute over property near the mouth of Lopez Canyon.

Decades earlier, Branch and *alcalde* John Price had inspected the grisly murder scene at Mission San Miguel, where a band of military deserters and ship-jumpers had murdered their host, John Reed, and ten members of his family and household. The bodies had first been discovered by famed mountain man Jim Beckwourth; within days, a Santa Barbara posse would confront the murderers in a gun battle in the surf near Summerland. Two would die that day. The others were executed by military firing squad led by Lt. Edward Ord, later a Civil War general; the fort later founded near Monterey was named for him.

One hundred fifty years later, Francis Branch's legacy is strong in San Luis Obispo County: streets and schools are named for him. The Talley Vineyards tasting room is the former home of Ramon, their eldest son. The millstone from the family flour mill is now part of the Heritage Square Park in downtown Arroyo Grande.

But time has not treated the little cemetery well. Generations of cattle have scratched itches against family tombstones, knocking them over and shattering them.

In 1971, Eagle Scouts repaired the cemetery, replacing the damaged marble tombstones with wooden ones that are now increasingly weathered, and their lettering faint.

Ironically, the lovely remoteness of the cemetery, on private ranchland, has contributed to its disrepair.

The silence there is arresting. It is broken, each morning, only by the distant rattling of tractor engines as they turn over and begin the workday on the farmland owned by the Ikeda family. The colorful patchwork fields of row crops stretch for miles on the valley floor beyond the graveyard and below the hill where Francis Branch's adobe once stood. It is as if the land itself inherited the energy of the man who first claimed it as his own.

The cemetery has since been enclosed and restored, thanks to the Ikeda family.

"It Takes Life to Love Life"

Degenerate sons and daughters,
Life is too strong for you--
It takes life to love Life.

"Lucinda Matlock," from Edgar Lee Masters' *Spoon River Anthology*

Arroyo Grande's modern starting point was 1837, when Francis and Manuela Branch arrived with their little daughter. The valley soon proved, even for a young woman as strong and loyal as Manuela, too wild to bear her second child. Eight months pregnant, she rode home on horseback over the San Marcos Pass to Santa Barbara to deliver her baby, a little boy they would name Ramon, where her parents would be close by.

What her husband first encountered were monstrous grizzly bears that carried off the seed of his hoped-to-be-fortune, bawling calves, so he began to kill the bears. His neighbor in the Huasna, another

Francis Ziba Branch. South County Historical Society.

former mountain man, George Nidever, gave up cattle ranching after he'd killed his one hundredth grizzly. (His successor there, Isaac Sparks, lost an eye to a grizzly.)

Branch's Upper Valley then was thick with willow scrub—the *californio* word is "monte"—so dense and so punishing that leather chaps were needed to protect *vaqueros* like Branch's from having their legs slashed to ribbons when they plunged into it to rescue strays. Branch cleared the monte and planted the crops he knew from his native New York: Wheat and corn, apple and peach trees. An Eastern corn-sheller was his proudest possession, and the base of the grindstone he used to mill the Valley's flour still sits in Arroyo Grande's Heritage Square. Both of them were landed at Cave Landing-- what is today Pirate's Cove, near Avila Beach.

The more I learn about him, the more I respect Branch. He had some of Lucinda Matlock's toughness, her willingness to embrace life.

He and his ranch hands—most of them Chumash, others *mestizo*—worked hardest at roundup in June, when the cattle were slaughtered, not for beef, but for their hides. The hides were stretched on racks and soaked with seawater until they were cured and as stiff as plywood. Then they were hauled, by cart, or *careta,* to Cave Landing, where they'd be tossed into the surf to be fetched by fearless men, often Hawaiians, who would haul them into longboats to hoisted up into the holds of Yankee brigs bound for Cape Horn and then to Boston Harbor and New England shoe factories.

It was the Gold Rush that made cattle valued for their meat rather than their hides—there was demand for beef from hungry miners who'd come from New York and Sonora and France and Chile. All it took to get the cattle to market was your life: Branch's friend, John Price, didn't sleep for three days after the pair found the bodies of the Reed family and their servants. Ten people were murdered at Mission San Miguel by Gold Rush outlaws who stole the gold dust of William Reed, who'd just sold a herd of sheep in the north. Jack Powers and Pio Linares and "Zorro's" inspiration, Salomon Pico, waylaid cattle brokers in the Cuesta Pass and Gaviota and in Drum Canyon near Los Alamos for the gold they carried from beef sold to the miners. Pico is said to have collected their ears. To fight men like these, Branch became a member of the San Luis Obispo Vigilance Committee, which was different in two respects from San Francisco's: Ours was a little later. We hanged more men.

Four years later, in 1862, Branch was in San Francisco when he got a message from Manuela. She'd given shelter to a traveler, common to ranch families then, and what he'd given the family in return was smallpox. Branch rode hard to get home again and by the time he did, two of his little girls were dead and a third died soon after.

They are buried next to him today, three little tombstones, broken in the years since by cattle scratching itches, next to his big tombstone. Branch died twelve years after, so he would have given instructions to have his grave close to those of his daughters.

He lost his fortune soon after he lost them. The vast herds of beef cattle he'd tended with such care for twenty-five years died on yellow, stubbled hillsides. Thirst and coyotes and ravenous mountain lions winnowed them down until they were gone.

What he hadn't lost yet was his faith in himself. He was making the transition to row crops and tree crops and dairy farming. He then began to divide the Santa Manuela *rancho* into smaller farms, run by ambitious sons and sons-in-law, men who were founding schools and building roads and raising churches. The immense energy this small, wiry, ambitious man had always taken for granted was finally taken from him, by pneumonia, in 1874.

So we have a street named for him today.

Yesterday I saw a pickup truck rear-end a sedan at the flashing crosswalk on Branch Street between Rooster Creek Tavern and the Branch Street Deli. Dozens of gawkers gathered to watch the culprit and the policeman and the fire trucks and the ambulance, thankfully, unneeded, as it turned out. Soon the gawkers dissipated and the commotion evaporated.

What was left, once the accident was cleared, was the name of the street. The folks involved, and the gawkers, too, most of them tourists, are to be forgiven, of course, given the situation, for not knowing a thing about the man for whom the street was named. Neither do the customers or the young waitresses at Rooster Creek Tavern or the sandwich-makers at Branch Street Deli.

But the street where they work is named for the man who once brought grizzly bears down with a Hawken rifle to make his cattle safe enough to the graze the land where he would build the adobe to raise the family, eleven children less those three little girls, that would evolve into the beginning of the town that would name its main street for him. Yesterday, all that meant was headlight glass shattered in the crosswalk.

Pumpkins the Size of Boulders

When a just-graduated young Ohio physician, Edwin Paulding, arrived in Arroyo Grande in 1882 on the just-completed extension of the Pacific Coast Railroad, he was stunned by the size of the Valley's pumpkins, some approaching two hundred pounds. They look, in the old photos, like boulders.

Any town that could grow pumpkins that size, he reasoned, ought to be able to support a doctor, and he was right. He began a medical career here—he was considered the county's best orthopedist—that would last forty years.

The narrow-gauge Pacific Coast Railroad's arrival in Arroyo Grande in 1881 played a key role in the town's population growth, which would double to nearly 500 people by 1890. The newcomers, overwhelmingly farmers, included Civil War veterans like Erastus Fouch, who farmed along today's Lopez Drive, Gettysburg combatant Joseph Brewer, in Oak Park, and Medal of Honor winner Otis Smith in the Upper Valley and the Huasna Valley.

Almost as important as the PCRR's arrival was the nationwide publicity about the richness of Arroyo Grande's soil.

The July 14, 1887 Altoona (Pennsylvania) *Tribune* is typical of brief notices that appeared frequently in eastern newspapers, citing "ninety-pound cabbage and 300-pound squash." Three years later, the York, South Carolina *Enquirer* marvels at twenty Arroyo Grande onions weighing one hundred pounds, a nineteen-pound carrot, and "another that took the 'cake'…a beet five feet long that scaled 154 pounds."

Missouri Civil War veteran and farmer Thomas Hodges was an early settler in the Arroyo Grande Valley, arriving in the 1870s. Courtesy the Bennett-Loomis Archives.

Yes, I'm dubious, too, but there at least there were no reports of the Loch Ness Monster swimming contentedly in the Arroyo Grande Creek.

An 1890 Kansas newspaper report about a Kansan transplanted to Arroyo Grande boasts about a climate that's so uniformly mild that "persons cannot tell whether they are cool are warm."

Not all the news was good. The 1886 Hemmi lynchings—the father and son accused of murdering a neighbor over a land dispute in Lopez Canyon—and the 1895 robbery of over $7000 from the PCRR station agent in Arroyo Grande received coverage in newspapers across the nation.

There were more extensive articles, including letters to the editor, which were enormously popular in the late 1800s and early 1900s. One of them, written by another former Kansan, John Jones, who'd moved to Arroyo Grande for his health, was printed in the El Dorado *Republican* on August 10, 1894:

> *Arroyo Grande is a very nice town, five miles inland, in one of the richest valleys in the state. Here they grow apples, peaches, apricots, nectarines, prunes, plums and berries in all kinds of profusion, besides grain, beans, corn and most vegetables in great abundance. The hill lands, not suitable for agriculture, afford a very luxuriant growth of rich, juicy grass which is grown during the rainy season and cures on the ground during the dry season, which not only increases its fattening properties and obviates the necessity of putting up hay for stock except a limited amount for dairy cows and work horses. One [Kansan] whose acquaintance I have made and in whose magnificent prune and apricot orchard I have been, cleared over a thousand dollars last year and expects to do much better this year. . . Mr. Carpenter, of Chase county, [Chauncey E. Carpenter, for whom Carpenter Canyon is named] is on the highway to wealth, and many more might be.*

Mr. Jones suggests that the Arroyo Grande Valley is so rich that area farmers are tempted to be less industrious than their Chase County, Kansas, counterparts, but, he argued, if one can avoid the temptation to slacken, fortunes can be made, like the one being built by Mr. Carpenter.

Local farmers might've strenuously and fairly objected to that characterization. Farming in Arroyo Grande could be just as hard as it was anywhere else, and sometimes as dangerous as the war that the veterans who settled here had fought. Samuel B. Miller of the 24th Iowa survived Vicksburg and the 1864 Shenandoah Valley campaign only to be killed in 1902 by a bean cutter. While bringing in a crop in the Huasna Valley, the machine hit a snag, threw Miller forward, under his horses, which dutifully kept moving, pulling the bean cutter over him. It was a death as horrific as any on the battlefield.

Another letter from the Anderson, South Carolina *Intelligencer*, appeared in 1888, after its writer had been given a tour in a sulky headed north from Santa Maria:

> *About two miles above Nipomo we struck sandy soils again and moved right along. The squirrels here are a great curiosity, and I wanted to stop every few minutes to throw at them. Sometimes you can see 10 or 15 playing around at once. We have*

jack rabbits and quail by the thousand. These jack rabbits are about the size of a fox. Nothing but a grey hound can catch one.

Half way between Nipomo and Arroyo Grande we had a beautiful view of the Pacific. It is about five miles away. We could see the steamers moving slowly along to the great city of San Francisco…We reached Arroyo Grande about 2 o'clock. It is about 16 miles from Santa Maria, and is a beautiful little place. The population is about 600. The soil is very fine, and produces a great variety of crops. About the first person you meet is a Real Estate agent with tickets containing the following: 'Arroyo Grande Valley produces 60 to 80 tons of carrots, per acre; 40 to 50 tons of squashes, per acre; 2 ½ tons of beans, per acre; 300 sacks potatoes, per acre; 270-pound squashes, 100-pound beets, 5-pound onions, 10-pound potatoes, Irish…"

By the end of his letter home, South Carolinian A.T. Dunlap had made up his mind about Arroyo Grande. "I think I am going to like it here finely," he wrote.

The Lynching, 1886

The civilizing and the Americanizing of the once-wild Arroyo Grande Valley begun by Francis Branch should have accelerated with the 1881 arrival of the railroad, the narrow-gauge Pacific Coast Railway. It did, to a large extent, tying the Valley to the Pacific Ocean, where there was a commercial wharf at Port Harford, and to markets in San Luis Obispo, to the north.

The railroad's efficacy as a tool of civilization was dampened when the citizens of Arroyo Grande, in 1886, hanged a fifteen-year-old boy from the PCRR Bridge that forded the Arroyo Grande Creek in the heart of town. The lynch mob strung up the boy's father, too, and the bodies were left dangling for hours, prompting furtive but inevitable truancy as little boys slipped away from school and stood under the corpses to gawk at them, from the soles of their feet to their stricken, clay-colored faces.

Although a local pastor would praise the ad hoc Committee of Vigilance for its work that day, it didn't sit well with all the participants. One of them, Fred Jones, in great, great old age, talked to my brother's class at our two-room school, Branch Elementary, in the late 1950s. The victims of the vigilantes were Peter Hemmi and his teenaged son, Julius. or P.J. Mr. Jones, the man who told the story, must have been about P.J.'s age when this happened.

The PCRR bridge over Arroyo Grande Creek. San Luis Obispo Historical Society.

Mrs. Hemmi was sitting in the anteroom of what passed for a jail and when the lynch mob, many wearing handkerchiefs over their faces, burst in, the look on her face revealed that she knew exactly what was about to happen. Jones had never forgotten that face at that moment; it haunted him for the rest of his life.

47

They wanted to lynch a third man, Peter's nephew, but the elder Hemmi defended him. The mob let the nephew go, and he ran for his life with a noose still around his neck. Peter could not save his son. P.J. ended a long-running land dispute in Lopez Canyon between his father and their neighbors, the Walkers, with a rifle. On March 31, he walked onto their property and began firing. Eugene Walker died in his garden amid his vegetables. P.J. then shot the family's dog. When Mrs. Walker came screaming out of the house, he shot her, too. She would live, but not for long: She died in the care of family months later. Now, hours later, no amount of pleading could save the terrified teenaged killer. P.J. had shot a young mother, and this was beyond the pale. His death by strangulation after he'd been pushed off the little bridge was justice.

Even fifty years later, Madge Ditmas refused to call Peter Hemmi by name in her history columns in the local weekly, the *Herald-Recorder*, referring to the Swiss-born Hemmi as "The Frenchman."

There was not the slightest chance that the two would be allowed burial on sanctified ground, amid their neighbors. The 71-year-old Manuela Branch had their bodies brought to her family's graveyard, and the two were buried a few feet away from her husband, whose reputation was indestructible.

Saloon Days

Branch Street circa 1900. The Capitol Saloon is at left. South County Historical Society

One of the delights of history research is finding a cache of Sanborn Fire Insurance maps. They detail businesses and dwellings, so they're valuable historical snapshots of communities. The 1903 Sanborn map of Branch Street in Arroyo Grande includes notable landmarks: Churches, the Columbian Hall, the Ryan Hotel and no fewer than six saloons bunched near the intersection of Branch and Bridge Streets.

Longtime local teacher Ruth Paulding noted, according to historian Doris Olsen, that most frontier towns had a saloon on every corner but that Arroyo Grande was unique: Eleven saloons for only two or three corners.

To be fair, saloons, for working-class men, were an important source of refreshment beyond the liquid kind. New York *Times* reporter Jon Grinspan notes that

...saloons provided drinkers with a free lunch: cheese, crackers and bologna, but also pigs' feet and pretzels, liverwurst and sardines, more raw onion than any man would want. In a nation with no social safety net and chronic recessions, these snacks kept many laborers alive.

And, by the late 1800s, Americans' drinking habits had changed. In the early part of the century, when whisky was cheap, each citizen consumed the equivalent of 7.5 gallons of ethanol per year (compared to a still substantial 2.42 gallons a year today). By the time of that Sanborn map, a wave of immigration from Germany offered cheaper and lower-octane beer, so that beverage became immensely popular. And saloons frequently might be like modern hamburger franchises—they'd serve only one brand (Schlitz, Anheuser-Busch, Pabst Blue Ribbon), so that might help to explain this nexus of saloons in a town of only about 800.

Still, the presence of drunks unnerved newcomers like Dr. Ed Paulding, Ruth's father, who noted that "Sabbath is unknown and drunks are the rule." Historian Jean Hubbard describes Rev. Osborn, the Methodist minister, nonchalantly interrupting a sermon to escort a drunk out of his church by the collar. After the noise of "a brief scuffle," Osborn returned and finished the sermon.

Among the saloons were the relatively upscale bar at the Ryan Hotel, two establishments run by Pete Olohan, who gave his name to the alley that runs parallel to Branch Street, and Frank Cook's Capitol Saloon, where tragedy struck in March 1904. A local man, George Roberts, was firing his pistol into the air along Branch Street and ducked into the Capitol for a drink he probably didn't need. When Constable Henry Lewellyn appeared at the Capitol doorway to disarm the man who was disturbing the peace, Roberts shot him. Lewellyn died the next day in the Ryan Hotel. Roberts was eventually acquitted because evidently, there'd been bad blood between himself and Lewellyn. The jury ruled the killing an act of self-defense. If Arroyo Grande was not exactly peaceful, George Roberts died a peaceful death in Santa Ynez thirty years later.

The Peas of Wrath

Dorothea Lange took this photo of workers harvesting peas in Shell Beach.
Library of Congress.

I've always been interested in social history, including women's history, and military history. Now I've discovered how fascinating agricultural history is. That's a validation of the way I used to look forward to teaching the Agricultural Revolution to my European History classes

It wasn't true when I was growing up in the Arroyo Grande Valley, but twenty years before, sweet peas had been the dominant crop in southern San Luis Obispo County, from the foothills east of Shell Beach to, of course, the Nipomo Mesa, where Dorothea Lange immortalized pea-picker Florence Thompson, the "Migrant Mother."

Thomas Chalmers
Commissioner

TOTAL VALUATIONS
1929 - 1937

	ANIMAL INDUSTRY	FIELD CROPS	FRUIT-L.'T CROPS	VEGETABLE CROPS	TOTAL
1929	5,842,100	2,390,200	538,400	3,926,115	12,696,815
1930	4,063,100	1,827,400	603,000	2,529,000	9,022,500
1931	2,786,400	1,145,796	636,100	2,572,600	7,140,896
1932	1,777,600	1,550,800	480,300	2,634,600	6,423,300
1933	1,804,800	1,810,000	458,100	2,409,000	6,481,900
1934	2,216,600	1,762,900	365,800	2,519,100	6,864,400
1935	3,707,600	3,175,200	285,400	2,706,100	9,872,500
1936	4,174,100	3,539,600	571,100	2,815,000	11,098,800
1937	6,070,800	4,082,700	1,529,000	2,804,700	15,487,200

Despite that image, the Depression, I'd thought, couldn't have been as acute here as it was in the East, where unemployment in Detroit was 50% and, at one point in Toledo, 80%. But these figures, from the county agriculture department, tell an appalling story, too.

The total valuation of San Luis Obispo County agriculture fell by half between 1929 and 1933, with the collapse of crop prices. Peas were the largest vegetable crop--about 5,000 acres, nearly all in the South County, were planted annually. Lettuce came in second, at 3,000 acres planted. Peas were important to the point of absurdity. A photo from a World War I-era postcard depicts Arroyo Grande teen-aged girls, dressed in gauzy gowns, like twentieth-century vestal virgins, "dancing at the Sweet Pea Fair."

The 1929 pea crop was valued at $2.2 million dollars, but the harvest from roughly the same acreage four years later was valued at only $822,000. This collapse, prior to the arrival of AAA subsidies, contributed to another disaster.

Peas had been so enormously profitable during and after World War I that farmers, according to WPA Writers' Project accounts, practiced little rotation and intensified cultivation of peas and, quite naturally, even expanded their acreage as prices began to fall after the Crash.

This led to a crisis in soil erosion in places like Corbett Canyon. In 1937, the head of the Soil Conservation Service said the erosion in Arroyo Grande was among the worst he'd seen in the United States, and he'd seen Oklahoma. It would take intensive labor by CCC and WPA crews building check dams and terraces and planting windbreaks to prevent Arroyo Grande from looking like North Africa. It was an enormous effort and, I think, one of the most stunning achievements of the CCC, which employed young men 18 to 25 years old and paid them $27 a month, half of which they were expected to send home.

There were other kinds of crises. There were bitter strikes in the South County by migrant pea workers--Filipino, some Mexican, and poor white migrants from as far east as Vermont--in 1934 and again in 1937. In 1939, according to a migrant nurse's report, wages were still low for pea-picking, at one cent a pound, thirty cents a hamper, and wages were cut, by mid-season, to twenty-five cents.

Growers estimated that they needed to clear 3 1/2 cents a pound to make a living. What struck me wasn't the miserliness of growers, but the enormity of their shipping costs. A hamper of peas that sold for $3.45 on the East Coast cost $1.70 to ship there. It reminded me of the days of the Populist movement, when it cost a farmer more to ship a bushel of wheat from Kansas to Chicago, by rail, than it did to ship that bushel from Chicago to Liverpool, mostly by ship.

By 1939, good years were beginning to return. A regulated and relatively clean network of county camps housed 3,000 pea pickers at the height of the season, which ran from March through May. Most of these camps were on land owned by local farmers and operated either by labor contractors or camp bosses appointed by the contractors. According to a government accounting of the 3,000 workers in those camps, 426 of these harvest families were "white," 167 "Mexican" –the latter statistic shows that Mexican labor had begun to return after nationwide deportations in 1931.

Oklahoma migrants, Nipomo, 1937. Dorothea Lange photograph. Library of Congress.

There is no category for "Filipino," but they were there in large numbers, too, though not as families. Filipinas were not permitted to immigrate and California miscegenation laws barred Filipino men from marrying Caucasians. It would require them dying in World War II combat—the first all-Filipino infantry regiment was formed at Camp San Luis Obispo--to "earn" the right to marry. After the war, they began to bring home war brides from the islands and start families of their own.

There were also 569 children in the camps. Teachers were brought in to give lessons in one of the camps and in a schoolhouse that is today's Nipomo Men's Club. A migrant nurse devoted to these farmworkers noted that older children looked wistfully every day as the Arroyo Grande Union High School bus passed their camp, slowed, and kept going. This woman had sand. She marched into Principal Clarence Burrell's office--Burrell was a good man— who in turn took up the issue with the Board of Trustees. They directed the bus driver to pick up the kids at the camp and bring them to school.

There were only four weeks left that school year and you wonder about those kids, both at how enormous it must have been for them have classes in a "real school" and you wonder, too, about how they were treated. I remember how cruel children can be. When I was in elementary school, we once called a poor white family "Okies." The peas were gone, then, replaced in my time by new valley crops, but bigotry has a long growing season.

Power Struggle in the Fields

I've been reading a history of California in the 1930s, when the state's politics were dominated but an alliance of reactionary forces that fought the New Deal and the state's farm workers with all their strength, which was considerable.

What made up that coalition? To borrow Renault's quote from *Casablanca*, they were the usual suspects: Harry Chandler's Los Angeles *Times*, the Hearst newspapers, the L.A. District Attorney and the Los Angeles Police Department, the Chamber of Commerce, Pacific Gas and Electric Co., and Associated Farmers, a powerful anti-labor lobby. They blocked literally hundreds of bills in the state legislature that would have provided laborers with a minimum wage and with decent housing. LAPD officers were sent to the Arizona border to block migrants from entering the state. Growers intimidated labor organizers with professionals whose specialty was busting strikes. Some wore revolvers on their hips, like Henry Sanborn, a National Guard officer who organized hundreds of paramilitary "deputies" in the 1936 Salinas lettuce strike This strike had been provoked by the growers themselves when they locked workers out of the packing sheds. They had already built a big stockade, complete with concertina wire, in anticipation of a strike. "Don't worry," they told alarmed packing-shed workers before the lockout. "That's for the Filipinos."

The one dissident in the state's economic power structure, an ardent New Dealer, was A.P. Giannini, founder of the Bank of Italy, today's Bank of America.

In the history of American labor disputes, like the 1894 Pullman Strike, the role of the government had been to uphold capital and suppress labor. Theodore Roosevelt's intervention in the 1902 Pennsylvania Coal Strike represented a rare departure: He demanded that both sides come to the bargaining table or he'd use the army to take over the mines. Neither management nor labor were pleased with the president, but the strike was settled. When Franklin Roosevelt became president, capitalists, including California growers, were outraged that the government seemed to side so clearly with workers in the pro-union Wagner Act. But that law did not extend to agricultural workers. FDR didn't want to alienate powerful Southern Democrats.

Still, there were now health inspections of labor camps, and occasional attempts by the federal government to settle strikes. One such attempt led to retaliation: A Labor Department official was beaten, stripped, and left in middle of the desert of the Imperial Valley. The Arroyo Grande *Herald-Recorder* at this time regularly railed against the excesses of this activist government on its editorial page while its news page primly reported another schedule of AAA subsidy payments.

Meanwhile, the big growers had to confront labor disputes. The easiest way to sanction strikers, and to make labor organizers "disappear" over the county line, was to arrest them for vagrancy, since they clearly weren't working. That was the pretext used by SLO County Sheriff Harry Haskins, backed by 200 instant deputy sheriffs, in the April 1937 pea strike. It worked: That strike, centered in Nipomo, ended pretty quickly. So had another one farther north, in January, in and around Pismo Beach, organized by Filipino farm workers. It was over in three weeks, with some violence--fights between strikers and scabs—but this strike ended with a negotiated settlement. The growers didn't negotiate with the strikers. They negotiated with the Chamber of Commerce, which dictated the settlement.

California Filipinos were militant and angry, for good reason. Several sources I've read place them at the bottom of a kind of racist hierarchy with whites at the highest level, followed by Japanese, then Mexicans, and finally Filipinos, who were housed in filthy camps. They were frequently harassed by police, and were seen in the popular press as sexual predators, with their invariable target, of course, white womanhood. This sounds like 1930s Mississippi as much as 1930s California.

Even the local weekly paper, the Arroyo Grande *Herald-Recorder,* comes off badly. Its news columns, before longtime editor Newell Strother's time, are openly racist, especially in their coverage of Filipinos.

One 1937 story details an Oceano raid on a hall holding taxi dances-- Filipino men would buy a ticket and dance with a woman, invariably Caucasian, since Filipinas were not allowed to immigrate. The raiders were more of those instant deputies. Several dancers, including the girls, were arrested. The *Herald-Recorder* reported that one Filipino laborer had bought more than 200 dance tickets from one of the arrested taxi dancers.

I guess this detail in the story was meant to provoke a sharp intake of breath on the part of its white readers.

Tensions began to ease by 1938, partly because the economy was beginning to recover, partly because a reactionary governor, Frank Merriam, was replaced by a more moderate one, Cuthbert Olsen. In the meantime, a state investigating committee (one young attorney-investigator was Clark Kerr, the future UC President) and a federal one, led by Sen. Robert LaFollette, embarrassed Associated Farmers. The investigations revealed that they'd denied their workers basic civil rights, relied on violence, were indifferent toward inadequate and unhealthy housing conditions, used industrial espionage on a large scale, and frequently cut wages, continuing to claim that they could only pay what the market would bear even when, by the later 1930s, crop prices had begun to recover.

So history does not judge this alliance of big business, big agriculture and police power well. The powerful brought that judgment, in their seeming victory over the strikes of the mid-1930s, on themselves.

The Azoreans

In growing up in the Upper Arroyo Grande Valley, one of my favorite sights was looking down Huasna road to see two farmers, Manuel and Johnny Silva, who probably had breakfast together just two hours before, stopped in the middle of the road, pickup cab to pickup cab, to talk while sprinklers described vast arcs in the fields alongside them. It was a mystery what they would have to talk about so soon after breakfast, but if a motorist had come up behind the trucks, the men inside would instantly pull off to the side to let him by. Then they would wave cheerfully. Two hundred yards later, if that driver had looked in his rearview mirror, the trucks would be together again and the conversation would have resumed. Moments like those, seventy years after their ancestors had come to America, demonstrated that the secret to the success of Portuguese immigrants in the Arroyo Grande Valley was their devotion to one another.

Festa *parade, Arroyo Grande, 1913.* South County Historical Society.

It was a series of earthquakes and volcanic eruptions, along with economic stagnation and political unrest, that led nineteenth-century Azoreans to leave for Brazil or the United States. Today, their American descendants outnumber the remaining Azoreans four to one. They settled continental America from Boston to San Luis Obispo County to take up a familiar trade, whaling, in New Bedford, in Hawaii and along the California coast. Portuguese immigrants to San Luis Obispo County launched boats from San Simeon, where they harvested primarily gray whales and occasionally humpbacks. But by the 1870s, harvests were dwindling. At the same time, John D. Rockefeller was harvesting lesser oil companies to build Standard Oil. Rockefeller's kerosene and Edison's incandescent light bulb replaced whale oil and forced the seafaring Azoreans to look inland.

In Arroyo Grande, Portuguese immigrants turned to truck farming and to dairy farming. In researching the book *World War II Arroyo Grande*, I turned to an old friend and Branch School classmate, John Silva, and he modestly offered that he didn't know all that much about local history. Then he began to recall the name of every Portuguese dairy farmer from Lopez Canyon to Corbett Canyon. He was amazing.

The immigrants were both skilled farmers and devout Catholics, so their *festas*—including the Festival of the Holy Spirit, which commemorates the miracles attributed to thirteenth-century Queen Isabel of Portugal—became a regular feature of the growing town's life. Parades down Branch Street and barbecues and dances organized by the religious fraternity IDES (*Irmandade do Divino Espirito Santa*) made the Portuguese a highly visible minority and might have hastened what seems like a relatively rapid period of assimilation into the community.

The *festa* remained an annual event centered at the IDES Hall just outside town, and Portuguese Americans from the San Joaquin Valley descend on nearby Pismo Beach in the late summer for the St. Anthony Festival, a tradition that began in the mid-1950s. In Arroyo Grande, while parish priests were Irish, it was the Portuguese who were the backbone of St. Patrick's Catholic Church, which stood, in ecumenical harmony, within a few feet of the Methodist church that flanked it to the northeast.

Festa celebrants before the war years would have included the Brown family. Antonio and his wife, Anna, were both born in the Azores, became citizens in 1906, presumably had their names Anglicized and produced two sons widely apart in age. Lionel was born in 1904 and his younger brother, Louis, in 1924, when his parents were approaching middle age. Louis must have seemed like another one of Queen Isabel's miracles.

The Browns were farmers and settled just outside Arroyo Grande in Corbett Canyon, narrow and dense with oaks but with pockets of good soil that the immigrants began to cultivate.

They must have known a nearby family with difficult circumstances. Their neighbors, Joseph and Clara Gularte—John Silva's maternal ancestors-- came from the Azores early in the century and married in San Luis Obispo in 1906. In the 1920s, Joseph Gularte began to cultivate strawberries, pioneering what became an important area crop. The berries were harvested by a platoon of his daughters, and their father made sales rounds to the Portuguese groceries in San Luis Obispo. Joseph died suddenly in 1934, and Clara became the head of a family of ten children: four boys and six girls. Clara's burden would have been lightened by her elder sons, who took over the family's farm at the mouth of Corbett Canyon; the 1940 census also shows that the girls were beginning to marry and establish households of their own. Meanwhile, a younger son, Frank, was working for one of the most important businesses in the valley, E.C. Loomis and Son, vegetable brokers who kept a farm supply and feed store at the base of Crown Hill in Arroyo Grande.

The immigrants' sons would play major role in turning me into a writer: When I found Louis Brown's grave in the Arroyo Grande District Cemetery, a Marine killed three days before he turned twenty-one, I realized from the date of his death that he'd been killed on Iwo Jima, one of the most famous battles of World War II. I would find out he died in an assault on Hill 362A—cause of death, "burns, entire body"—no more than 48 hours after he'd gone into combat the first time.

Frank Gularte, by comparison, was a combat veteran. His tank destroyer battalion had fought across France, playing a role in the attempt to close the Falaise Gap and so bag the German army in Normandy. The unit, part of Patton's Third Army, then drove toward Metz, on the German frontier. Metz is an old Roman garrison town that town my students and I once visited, and it's marked in our memories by a Romanesque Cathedral that stands alongside the Moselle River's impossibly blue water. Frank died nearby, and his death was every bit as tragic as Louis Brown's and his family's tragedy was every bit as painful. A German sniper killed Sgt. Gularte on November 28, 1944 in Merten, a French border town in a beautiful little valley.

Five days later and more than 5,000 miles away, his first child, Frank Jr., was born.

Chapter 3. Grands and Great-Grands

A tintype with (l-r) an unidentified woman; my great-grandfather Taylor Wilson; my great-grandmother Sallie McBride Wilson.

Grandma Gregory and the
Pendergast Machine

Somewhere we have a penciled thank-you note from John W. Davis, who is about as famous as whichever team finished third in the National League pennant race in 1939. (It was the Brooklyn Dodgers, 12 ½ games out.) Davis was the Democratic nominee for President in 1924, and he did far worse than the 1939 Dodgers.

He was trounced by Calvin Coolidge. Coolidge's workdays at the White House were at most seven hours, punctuated by summer naps in his rocking chair on the portico. Sadly, these had to be suspended when Coolidge began collecting dense crowds, silent tourists, watching gravely and debating among themselves in urgent whispers over whether the president had died. After all, Harding had pulled *that* trick.

To be fair, the White House staff frequently had the same debate when the president was conscious.

Meanwhile, John W. Davis would go on to a distinguished career, arguing 150 cases before the Supreme Court. Today, Davis is noted mostly for being on the wrong side of every one of them. If it was racist, reactionary, or repressive, he defended it passionately, with the conviction and confidence of one who knows that God Almighty is his co-counsel. The crowning of his legal career— thank the aforementioned Lord–came when he lost *Brown v. Board* before the Warren Court.

But the Democrats could've run the killers Leopold and Loeb in 1924, and I think Grandma Gregory—Dora Wilson Gregory-- would've worked her heart out for them as long as they were Democrats. She went to the national convention at Madison Square Garden as a delegate that year, only four years after women had gotten the vote. It took two weeks and 103 ballots for the Democrats to get their candidate, who certainly *looked* presidential, if he didn't poll that way. Having survived the convention, Grandma would later become the Texas County, Missouri, Party Chairwoman and a powerful figure in downstate Missouri politics.

She is undoubtedly why, when I watched a national political convention for the first time, when I was 12, in 1964--and when conventions actually meant something– I was entranced. Barry Goldwater of Arizona would prevail over Pennsylvania moderate William Scranton for the Republican nomination, and I couldn't tear myself away from the television.

It was a different Democratic party—both in its conservatism and in its discipline-- in Depression-era Missouri. Before every election, my Dad remembered, a new car, a little of its shine visible under miles of road dust, would pull up outside my Grandfather's farmhouse. Two city boys in three-piece suits--usually reserved in rural Missouri for funerals, and for the deceased-- would deposit a bank-bag full of cash on Dora Gregory's kitchen table. For them, it was but one more stop on a kind of purgatory circuit where they would drop off dozens of bags in dozens of homes. This part of the state was remote and thinly populated, and city boys might not have had all that much appreciation for the natural beauty beyond their car's windows.

Dora Wilson Gregory during the 1940s.

They were bagmen for the Kansas City Pendergast Machine. Boss Tom Pendergast's Kansas City was a kind of cultural hub for the Depression-era Midwest. It was, for example, a city that Louis Armstrong, Count Basie and Duke Ellington played during Prohibition, since Pendergast made sure liquor flowed freely in local jazz clubs. Pendergast's Kansas City sometimes resembled Capone's Chicago. A pitched 1933 gun battle there, an ambush in Union Station that had been planned by "Pretty Boy" Floyd, claimed the lives of four lawmen and the prisoner they were escorting.

In contrast to modern, cosmopolitan Kansas City, Texas County was a place where Civil War violence had not yet ended. When my father was a teenager, there was a Confederate veteran still alive in in Houston, the county seat. There also was one Union veteran in the same town. The two had not spoken since 1865.

FDR's first term was past its midpoint when, on July 4, 1935, the county band was playing the National Anthem. The old Confederate finally snapped: He leaped on the old Yankee, and the two rolled around on the courthouse lawn, knocking over potato salads and tubs of sweet tea in bitter personal combat. It was a small-scale Battle of Antietam. When six young man finally pried the two apart, the old Confederate triumphantly held up a generous portion of the Yankee's ear, which he'd removed with a Barlow knife.

Most of the people of Texas County were considerably calmer and much kinder than the old Confederate, especially if you happened to be a Democrat. Tom Pendergast's Democrats had Texas County sewn up. Proof of this came on Election Day, when my pre-teen Dad handed out fives to waiting voters, murmuring, "The Democratic Party thanks you," over and over. The five-dollar bills came from the bank bag on my grandmother's kitchen table.

To be fair to the Machine, it distributed food, not just bribes, and people in the hills were hungry in the depths of the Depression. A young Dad also helped distribute food to the needy. Grapefruit stymied them. "We boiled it, Bob," they told him apologetically, "an' then we fried it, but it still tasted putrid."

These were not ignorant people, not by any choice. They were immensely proud and largely self-sufficient, but life had changed little for them since the Civil War. The Depression had propelled them backwards. No one seemed to care. What Dad came to realize was that Ozark hill people were victims of isolation. And of neglect, which even a cynic like Pendergast and, much more effectively, Roosevelt, sought to overcome.

The miracle that began to break that isolation down was rural electrification. This was a life-changing event that meant for Ozark housewives the advent of electric washing machines and electric irons. Laundry day and ironing day, as historian Robert Caro noted so movingly in the first volume of his magisterial biography of Lyndon Johnson, tortured women like those who lived on the Ozark Plateau. It bent their backs, ripped intestinal muscle, burned them with blisters and the lye burned away the skin on their hands and forearms. The kind of work they did, without electricity, would eventually wear them down; women who worked that hard died relatively young. Not even a powerful man like Boss Pendergast could help Ozark women, but the New Deal's funding of rural electoral cooperatives would.

Thanks to Pendergast, FDR and Grandma Gregory, my Dad was a lifelong Democrat. My Mom was an Eisenhower Republican, so my parents had lively political discussions when we were growing up. One of them doomed dessert, because the colander of fresh strawberries, washed for strawberry shortcake, wound up on upside-down atop my father's head.

JFK's nomination brought political harmony to the marriage: Dad voted for him because he was a Democrat; Mom because he was Irish Catholic.

So politics, thanks to my grandmother, meant a lot in our family. I wish I could say I loved my Grandmother Gregory, but she was a steel-spined schoolmarm who didn't tolerate foolishness, by which she meant consciousness, and she used to whack us absently with her cane. We stole her eyeglasses in revenge. And, sadly, by the time I knew her, she was edging into dementia, and though she couldn't locate her dentures, or her eyeglasses, she could remember in vivid detail how every person in Texas County, Missouri, had died between the Civil War and the 1939 Dodgers.

It didn't take a lot to prompt a Grandma Gregory death story, and, looking back in the fullness of my own years, I realize that some of them were humdingers.

My favorite, and I use that word ironically, was the neighbor who suddenly disappeared. The family and the authorities and happy coonhounds–they like to be kept busy, or they get saucy– looked for several days, to no avail. When one of the kids finally did find him, he was at the bottom of the family's well, where he'd plummeted after a massive coronary.

Oddly, these stories were poignant because they showed my grandmother was already living in the past; her connections to modernity would grow more and more fragile. But, as a younger woman, she was shrewd and powerful. For that, I admire her.

70

Kentucky Gentleman

My grandfather, John Smith Gregory, was born in Shelby County, Kentucky, in 1862. He was a father of eight, a farmer in south-central Missouri, a lumber estimator, outdoorsman, and a fine dancer. Harry Truman was a fan of my grandfather's blackberry wine. On campaign swings downstate, he made it a point to pay court to my grandmother, the local Democratic powerbroker, but after those formalities, the heart of the Senator's visit was a sip or four of John's blackberry wine.

That wine may have made me possible. My father was a kind of miraculous afterthought, the last of eight children, born when my grandfather was fifty-six. When Dad went into the Army in World War II, he stood as good a chance as any other country boy of being vaporized by a German 88 shell somewhere in the dark canopy of the Ardennes. Instead he spent the war in London protecting pubs from the Nazis, thanks to Truman's nomination of him to Officers' Candidate School.

John Gregory at ease in front of his home near Raymondville, Missouri. The farmhouse still stands.

My family's forebears were Virginians. In the wonderful book about early American folkways, *Albion's Seed*, historian David Hackett Fisher reveals that teaching dance had been central to the way Virginians socialized their children.

My family must have raised their children that way from the days they'd emigrated, in the 1690s, from the Midlands of England to the banks of the James River. So it was no accident that Grandfather's most formidable talent may have been his dancing. By the 1930s, John Gregory had become kind of Ozarkian version of Fred Astaire.

My grandmother was not amused by the line of pretty teenagers at barn dances who shyly waited their turn to waltz with Mr. Gregory. She suspected, too, and I'll bet she was right, that those girls liked also his twinkly eyes and the soft smile beneath his silky white mustaches. My grandmother was not given to smiling. She had a temper and, with it, a strong and wide body: she was a hard woman to knock down in a windstorm. Years later, we regarded her visits to us in Arroyo Grande with the same enthusiasm that an Irish monastery might muster for a Viking raid.

Her grandfather, by the way, had been a Confederate brigadier general of modest accomplishment and minimal talent–I was named for him, and for his son, a staff officer killed in action by an artillery shell in 1862 Arkansas–so that branch of the family saw themselves as gentry. They were insufferable. Despite that, John Gregory indulged my grandmother; he was a tolerant man.

He had a genius for math. My Dad inherited this gift. I, as my geometry teacher at Arroyo Grande High School noted ruefully, had no talent in that line, nor in any plane. But lumber companies sought out Grandfather because he could eye a stand of Missouri hardwood and calculate, with eerie precision, how many board-feet it would yield.

He was a competent but unorthodox farmer. In the Ozark foothills any money there was to be made–and there wasn't much–was to be made in tobacco and corn and hogs. John accepted that reality but his real passion was ginseng. Cultivating ginseng was to John Gregory was what stamp collecting was to Franklin Roosevelt: It was his outlet. He was not a talkative man, but I can imagine him, almost poetic, winning over dubious neighbors at the local grocer's about the miraculous attributes of ginseng. He won them, too. In a little shirt-pocket notebook I still have he has meticulously recorded his sales figures: *J.K. Davis, $250; John Helsey, $50; W.T. Eliot, $62.50.*

But his hallmark, the essence of his character, was his kindness. My father remembered this most of all: During the Depression, there'd be an occasional knock on the farmhouse door. It'd be a jobless man on the move.

--May I sleep the night in your barn, sir?

--Young man, you may not. Grandfather would eye the stranger coldly, for dramatic effect. *However, we* do *have a spare bed. How about some bacon and eggs?*

It was these visits that so impressed my own father with the cruelty of the Great Depression. These strangers who wolfed down my grandmother's meals (beneath her stony exterior there was a deep humanity she didn't like to let out much) were not "bums:" They were college students, engineers, veterans of the Great War, and one, a violinist, paid for his supper and bed with a solo concert in a kitchen warmed by a wood stove and lit by kerosene lamps instead of footlights.

When they hung a ne'er-do-well –the local bully–at the Missouri State Penitentiary, the barbershop crowd bet that not even John Gregory, in town for his every-other-day shave, could find anything nice to say about him. There was a pause, but not a long one, underneath the hot towels: "The man," he said, "had a beautiful set of teeth."

My grandfather was killed by a driver from Wichita Falls, Texas. Grandma had called Dad back to the house because he was barefoot and no son of *hers* was going to make a social call to Mr. Dixon's looking like a hillbilly. Dad never forgave her because if he'd been there, he would have heard the roadster that hit my grandfather as he crossed the road.

The impact broke both of John's legs. But even at seventy, he had an athlete's body and he fought hard to live in a Catholic hospital that must have caused my Church of Christ grandmother intense anxiety, looking out for Grandfather while listening intently for any Papist heresy.

As a teenager, Grandfather had accepted a dare from two friends to swim across the Red River in flood, and John was the only survivor. Not this time, not in the hospital in Springfield. This time, the river was too strong and he finally made the choice to let the current carry him away.

After they drove him back home from Springfield, there was a big funeral. I still have the yellowed obituary. Despite the fact that it was the darkest year of the Great Depression–1933–there would have been big honey-cured baked hams and fried chicken and candied yams and mashed potatoes and a battery of salads, casseroles, and pies, dusted with sugar, from every farmhouse in a twenty-mile radius.

Both my father and his sister, my Aunt Mildred, talked about him always in Homeric terms. He was their father, and he was their hero. They found it hard to let him go, so they never did.

Leaving Ireland: The Ship
Dunbrody

*Fox a) Coolboy b) Coolboy c) Carnew d) 1847 e) 258 f) Denis, 50, Bess 49,
Pat 28, Michael 26, Catherine 24, Denis 22, William 20. Mary 16. Peggy 14,
John 12, Nessy 10. j) 1 acre from Lord Fitzwilliam*

The folks in this list are distant ancestors, fleeing the Famine and bound
for Canada. When the Fox family got settled in Ontario, Denis's son,
Patrick, fathered a little girl named Margaret. Margaret was my mother's
grandmother. So my mother's name was Patricia Margaret.

.

Dunbrody. Photo by Pam Brophy.

The photograph shows a replica of a ship, the *Dunbrody*, like the one that would have brought them to Canada. But *Dunrbody* was the ship that brought another Patrick to Boston—Patrick Kennedy, John F. Kennedy's great-grandfather, from County Wexford. My ancestors were close by, in Wicklow, near the Wexford border.

It must have been terrifying. It would have been a two-day walk for these hungry people from Coolboy to the port at New Ross and few Irish ever traveled beyond the sound of their parish church's bells.

The sea voyage took two weeks, and the ships carrying Famine refugees became known as "Coffin Ships" because sometimes half or more of the passengers died in transit or, in Canada's case, in quarantine in Quebec. *Dunbrody*, thank goodness, was an exception: the owners seemed to actually care for their human cargo, and she made dozens of passages between New

Ross and the New World (New York, Boston and Quebec) with a very low death rate.

The Fox family left New Ross at the same time when two Famine ships foundered on icebergs during their passages: One was lost with all souls and sixty drowned on the other. It remains amazing what immigrants facing certain death at home will risk to stay alive.

There's an absorbing book about these migrant people, Thomas Gallagher's *Paddy's Lament.* The emigrants bound for America were feted, with what food and drink families and neighbors could get together, with a farewell party. But these little parties, celebrated, of course, with music—a fiddle and a tin whistle, perhaps--were shot through with sadness. They inevitably ended with tears.

The Irish called them "American wakes."

Patricia Keefe Gregory at twenty-two, with her daughter, Roberta.

Two Patricks in America

I just found my Mom's maternal great-grandfather, Patrick Fox, in the 1880 Pennsylvania Census. He was a coal miner. Mom's paternal great-grandpa was also named Patrick, and his last name was Keefe.

The two Patricks were Famine immigrants from the same village in County Wicklow, tenants to the same landlord, Lord Fitzwilliam. Fitzwilliam paid their passage to the New World because he was a humanitarian and because he was a man of business.

Hazelton, Pennsylvania coal miners, 1905. Library of Congress.

Fitzwilliam replaced them with sheep, easier to get along with than Irishmen and slightly cheaper to feed, although the variety of potato the Irish ate was so inferior that any self-respecting sheep would have turned it down.

The vast majority of the Irish, in the 19th century, lived their entire lives without ever eating meat. They were the poorest people in Europe before the potato blight hit—it turned a cellar-full of potatoes overnight into something resembling tar--when they were transmuted from poor people into statistics.

Meanwhile, every Irish family kept a hog, which had run of the place. They sold it to market to pay their tithes to the Protestant Church of Ireland, to which none of them belonged. It was the law, you see.

As was the case in many immigrant families, children in large families were named for ancestors: My mother's name, Patricia, is the feminized version of the Patricks among her ancestors. I guess your imagination for names runs out, for example, when you hit child #11, so the old standards serve best, and the families the size either the Foxes or the Keefes would've easily filled the entire floor of a city tenement.

Sister Loretta.

One of the Foxes, Sister Loretta—her birth name was Margaret--got a new name when she became a nun.

Her order wore the headpiece that vaguely resembles that of Sally Field's order in the 1960s television series, but evidently Sister Loretta did not fly. Nor does she look perky, as Sally Field did. In the one photo we have of her, she looks determined. She devoted over fifty years of her life to caring for orphans in what were called, in Victorian-era America, "asylums." The records in one orphanage where she worked show that there were hundreds of little girls, many of them with Irish surnames.

By the way, Patrick Keefe never would have stooped to working in a Pennsylvania coal mine like Sister Loretta's brother, Patrick Fox did.

He preferred the Pennsylvania oil fields.

So did my Dad's side of the family. The top three roughnecks in the photograph, we believe, are among his many uncles at a field in Taft or Bakersfield. One of them got mad at a camp cook and shoved him into a boiler.

We're not sure whether it was lit.

I'm reasonably sure this is true of every family: our ancestors were tough people.

The Californian

What's hard about doing your family tree is finding some branches you'd rather break off, the one that comes to mind is the ancestor with 19 slaves in the 1850 census, identified only by gender and age, as if they were machine parts rather than human beings. That's not the case with my Grandma Kelly. When she died in Cambria in 1974, I think she'd finally found some happiness in that beautiful place. She deserved it. Her life, I now realize, represents a significant slice of California's economic history, and the wealth the Golden State has generated came because of people like her, proud independents whose only wealth was their determination to keep going.

When I was little she took us out to lunch at a restaurant, now torn down, where the College Square shopping center is today on the northern edge of San Luis Obispo, off Santa Rosa Street. When the waitress handed out the menus, her eyes widened and locked on Grandma's bracelet: It was made of gold nuggets.

That bracelet was a reminder that Emma Martha Kircher, my Grandma Kelly, was born in a mining town now underneath Lake Shasta: Kennett, California. The nuggets on her bracelet were her father's. Charlie Kircher, the son of German immigrants from Baden-Wurttemberg, refugees from the humiliating collapse of the German revolution of 1848, was a restless Kansas farmer who came west in a lesser-known California Gold Rush near the turn of the century.

Kennett was at its epicenter: From the photographs it's a town that looks like a Universal Studio version of Dodge

My mother and grandmother, about 1924.

City; later photos, by the 1910s, show a huge and menacing copper smelter, the industry that sustained Kennett after the gold ran out, dominating the little town.

Charlie Kircher, my great-grandfather, was not the romantic figure I thought him to be, not a hardy 49er with shovel, pan, and cradle. He was a company man. The Uncle Sam mine where he worked eventually would yield over a million dollars in ore. One of his jobs, as a chlorider, was to separate the gold ore from the rock in which it was embedded. It wasn't romantic at all. It was tedious, smelly, but important to an industry that could be immensely destructive. The photographs of what hydraulic mining, for example, did to

84

the land of Shasta County are as shocking in their way as the photographs of bombed-out German cities at the end of World War II.

But it's here where Charlie seems to have found his vocation, and it's in Kennett's gold fields where he set down his roots. He married a 14-year-old native Californian, Nellie Wilson, in 1894, and the couple promptly produced three children: my grandmother, Emma Martha, born in 1895, Violet, in 1898, and Charlie Jr., in 1900.

My grandmother's earliest memory was of "a house on stilts." I had visions of her living over the Sacramento River — I seem to remember an urban legend that the late country-western star Merle Haggard owned a house like that over the Kern River with a trap door to facilitate fishing. That wasn't Emma's situation at all: Her house was terrifying. It was a Company house for a Company man, built flush into the steep sides of Iron Mountain, and below the stilts is a sheer drop, seen in an old photograph, that makes it a miracle she survived her childhood.

A miner's "house on stilts." Courtesy Shasta County Historical Society.

She attended a school, a little steepled building, in Kennett, which was also graced with a Methodist Church and the two-story Diamond Saloon and Hotel. Kennett was a tough town. Charlie Kircher was a tough man. The records note a "crippled right hand," but he may have used the good one liberally. Nellie divorced him and had remarried by 1906.

Although the three children followed Charlie to Burbank in 1910, the youngest, Charlie Jr., would lie about his age to join the World War I navy, perhaps to put some ocean between himself and his father.

That's when Charlie Kircher's trail disappears. I can find no record of his death and my grandmother never discussed him and very rarely discussed her early life.

I can pick up the thread of her life again in Taft, a town just over the San Luis Obispo county line that resembled Kennett in every way except for one: the source of wealth was oil, not gold.

Emma Martha Kircher met my grandfather—they'd married in July 1920 in Bakersfield—whose job descriptions over the years more or less connect with the oil industry and also with the fact that he couldn't seem to hold a job for very long.

Mattie's, 1940. The Huntington Library.

"He was a bad man," my step-grandfather said of Edmund Keefe, who liked to drink and to "borrow" cars. The Taft Police Department and the Kern County Sheriff knew him far better than I ever will. His disappearance, it turned out, was linked to a woman who lived in Taft, Mattie Smyer. When she moved to Pismo Beach, she would become a famed restaurateur—today, Mattie's old place is McLintock's Restaurant. When World War II came, Mattie's contribution to defeating the Axis was a stable of girls behind the restaurant and in little multi-doored houses across Highway 101, near the sea.

The Mattie connection was something we discovered years after, when my parents made the innocent mistake of taking my grandmother to Mattie's Restaurant for her birthday dinner . Midway through the main course, after an epic personal struggle, her face began to twitch and tears began to run down her cheeks. She turned to my mother. "That woman," she blurted, meaning Mattie, "is the one who ran off with your father." Edmund Keefe may have been a bad man, but my grandmother had been badly in love with him.

With Ed gone, Emma Martha Keefe was a single mother in an oil boomtown. She and my mother lived close to the bone; their poverty is revealed in an old school picture of my Mom, a jaunty little beret on her head, sweater and pleated skirt, but her shoes are beaten and scuffed.

Emma resisted, but not for long, the courting of Taft police officer George Kelly, my step-grandfather, our Gramps.

It was Gramps who, at lunch one day, casually mentioned that Mattie was leaving Taft for the coast, and she was putting on a big yard sale. The furniture was elegant. Grandma wouldn't hear of it. "Not," she sniffed, "from *that* woman."

Later, she surreptitiously drove by the yard sale. She made a few more passes. Very slowly.

Fifty years later, when I spent the night at my uncle's house near Sacramento, I slept on a Mattie Smyer couch in a living room surrounded by Mattie Smyer end tables, lamps, china cabinets and easy chairs. It was beautiful stuff. If one can use the word "voluptuous" to describe an elegantly curved floor lamp, then this was libido-driven furniture.

The Kellys eventually moved to Williams, in Colusa County, to raise almonds, where the earliest memory I have is of falling down Gramps's ranch-house steps. I still have the scar on my knee.

When the pair came to visit us in Arroyo Grande, there was inside me the kind of excitement a little kid feels on Christmas Eve. Grandma talked about politics, but also about Hollywood scandals–Elizabeth Taylor and Richard Burton seemed to share equal time with the Berlin Wall and the Mercury astronauts–and teased Gramps, a quiet man but a remarkably funny one, without mercy. He had learned after years of marriage how to be her straight man, Burns to her Gracie Allen.

The only part I hated about their visits was when it came time for them to leave, and I would watch their car until it was gone, and still watch awhile after. Maybe, I thought, they've forgotten something and will have to come back.

They retired to Cambria in a house built in large part by Gramps, then in his sixties. They lived quietly and putting on the Ritz consisted of going to an all-you-can-eat family restaurant, the Chuckwagon, just off Highway 1. It wasn't fancy, but the fried chicken was memorable, and Grandma Kelly had no need for fancy. The wealth she had was in living life, in enduring bleak poverty and in putting heartbreak behind her, and through all of that, she was most truly herself in those moments I caught her smiling at Gramps when he went back for seconds.

Chapter 4. Strong Women

Japanese mother, American daughter in a Guadalupe broccoli field, 1936. Dorothea Lange Photo. Library of Congress.

Sheila Varian's "Perfect Horse"

The Polish-born Arabian stallion's name was Witez II—"Chieftain" or "Hero" in translation. He was at sea, bound for a new home in post-World War II America. But as his ship entered the Bay of Biscay, it was hit by an intense storm that produced monstrous waves. Its cargo—Witez and 150 other prized European horses—began to make noise below decks: The terrified animals screamed, kicked at the bulkheads and began struggling among each other, and wounding each other, in confusion and panic.

A U.S. Army officer, Capt. William Quinlan, was in charge of the Liberty Ship *Austin's* precious cargo. Quinlan and his soldiers worked frantically to separate and calm the horses—Arabians, like Witez, along with Thoroughbreds and Lipizzaner from Vienna's famed Spanish Riding School.

Quinlan lurched toward Witez and found him quiet and unafraid, focused fiercely on maintaining his balance as the ship straddled another wave. Writer Elizabeth Letts describes the encounter:

Quinlan stroked the horse's nose for a moment, whispering a quiet word of thanks. Witez, the chieftain, had been bred to maintain his composure in the fury of battle — and here on the Stephen F. Austin, he had won his warrior's stripes.

Witez II. Wikimedia Commons.

Sixteen years later, another horse demonstrated the same composure and focus that Witez did that day in the Bay of Biscay. She, too, was an Arabian. She, too, was a warrior. The smallish, hard-muscled mare, named Ronteza, was Witez's daughter. Her home was Corbett Canyon, near Arroyo Grande, and in 1961 she proved herself to be her father's daughter in front of 20,000 spectators who watched, momentarily hushed, as the little horse stumbled and fell in competition.

Her rider was Sheila Varian.

* * *

It was, of course, Walter Farley's classic book *The Black Stallion* that first made Sheila Varian, along with many generations of little girls, fall in love with horses.

Varian was raised in Halcyon in a family marked by brilliant individuality: Two uncles were the founders of one of the first electronics firms in what is now known as Silicon Valley. She learned to ride during gallops on the beach at age eight on Judy, little Ronteza's opposite. Judy was a sixteen-hand Morgan/Percheron cross, so it was a long way to the ground. Varian wouldn't be gifted with her first saddle until she was twelve, but she, wearing feathers in her hair, in her imagination a Plains Indian, would gallop for miles on Judy, the horse her father rode hunting deer in the hills above the Arroyo Grande Valley. She was fifteen when her parents bought her first Arabian, a mare named Farlotta. Varian describes the intensity and the symmetry of that relationship:

I don't know if I've ever loved anything as I loved Farlotta. She was frightened, belligerent, thin and wormy when I got her, but nothing mattered except that she was mine. I ate my dinner in her manger. I dreamed in the sun lying stretched out on her back. For a long time she bolted and ran, half a dozen times every ride.

It was a tribute to Varian's emerging gift as a trainer when she and Farlotta, a few years later, began winning awards up and down the state— including the All-Arabian Show at the Cow Palace, where another Varian mare, Ronteza, made her debut a few years later, in 1961.

By then, her parents had surrendered to the realization that this particular Varian's genius lay with horses. As Sheila finished her education at Cal Poly and began working as a P.E. teacher at Arroyo Grande High school, the Varians acquired the twenty-one acres in Corbett Canyon that was the nucleus of today's 230-acre Varian Arabians, now home to over 150 horses. Her parents' support was unswerving. Her father, Eric, built fencing and did the ranch's maintenance work; her mother, Wenonah, became a self-taught expert researching the pedigrees of the Arabians that were potential Varian horses.

They decided to buy a "the blocky little mare," as Varian described her affectionately, with a near-flawless pedigree: Ronteza's dam was named Ronna; her sire was the stallion who had stood so calmly on the heaving deck of the *Stephen F. Austin*, Witez II.

* * *

The horse whose life almost ended in the Bay of Biscay in the fall of 1945 was foaled in the spring of 1938. Witez was born at Janow Podlaski, a farm that bred horses for the Polish cavalry. Elizabeth Letts describes a foal whose beauty was recognized almost instantly. He showed from his first wobbly moments a potential for perfect proportions and, fittingly, he was marked by a large white star on his forehead "that looked remarkably like an outline of his native Poland."

*Arabians graze peacefully today at Janow Podlaski, the onetime home of the Polish champion Witez II.*https://pxhere.com/fi/photo/714332.

Poland was swallowed by the first act of World War II in Europe the next year. As Witez's homeland was invaded by Hitler's Germany and Stalin's Soviet Union, Witez almost became a casualty of war.

On September 11, 1939, ten days after the outbreak of war, the staff decided to evacuate the 250 Arabians at Janow Podlaski and drive them east, away from the German blitzkrieg that had been unleashed for the first time in history on Poland. Their destination was a refuge in Romania—500 miles away.

The trip almost claimed Witez. After days of a forced march—mostly at night, to avoid strafing by Luftwaffe fighters and Stuka dive-bombers—the colts began to tire, including Witez and two of his brothers. When the procession blundered into a vast Polish military convoy in the middle of the road east, Witez was among some eighty horses who panicked. He and his brothers disappeared into thick forest.

Their handlers were despondent. They pressed on, but, by September 20, their way blocked by artillery fire and by the news that the Soviets were advancing from the east, they turned back to Janow Podlaski.

Eventually, Witez returned to the farm, as well. Emaciated and exhausted, he was among some thirty of the runaways who'd been found and sheltered by Polish civilians, horse-lovers, as foreigners subdued their country.

For the next six years, Witez's life was dominated by German authorities, including a self-proclaimed Nazi expert on breeding, Gustav Rau, who became the master of Janow Podlaski. Rau was determined to produce prize animals— including Arabians and Lipizzaner—that would constitute, in the Nazis' sinister view of genetics--"the perfect horse." This would be the kind of animal that could, for example, tirelessly pull an artillery piece for miles on European roads and then rush it into combat. Rau's breeding program, he believed, grounded in stallions like Witez, would lead the *Wehrmacht*, the German Army, to ultimate victory.

* * *

Sheila Varian was seeking a victory of a different kind. As Varian Arabians began to grow in Corbett Canyon, the California native was learning *californio* horsemanship from another woman, a widow, Mary "Sid" Spencer, who bred Morgans and ran Herefords on the ranch she and her late husband had established in Lopez Canyon. Spencer was an archetype, not just a rancher. She was a widow who ran a ranching operation on her own and so was fiercely independent and fiercely protective of the land she'd worked so hard to develop. In the early 1960s, my father and some friends went dove-hunting in Lopez Canyon when they inadvertently crossed onto Spencer's property. Their first encounter with Sid was at the business end of a 30-30 carbine. "Why don't we just sit here quietly," she told the trespassers, "until the sheriff gets here?" All the parties involved thought this was a sound idea.

Spencer was also a masterful teacher, generous with her time to those who rode into her life on horseback. She introduced Varian to a gentle kind of horsemanship—the California *vaquero* tradition—that her student believed could work as well for Arabians as it did for Spencer's Morgans or the more common California working horse, the Quarter horse.

"Working" at the Spencer ranch was frequently celebratory. Photographer and writer Jeanne Thwaites described a typical calf roundup—an all-female occasion—at Spencer's 1,900-acre ranch in the 1960s:

Sheila Varian and Ronteza in competition. Photo Courtesy Varian Arabians.

While men may make a roundup into a serious and even dreary business, the girls turn it into a riotous picnic. They try their roping techniques without inhibition, race after and throw the calves, and with gleeful gloat that no man is present to witness their shrieks, giggles and other unprofessionalisms. They wail about their bumps and bruises and make a lot of their own lack of brawn, but at the end of the day the job is complete and they are still full of fun.

Varian incorporated the kind of light-hearted approach to training her horses that typified Spencer's ranch. "All good horses," Sheila remarked, "like smart children, need good instruction, but they don't need harsh instruction." The vaquero way of training a cattle horse fits that philosophy, and Varian adapted it to training Arabians, beginning with them about age three with a bridle and snaffle bit in a process where the horse would eventually graduate, as a full-fledged cow horse, to a spade bit. It is training that emphasizes, in every stage, patience, gentleness, a light hand and the development of intuitive communication between horse and rider. What Varian insisted on doing, in 1961, was proving a point: Her Arabians, with the proper training, could compete with any other breed in cattle work.

* * *

Nearly six years after the opening of the war, Nazi Germany was crumbling, ironically, under the same kind of pressure—pressure from vast armies on both the nation's western and eastern borders—that had crushed Poland in the fall of 1939. By the spring of 1945, Witez had been moved by the Nazis to Hostau, a farm in the modern Czech Republic.

But as the war turned rapidly against Germany, Witez was once again in danger, as he had been as a colt. The Soviet Army was approaching and destroying everything in its path, including horses, which they either expropriated as draft animals or shot on sight to provide meat for hungry soldiers. Conditions to the west were not necessarily safer: 200 Arabians fled Janow Podlaski and headed west, away from the Soviets. Among them were Stained Glass and Grand Slam, two of Witez's brothers. The exhausted horses arrived in Dresden on the night of February 13, 1945, just as the Allied command unleashed the notorious fire raid, involving over 700 British and American heavy bombers, on the ancient city.

Dresden, 1945. Deutsch Phototek, Saxon State Library.

After a wave of bombers had dropped its incendiary bombs, one of the Polish handlers watched, horrified, as Grand Slam's tail burst into flames. He held on as best he could to the powerful horse and closed his eyes. When he dared to open them again, the flames that had engulfed Grand Slam's tail had sputtered out and the bombers were gone. So were over half of the Polish Arabians, incinerated in the fires or asphyxiated by the oxygen-consuming firestorm the incendiaries had been intended to produce. By the time the surviving animals reached their ultimate destination in western Germany, fewer than fifty remained.

By now Witez II's survival at the Hostau farm in Czechoslovakia also was in doubt. In late April 1945, he was among some 1,200 horses kept there, including Arabians, Thoroughbreds and the Lipizzaner brood mares and their foals, the breeding stock for the Spanish Riding School. Ironically, it was the imminent end of the war that now endangered the Hostau horses: the Soviets were closing in.

Meanwhile, just to the west, it was the surrender of a German general to the Americans that began the remarkable rescue of the Hostau horses. Sensibly deciding that his chances were better in surrendering to Americans rather than to Soviets, the general began chatting amiably with an American Third Army officer, Col. Hank Reed, and the subject turned to horses. The German loved horses. Reed, the prewar commander of the famed 10th Cavalry—the "buffalo soldiers" who, in 1940, were still a mounted regiment—loved them just as much. The German officer made an emphatic plea to Reed: Might not the Americans rescue the animals before the Red Army turned them into "horseburgers?"

Gen. George Patton, center, seems to be on good terms here with two of his commanders here: Eisenhower, at left, and Omar Bradley, just behind Patton. U.S. Army Photo.

When word of the situation at Hostau reached Third Army's commander, Gen. George Patton was both sympathetic and peeved. The controversial officer, so frequently disciplined by his commander, Dwight Eisenhower, was in no position to authorize what most would see as a fool's errand. When Patton made up his mind, he promised to disavow what was called "Operation Cowboy" if anything went wrong.

"Get them," he ordered Col. Reed. "Make it fast."

* * *

Sheila Varian's first Arabian, the two-year-old named Farlotta, had represented a different kind of rescue. Although the pair triumphed in 1956 at the All-Arabian show at the Cow Palace, the mare died soon after, at seven, the victim of the poor care that had plagued her early years. Farlotta's death—the angry and mistrustful horse had become Sheila's friend—left her despondent. Varian's depression began to lift only when she noticed that she wasn't alone in her grief: Standing with her head down in one of the ranch's corrals was her second Arabian mare, Ronteza, who had been the horse closest to Farlotta. Sheila's therapy, for both horse and rider, biographer Mary Kirkman noted, was to begin working with Witez II's daughter.

At first, Ronteza was no replacement for Farlotta. The mare was quiet and seemingly passive, especially when compared to the spirited Farlotta, who had even learned to enjoy games of "fetch" with the sticks Varian tossed for her. Gradually, Sheila began to realize the that the quiet little filly "was just a very serious, kind and sweet horse that didn't beg for treats and didn't come when called."

Ronteza would come into her own at Sid Spencer's ranch, where the mare began to show an instinctive feel for working cattle. Varian began entering her, still in her hackamore bit, in competition against other Arabians, and the pair began winning. They then graduated to open shows, working cattle in an arena against competitors that were almost always Quarter horses. Ronteza was an interloper: Arabians, it was believed, were too delicate and fine-boned and lacked the toughness necessary to any cow horse. In the fall of 1961, Ronteza was finally "a finished spade bit reined cow horse," and Varian decided to disprove the canard about Arabians in the most audacious way possible—at the reined cow horse championship, part of the Grand National Rodeo, at the Cow Palace in San Francisco.

* * *

In the spring of 1945 at the Hostau farm in Czechoslovakia, the men who cared for Witez and the Lipizzaner knew that the war was ending when the local *Wehrmacht* commander had a mountain of luggage piled into his chauffeur-driven Mercedes and promptly disappeared. He was followed by the teenaged soldiers of the *Volkssturm*, the youthful militia who were jubilant at being relieved of their ostensible duty, to stand and fight in defense of the horse farm.

When American trucks and armored vehicles began to appear—they were the vanguard of the mechanized 2nd Cavalry, a component of Gen. George Patton's Third Army—the stablemasters walked carefully toward the column with a large white sheet as a token of surrender. The Americans, though, had come in peace: Their mission was to secure the horse farm and protect the horses, and the man who ordered them there was the 2nd Cavalry's commander, Col. Reed, the one-time horse soldier of the 10th Cavalry.

His soldiers understood their mission. At 71, Louis Holz, a 2nd Cavalry lieutenant in 1945, remembered his motivation: "We thought we had a chance to save a sliver of culture for the rest of the world. We sensed the end [of the war] was in sight, and we were in a frame of mind to give credence to beauty once again."

If Hostau was secured, the beautiful horses there were not yet safe. They would have to be evacuated to German soil now under Third Army's control. The Czech farm lay within what was to be the postwar Soviet sphere of influence and the presence of American troops would constitute an opening shot in what would become the Cold War. Col. Reed began organizing Operation Cowboy, and the improbable convoy of jeeps, trucks—the latter carried mares about to foal and colts too fragile for a long journey—began to head west, for Germany. The 2nd Cavalry soldiers, after a war spent mounted on trucks and jeeps, not horses, had become actual cavalrymen. They were jubilant. So was the Arabian stallion under their care, Witez II, happy to leave Hostau behind. Elizabeth Letts describes the leave-taking:

Witez set off eagerly, eyes bright, tail aloft. On his back, one of the cavalry riders, a cowboy who hailed from Idaho, looked like he was having the time of his life. Few of the horses stabled at Hostau, horses used for breeding, were trained to be ridden under saddle, but Witez was one. The bay had been given the important job of riding herd on the young stallions, the group that would be the most excitable.

On May 16, four days after leaving Hostau, Witez and his traveling companions were safely inside Germany. But the stallion's travels had just begun. By then, Gen. Patton, a veteran polo player and Olympic pentathlete, had been graced with a performance by the Spanish Riding School's stallions, who'd spent the last days of the war in rural Austria. It was the riding school's master, Alois Podhasky, who asked the mercurial general to officially place both the performing horses and the animals at Hostau under American protection. Podhasky could not have known that Patton had already authorized Operation Cowboy.

The surprisie rescue of his breeding stock so pleased Podhasky that he allowed the Americans to claim some of the horses for their own. Witez II was among the 150 animals the Army chose, the spoils of war, for shipment to the Quartermaster Remount Depot at the Kellogg Ranch in Pomona. It was this voyage that had nearly claimed Witez and his traveling companions in the vicious storm that overtook the *Austin* in the Bay of Biscay.

In 1949, when the Army Depot closed, California breeders Earle and Frances Hurlbutt bought Witez at action for $8,000. When the couple began to show him, he won championship blue ribbons up and down the Pacific Coast. His main business remained at the Hurbutts' Calabasas ranch, standing at stud and so producing a new generation of Arabians with Polish bloodlines. In 1954, Ronna, a mare bred to Witez, gave birth to the filly who would mature into Sheila Varian's cow horse.

* * *

Ronteza, according to conventional wisdom, had no more business competing at the Cow Palace than the 2nd Cavalry cowboys had riding through Czechoslovakia. By now—the fall of 1961—Varian had the equivalent of two full-time jobs, teaching P.E. and working intensively with her mare every day after school, running laps in a nearby hay field to build her endurance. In October, the pair began working with cattle on a ranch near

Oakhurst. Late in the month, Varian, her mother and Ronteza arrived in San Francisco for the Grand National Rodeo and the reined-horse competition.

Ronteza and her competitors were expected to show their skill at riding patterns—in 1961, "anything the judge thought up, and they were given to you just before you entered the arena," Varian remembered—that demonstrated the rider's ability to maneuver the horse in turns, spins, figure-eights and sudden stops, where the horse is virtually sitting down in a dramatic cloud of arena dirt. The second part of the competition involved cow work, in chasing, heading and turning a steer.

In the competition's first round, against thirty horses in the lightweight class Ronteza, was ready to go—she disliked warmups and practice runs. She did well. The pair were selected for the next round, against four other lightweight finalists. Varian, by the time that first round was finished, was emotionally and physically spent—she was too tired to stay and watch the heavyweight competition. She left the arena without understanding that because Ronteza's number had been called first in the lightweight division's first round, she had won.

What the pair had done so far was stunning. Ronteza was the only Arabian competing in the championship. Sheila Varian was the only woman. They weren't done making their point.

In the lightweight finals, Varian and Ronteza rode a new pattern, seemingly without effort. But when it came to cow work, the pair faced imminent disqualification. This is what Varian remembered in the pursuit of their steer:

Ronteza drove grittily and hard, pushing between the fence and the cow. She was galloping all out with her head down, charging for the shoulder of the cow to finish the circle. Suddenly her feet hit the hard-packed dirt from the horses' buggies [a harness competition had preceded theirs] and in one motion she was falling. I was standing over her, feet on either side, the reins still in my hands. The rules echoed through my mind in slow motion: Go off your horse and you are eliminated.

A dramatic photo captures the moment: Ronteza is nearly flattened on her left side, her head still upright and her neck arched while Varian is being propelled forward with the reins still in her widely-splayed hands. The photograph suggests exactly what happened next: The position of Ronteza's head shows that she's already beginning to stand up; Varian, nearly over her mount's neck, is refusing to stand down. The pair recovered—by now they had the audience on their side—and the determined little mare showed the same seriousness and focus that her father had shown below decks on the *Stephen F. Austin:* She circled and turned her cow.

Near disaster at the Cow Palace. Photo courtesy Varian Arabians.

It was now their turn to wait for the other four horses to compete. When they had finished, the judges called Ronteza's number first.

* * *

That was Friday night. On Sunday afternoon, Ronteza and Varian competed against the finalists in both the lightweight and heavyweight classes. They defeated all comers and were national champions. Varian remembered a moment from the Cow Palace competition vividly: at the start of one round, she could feel distinctly Ronteza's heartbeat through the panels of the saddle. She knew then that her mare was ready. When the signal was given, when horse and rider entered the Cow Palace arena, two hearts beat as one.

Sheila Varian, 2002, with her stallion Jullyen El Jamaal. *Lisa Andres photo.*

Transcendence

Anoushka Shankar is beautiful. She is by the way, the sister of another beautiful woman, the singer Norah Jones and, of course, they are the daughters of Ravi Shankar, the master of the sitar, the instrument that so entranced Beatle George Harrison. Anoushka herself has mastered the incredible instrument. It sings for her.

There are so many kinds of beauty. With Shankar, the self-discipline she has---the mastery of her Self---is a what is truly beautiful. In concert, that's evident in her attention, riveted on the sitar, a massive and complex instrument that can have up to twenty-one strings. I've never seen concentration like hers.

Shankar in concert, 2014. Photo by Didier Chérel

There is a grace about her, a generosity, too. In one concert video, she gives each of her backing musicians—violin; a percussionist, on the *tabla* drums; the *shehnai* player, whose wind instrument resembles a clarinet--a chance to solo and to shine, and each is stunning. During their solos, she softly claps her hands in time; she's smiles at her musicians and friends. Sometimes she closes her eyes as they play: It's a beatific look, even the look of a proud mother (which she is, offstage.) She has given herself over to the other musicians, entered into *their* performances, and it is the most perfect kind of praise.

At other times, she is almost by herself. She's *gone* in a raga, a form marked by complexity and improvisation—the latter accounts for her popularity at jazz clubs. She is so fast and so nimble and the notes tumble as if they were droplets in a great waterfall. And, every once in awhile, a small smile crosses her face, and now her eyes begin to close as if she were listening to a stranger.

Something wonderful is happening, I think. Athletes refer to it as being "in the zone," where, for example, every pitch hits the corner for which it's intended because the pitcher realizes he can release the desire to *aim* the pitch. Throwing suffices. My hero, Sandy Koufax, had games like that. He was untouchable then.

So is Shankar. When you see that smile, she is in a special place where the playing is fluid, effortless and joyful. It's all right, I think, for her, let alone her audience, to enjoy moments like this, after all the years of rigor and denial and endless, endless practice (her father was a stern teacher). Those moments, after all, aren't meant for her alone, or even for her audience alone. When Shankar smiles, it's because she's fully aware that God is listening to her, or, even more important, that God is playing *through* her. There's where the joy is, in the surrendering.

Clara Paulding, Teacher

Miss Ruth Paulding had retired by the time I met her. She taught languages for many years at Arroyo Grande Union High School, just across the street on Crown Hill from the house where she was born. She became an institution. So had her mother, Clara Edwards Paulding, a lifelong teacher who decided to teach one more year, in Oceano, when she was seventy-one, so that she could splurge a little on herself. Her teacher's salary that last year bought her a porcelain kitchen sink and a new set of dentures.

I got to see that sink, among a houseful of minor but precious treasures, during a tour of the Paulding home.

I'd met Clara's daughter Ruth, or Miss Paulding, when I was a little boy. We were both parishioners at St. Barnabas Episcopal Church, then in a surplus World War II chapel on what was once Barnett Street; the street's gone and so is the church, replaced by a gas station. The new St. Barnabas stands on a hill overlooking Arroyo Grande. Memories have more staying power than mere buildings, especially if they're of women like Miss Paulding. She was by then in a wheelchair but had a kind of

Clara Edwards. County Historical Society.

elegance about her, dressed as she was for Grace Cathedral instead of an old army chapel, and if her body was betraying her, her spine curved cruelly, her spirit was graceful and even youthful. If you got a little smile from Miss Paulding on returning to your pew from the communion rail, it carried the same freight as a priest's blessing.

Ruth was born in that house on Crown Hill and she would die there in the aftermath of the 1960s, when the nation seemed to be coming apart at the seams, because that was exactly what it was doing. Her mother, a great student of history, would've recognized that instantly had she still been with us then.

Clara Paulding taught at Branch, Huasna, Santa Manuela, Oceano, was the principal of the Arroyo Grande Grammar School and one of the founders of the high school--and she might have been able to give us all some perspective then, perspective we need today, about the durability of America and of Americans.

Clara was durable. She and her doctor husband, Ed, buried a little boy in the front yard, under a white rosebush, who should have been Ruth's older brother. He died a few hours after a birth that nearly killed Clara, as well. But this was a woman who had homesteaded in Cholame by herself. She visited friends by coming down the Cuesta Pass in her trap and pony where there were no turnouts and the road edged sheer drops of hundreds of feet.

She must have inherited that tough-mindedness from the ancestor whose name she cites on her own tombstone in the Arroyo Grande cemetery. Jonathan Edwards was a famed New England Puritan divine, a powerful preacher whose "Sinners in the Hands of an Angry God" is still taught in high schools for its vivid use of metaphor: *[God] holds you over the Pit of Hell, much as one holds a Spider, or some loathsome Insect, over the Fire.* The poor parishioners who fainted in the pews when Edwards first delivered this sermon in 1741 took those metaphors literally.

Clara was mild compared to the ancestor she was so proud of. She was an enthusiastic churchgoer and ecumenical, as well: She played the organ and directed the choirs for Methodists, Presbyterians and Episcopalians.

However, she was an agnostic. She wanted to believe, but she couldn't make that leap.

She was also a suffragist.

Jonathan Edwards would've been horrified.

Once I learned about Clara, I became an admirer. She had an active mind. Near the end of World War II, Clara and Ruth decided to take summer courses at Clara's alma mater, Mills College. Ruth took classes for the extra money it would mean in her teacher's pay at the high school; Clara, at ninety-three, took her class for pleasure. Naturally, it was a history course: "The United States to 1865." She chose that one, she said, because she remembered all the rest.

One of Clara's assignments during nearly fifty years in the classroom had been at the school I attended, Branch Elementary. There is a photo of her in front of the school. Behind Clara and her bicycle in 1898 is the same doorway I would enter on my first day of formal education sixty years later. She looks severe in the photograph. She wasn't. She *was* incredibly tough: At Branch, when a teacher quit, Clara taught, by herself, sixty children in eleven different grades. Not only did she juggle all those grade levels and the subjects she taught those children artfully, but she loved teaching them, too. Branch kids were among her favorites.

In 1898, the year of the bicycle photograph, Arroyo Grande was a bustling little town of several hundred people. Beyond the town, to the east in the Upper Valley, and to the west, bounded by the sand dunes at the edge of the Pacific, in the Lower Valley, there were patchworks of farms worked by ambitious settlers. Arroyo Grande men and their teams of heavily-muscled draft horses, their necks arched in effort, turned some of the richest soil in the world to prepare it for planting. They might have been plowing to sow pumpkins or carrots, onions or beans, or one of the most important products in the many cycles of agriculture the Valley has seen: flowers, cultivated for their seeds.

Clara Edwards Paulding, Branch School, 1898. South County Historical Society.

What must have delighted Clara Paulding on her two-mile bicycle commute to her sixty students every morning would have been the sight of brilliant fields of flowers. She would have smelled the delicate fragrance of sweet peas. It's easy to visualize her waving to the men who worked those fields as she bicycled to school.

Clara's spirit suffuses the Paulding House even today.

You're met with an unpretentious kind of homeliness and you are honored to be its guest. The house seems a little insistent, as Clara was (since she *was* descended from the straight-and-narrow Jonathan Edwards) that you wipe your feet.

That's why the bathtub, one of Clara's more prized possessions, adjoins an exterior door that overlooks the garden where Ed loved to putter. Ed was by nature a putterer. Clara was by nature a pragmatist, and Ed was not allowed back into the house after his gardening until he'd cleaned himself up in the bathroom first. And the bathtub was no trivial thing: people would drive out to the Coffee Rice home in the 1890s just to stare at a bathtub. It was the equivalent of a Disneyland ride. People just didn't *have* them, and the Pauldings had Arroyo Grande's second.

The tub's a long one. It was made for leisurely baths accompanied by books or magazines and maybe a cup hot of chocolate, restoratives good teachers need at the end of the day.

The Girl in Her Prom Dress, Camp Cooke, 1944

This photo, from the Santa Maria Museum of Flight, is one of my favorites in the book *Central Coast Aviators in World War II* . These young women were more than likely USO guests of the Army Air Forces cadets at Hancock Field,

Santa Maria, on the site of today's Hancock College. I see at least two girls–one of them looks a little like Betty Grable–with whom I would've fallen in love more or less instantly.

The poignant part is that many of the young men in this photo will die. For every American infantryman killed in World War II, three were wounded. For every American airman wounded in World War II, three were killed.

When I gave a talk in Grover Beach on the book to the volunteers at the Five Cities Food Bank I noticed an older woman looking at me narrowly. I thought I was doing terribly. I stopped looking at her for fear of breaking out in the flop sweat so familiar to standup comedians. I was wrong.

She came up to me after the talk and told me that she'd lived in Los Angeles during the War, and she was part of a visit to Camp Cooke, today's Vandenberg Air Force base. In her time, in World War II, it had been a U.S. Army armored training base. She was one of the young women like the young women in the photograph. Densely chaperoned, they were brought to military bases by the USO to socialize with the young soldiers destined to go overseas to fight.

"We had dinner with them, and we went out to a dance, and then we went to church with them. And they were so happy to see us–I had a marvelous time!" Then she bought a book.

I'm well aware that wartime was not an Andy Hardy movie. Illegitimacy skyrocketed, and so, with fathers gone, did juvenile delinquency. And one of the civilian workers at Camp Cooke–voted a "Camp Cooke Cutie" in the camp newspaper in 1944–was Elizabeth Short, the "Black Dahlia" murder victim three years later, which sadly proves that a tradition of trivializing women, and of brutalizing them, goes deep in American culture.

This woman's experience was fortunately and obviously different, yet it was the same one I'd heard from a veteran Santa Maria *Times* reporter, Karen White, who once told me that she went to USO dances with her big sister at Camp San Luis Obispo. She, too had a marvelous time.

So I was gifted today with story of a woman who went to a dance with young soldiers seventy-five years ago. For just the briefest of moments, she was, in my imagination and in her memory, a teenager again. She was, as the faithful say, a blessing in my life.

114

My Tudor Grandmother

I have friends traveling to places like Edinburgh, Assisi and Dublin, so it's kind of stoking in me that powerful urge to travel.

Here's one place I'd like to see, at right, even though it's such an anomaly. It's a little 14th-century church set in a part of modern London that's all steel and glass and deeply unattractive. The church is homely, too, with an afterthought of a cupola, built without much thought to its place in architectural history.

St. Giles-without-Cripplegate, a name that befuddles etymologists, is where my ninth great-grandmother, Lady Elizabeth Gelsthorpe Gregory, was buried in 1585. Her husband, Sir John, a mere comma in English genealogy, was from Nottinghamshire. It wasn't far from where, in 2012, they found the little cache of bones that belonged to Richard III, with the deep puncture wound, inflicted post-mortem at Bosworth Field, in the royal rear end.

But that was far before Lady Elizabeth's time.

Her time belonged to *this* Elizabeth, the granddaughter of Henry VII, the victor at Bosworth.

What an exciting–and fearful– time to be alive for Lady Elizabeth Gelsthorpe Gregory. The year she was born, Henry VIII declared himself the head of the English Church. When she was five, Thomas More was beheaded.

A girl growing up faced a future nearly as bleak as More's. More's daughter, Meg, was a rarity: She could read and write and speak fluent Latin and passable Greek. Even a girl from a prominent family like the Gelsthorpes would have had just enough learning, including music lessons, to make her marriageable with not a lesson

Coronation Portrait, Elizabeth I. National Portrait Gallery via Wikimedia Commons.

beyond that. Yet not learning your lessons quickly enough, even in the case of noble girls like Lady Jane Grey, meant swift and painful physical punishment. The future "Nine Days' Queen" had her ears boxed frequently by her ambitious parents. Their ambition would lead Jane to the executioner's block when she was sixteen years old.

At puberty, Lady Elizabeth would've been enshrouded in clothing almost as barbaric as the not-yet-invented whalebone corset: Linen petticoat surmounted by a stiffened bodice, or kirtle, that mashed the breasts and stifled breathing and then, over that, the gown--for noblewomen, made of dense and elaborate fabric--velvet, or even cloth of gold for prospective noble marriages. A Tudor woman's gown would've been nearly as heavy as the chains sported by Marley's ghost. English or French hoods–the latter, Anne Boleyn's innovation–covered most of a woman's head. Lady Elizabeth and her sixteenth-century peers came of age in a kind of sartorial cocoon.

She didn't take long to grow up. She was fifteen when she was married, in the middle of the reign of Henry's sickly successor, Edward VI. It appears that she went to the altar pregnant with what would turn out to be a baby boy. This was quite common to the times, a story the parish registers tell us from all the weddings followed scant months later by all the christenings. Even Anne Boleyn was heavily and obviously pregnant when she married Henry VIII.

Lady Elizabeth would lose that son when she was twenty-five, in 1555, three years before Queen Elizabeth came to the throne. She would lose her husband that year, 1558. Another son would survive her by just two years.

It was a heartbreaking life because it was a time bereft of spiritual sureness, what with the Bible whipsawing back and forth between Latin and English and with scores of bishops--High Church, Low Church—taking their turns as kindling, burned at the stake.

More traditional English believers were so incensed by the Bible translator Wycliffe that they burned him at the stake forty years after he'd died.

So Lady Elizabeth must have spent much of her life holding her breath and mumbling her prayers, the way the Lollards did. Something in you wants to comfort her. That will have to wait, of course.

She's in the parish register, in the burials for March 25, 1585:

Elizabeth Gregory, wyddow

Three years later the Armada was blown clear 'round England to wreck on rocks far to the north, off Scotland and Ireland. I wish Lady Elizabeth Gelsthorpe Gregory could've lived to have celebrated news like that. We Gregorys have a fondness for underdogs, and the English were in 1588. What they had then was the richness and beauty of their language: Elizabeth I's Tilbury Speech, delivered as the Spanish approached the coast, is the equal to the words Shakespeare put in Henry V's mouth just before Agincourt or to the words delivered in Parliament, in Churchill's powerful voice, during the Blitz.

Thirty-five years after Elizabeth's death, Oliver Cromwell was married in St. Giles.

Eighty-nine years after, John Milton was buried here.

She would've been incensed, I bet, when, In 1940, St. Giles was set afire in the Blitz.

Lady Elizabeth's people remained staunch Anglicans. A great-grandson, John Gregory, an immigrant from Nottinghamshire, was a member of the vestry another church, St. Mary's Whitechapel, in Lancaster County, Virginia, the parish of Washington's mother. Yet another Gregory married Washington's Aunt Mildred, a name that has persisted for generations in my family, despite its homeliness, and he ceded Mt. Vernon to the future president's family. Do not take real-estate advice from anybody named "Gregory."

Washington County, Kentucky, of course, was named for the great man. And in the 1850 Kentucky census, here are the nineteen slaves owned by Godfrey Gregory, my second great-grandfather. He was, by Kentucky standards, a wealthy man. The slaves have no names in the census, a convenience that made them both legally and emotionally disposable.

I have no way, of course, of knowing this would be so, but I like to think Lady Elizabeth Gregory would have boxed Godfrey Gregory's ears. Life is cruel enough. Something in me believes she would've had little patience with the practiced cruelty that was slavery's bedrock.

NAMES OF SLAVE OWNERS.	Number of Slaves	Age	Sex	Colour	Fugitives from State.	Number manumitted	Deaf & dumb, blind, insane, or idiotic
1	2	3	4	5	6	7	8
Godfrey Gregory (nineteen)	1	64	M	B			
	2	32		B			
	3	27		B			
	4	25	B	B			
	5	10	M	B			
	6	28					
	7	24	M	B			
	8	23	M		✓		
	9	18	M	B			
	10	11		B			
	11	8	M				
	12			B			
	13			M			
	14	6					
	15	3					
	16	2					
	17	2					

The Photographer

In 1936, the woman's beret and vaguely mannish dress—oxford shirt, pleated skirt, sweater tied around her shoulders, high-topped tennis shoes— might have made her look a little like the outlaw Bonnie Parker. The car she drove was a powerful V8, the engine Bonnie and Clyde favored, but her car was homely and utilitarian, a wood-paneled Model C Ford wagon, not sleek and raked like the Ford Deluxe in which the outlaws had met their deaths two years before. The driver, nodding a little with each click of the seams in the two-lane concrete Highway 101, needed a wagon's room, not for bank-bags full of loot, but for equipment. She was hauling the boxy, awkward but fragile paraphernalia of the documentary photographer in her run north to San Francisco.

Dorothea Lange, 1936. Library of Congress.

She had a good six hours to go and so was taking a chance on dubious tires on the narrow coast highway. The road was littered in sad little Darwinian islets with expired possums, skunks, and ground squirrels. For her, the more menacing detritus was that of a nation in motion: fragments of glass, shredded and peeled truck-tire treads, oil slicks, fragments of cargo that included scraps of lumber and tenpenny nails. Her tires, nearly bald at the edges from months on the road, were vulnerable to the traps the 101 had laid for her, but she wasn't prepared for the trap the roadside sign presented.

PEA PICKERS CAMP

At first, she was strong enough to resist the seduction of the crudely-lettered sign. She had so far to go and had, after all, only reached the southern edge of San Luis Obispo County. Here the terrain was just beginning to reveal that she'd left the gravitational pull of Los Angeles, which ends at about the Gaviota Pass, with its severe rock outcroppings scattered with spiny yucca plants. She'd passed there, too, many times, where the light hits hard at noontime and yields to soft pastels at sunset, purples and pinks, all suggestive of aridity and drought in a country meant for lizards and not for farming.

She knew the farmland she was entering now pretty well. She'd photographed its Mexican migrants and itinerant cowboys and the gypsy people mistakenly generalized as "Okies," "mistaken" because she'd met the same kind of people from as far away as Vermont. They lived in labor camps like the one the cardboard sign suggested. Now they were as hard and as stark and as dry as the rocks at Gaviota. Poverty and stoop labor and hunger and human hostility had dried these people out by 1936.

She kept driving north. On the seat and the floor beside her were hundreds of 5 x 7 negatives secure inside their wooden frames, stored in black light-resistant boxes. On those negatives she had captured the migrant people in their ramshackle camps or in the fields, where she'd photographed whole families working with the trailing bags they filled with cotton bolls or potatoes or with the tall wooden pails they filled with bush peas.

Sometimes their children were knock-kneed from rickets or their bellies were swollen from malnutrition. Now, in the hard rains that had come late this year, the dominant sounds that came from the tents in the migrant camps were the wracking coughs of migrant children. The coughing came in attacks that convulsed them and curled them like sowbugs until they could gather enough strength for another breath.

Some of them, some of those children, were going to die.

South of the Ontario Grade, to her left, was a stretch of the Pacific in a shallow crescent from Guadalupe to Port Harford; the sight of it must have hurried her north to where she would finally see the ocean again, and with it San Francisco.

But ten minutes later, impulsively, somewhere near San Luis Obispo, the driver pulled to the shoulder and stopped the car.

Then she sighed. There was only one thing to be done. She brought the Ford around in a U-turn and headed south to look for the sign she'd passed, where she would turn off the 101. She could not know it now, a little angry at herself for reversing course, but when she turned off she would meet a Madonna of the Sorrows, a mother in a tent in a muddy field who would leave even a master like Raphael rapt in her presence and powerless to capture her image. This image was meant for the photographer and for her alone.

Florence Thompson, Nipomo, 1936. Library of Congress.

At the Retirement Home

"You are from Atascadero?"

"No, ma'am. Arroyo Grande."

"Oh. I am from Paso Robles. My husband built us a house there. Now I live *here*." She meant, with disdain, the retirement home. "But I still have that house."

She was Japanese, and before I could show off my fancy-pants history knowledge, wondering if she had come from Kyushu, like the ancestors of so many of my childhood friends, I realized: She was *Japanese.*

She was a war bride.

She fished inside her purse and brought out some photos. The one that caught my eye was black and white, frayed at the edges from so much handling, and the image was that of a handsome young serviceman.

"This is my husband. He built us that house in Paso Robles."

"Air Force?" I asked.

"Yes!" she brightened. "Air Force."

You could tell, easily, that she had been a beauty sixty years ago, when her husband and she were young. She still is.

You could tell just as easily that there was more than a little steel in her personality.

There had to be.

Kimpo Field, South Korea, during the Korean War.
U.S. Air Force Photo.

She had made the leap from postwar Japan—they must have met during the Korean War-- to the United States when this nation was at full tide, in the boom of the 1950s and 1960s, and she'd left everything she'd known behind to take up a new life in a very strange place with a very Byzantine language.

And she'd stayed.

She must have loved him dearly.

She the only Asian in the retirement home. Was she lonely because of that? You remember Filipino soldiers in 1943, many from our county, on short passes into Marysville, where the first place they hit wasn't a bar. It was a Chinese restaurant. They were lonely for *rice.* They were, of course, refused service, because they were Asians.

She must have made him rice. Maybe, in the years after the war, he got odd looks from his co-workers when he opened up his lunch box and contentedly ate the rice balls she'd made for him that morning, flavored with *nori* paste.

Kimi Kobara had made a similar cultural leap when she came to the Arroyo Grande Valley in the 1920s, as a picture bride from Japan. After the young couple had settled in, she'd sit up stark awake, alone and silent, every morning for weeks as soon as her husband, Shig, was out of the house and into the fields, where it was just light, with his horses and their plow, or their cultivator, or their harvester.

She cried every night.

Kimi, a middle-class girl from Kyushu, had no idea that life could be so hard in California.

But she must have loved Shig dearly, because she persevered, and she raised a beautiful family. Kimi had steel, too.

So this woman was a great beauty with great courage, and her husband had built her a house and she kept photographs from as far back as his service days, their courting days. You hope, and you know, that they will meet again.

Union Army Nurse

Lauretta H. Cutter Hoisington, buried in the Halcyon Cemetery, was among the Americans swept up in the great reform movements—temperance, women's rights, and her cause, abolition—in the years before the Civil War. She came from Ashtabula County, Ohio, a place that was sometimes visited by the firebrand John Brown. Brown was the abolitionist who'd used a broadsword to hack slaveowners to death in "Bleeding Kansas," in the violence that presaged the nationwide Civil War. In 1859, hoping to spark a slave rebellion, he tried to seize the federal arsenal at Harpers Ferry, Virginia. Barricaded in the town's firehouse, Brown and his followers fought United States Marines commanded by the former West Point Commandant, Robert E. Lee, before he was captured and later executed—to become, depending on one's region, either a great martyr or one of history's greatest villains.

Cutter's contribution to the Civil War and so to the abolition of slavery was her decision to become a volunteer nurse in the Union Army. Although she was well behind the lines, nursing was hazardous anyway: Many "matrons," as they were called, contracted diseases, as Cutter did. Some literally worked themselves to death. The most famous nurse of all, Clara Barton, worked much closer to the battlefield. At Antietam, a bullet passed through her sleeve and killed the soldier she was treating.

Lauretta H. Cutter Hoisington

Cutter was dispatched to Union Army Hospital No. 1 in Chattanooga, Tennessee, and her patients were among those campaigning with Sherman in the March to the Sea. They came to her hospital via a rickety railroad, frequently cut by Confederate cavalry, and arrived exhausted, in great pain, and filthy. The first thing a wounded soldier got was a bath, something accomplished with great professionalism despite Victorian mores, and the second was a bed. It might've been the first bed many of them had slept in for over a year or more, and one of the first signs of a soldier's recovery was the contented sigh that sometimes escaped when he nestled his head on a feather pillow.

So a matron's job was to give these soldiers as much comfort and care as possible: Changing their bandages, feeding them, moving them from one position to another, more comfortable one in their beds, writing letters home for them and, most painfully, holding their hands and talking to them softly as they began to die.

Cutter's hospital was divided into wards by the disease the soldier was suffering, and it was disease that killed more Civil War soldiers than battlefield wounds. She later wrote of gangrene wards, measles wards (measles could be fatal; it killed some 7,000 Union soldiers) and a typhoid ward. It was the last that nearly killed her. "In passing [the typhoid ward] the groans, and calls for lemonade impelled me to enter and minister to their wants as best I could." Her sympathy led to her contracting typhoid fever, the disease that had killed Willie Lincoln, the son whose intellect and sensitivity most reflected his father's. The eleven-year-old's White House death had unhinged his mother, Mary. Cutter came close to dying, too. She became so sick that she was removed from her tent to a private home. She didn't remember much after that except for the kindness of the matron who nursed her back to health—a woman from, of all places, Pasadena, California.

She continued her nursing career after the war, in homes for unwed mothers in Cleveland. She married a minister, William Henry Hoisington, in 1880, when she was fifty-four. She became a convert to Theosophy, the faith whose adherents founded the Temple of the People in Halcyon. She came to Halcyon in 1905 and became a "devoted member of the staff;" one senses, in her photograph (taken during a reunion of Civil War matrons) a penchant for organization and for order. There was, however, a great tenderness within this formidable woman: She would remember, to the end of her life, what she called "her brave soldier boys." Her time with them was difficult; she would later write:

To steel the heart to suffering, and endeavor to comfort those I could not cure, was my experience as an army nurse. It is not pleasant to recall the time when glory was bought with the mutilation and suffering of brave and patriotic men; and the labor I performed in hospitals Nos. 1 and 2, at Chattanooga, Tenn., during the years 1864 and 1865, oftimes comes to me as a horrid nightmare.

Chapter 5. Arroyo Grande's Civil War Generation

Gettysburg veteran Erastus Fouch.
. Courtesy Jack English

Starting a Book: Our Yankees

Since I grew up during the centennial of the Civil War, it's a conflict that has always fascinated me. I didn't know how *much* it had fascinated me until Elizabeth and I took our boys to Gettysburg when they were little. I surprised myself—this wasn't the product of some kind of clairvoyance; it was years of reading instead—because I knew exactly where we were and what had happened in each place on the battlefield, from the bulldog resistance of Buford's cavalry and their Sharps carbines on July 1 to the 20th Maine's counterattack on Little Round Top on July 2, which was one of the most decisive moments in American history.

Then we stood in the tree-line where Pickett's division shook itself out into lines of assault on the afternoon of July 3. When they emerged into the sunlight and began marching ("Deer-stepping," the poet Stephen Vincent Benét called it) across the farm fields, the Union soldiers on Cemetery Ridge marveled at the precision of their drill. I was lucky enough to be able to remember all of this for my sons.

Yet I never expected that this war would have such an intimate connection to my home town, like Gettysburg, a farm town, but one on the other side of the continent.

Nipomo veteran Charles Bristol with his cavalry saber. Courtesy Blake Bristol.

But there are 57 Union veterans in the Arroyo Grande District Cemetery. There are Confederates there, too, a scattering, but their service is harder to confirm; one, I think, is buried in an unmarked grave.

So what I've done in the last two days is to link each soldier to his regiment, noted on his tombstone, find his service dates and then link his regiment to a particular battle-- or more than one, since most fought in several battles. A slight majority seems to have fought in what was then the "West"--the war west of the Appalachians, and I was amazed to find at least four who fought in the Indian conflicts that paralleled the fighting in the east between North and South.

I've already found the regiment I would have wanted to serve with--surprisingly, a regular

U.S. Army unit. They were held in reserve at Antietam, were on the *other* side of Little Round Top at Gettysburg, idly watching artillery bursts blow up caissons and their horses, and arrived in New York City just *after* the draft riots. I like their sense of timing.

Now I need to start tracking these men on sites like ancestry.com to see if I can find primary sources about them and photographs of them. I've already found a letter written by one--a woman who served as a Union Army nurse in Tennessee. Then I have to get into my Myron Angel, Madge Ditmas and Pat Loomis histories and track down the veterans' obituaries to discover what they did here in Arroyo Grande in their mature years. I've also ordered a book, *Marching Home,* that's a kind of postwar psychological portrait of Civil War veterans, so maybe that will help me figure out what brought them to our little valley. I suspect they wanted the distance between themselves and the things they saw as young men.

Then I need to go a little deeper, to locate each regiment (and company, because those, too, are noted on their tombstones) in combat reports and first-had accounts as well as secondary sources to see if I can pinpoint these men and what they would have experienced at Shiloh, or Antietam, or Spotsylvania. And I've got a Medal of Honor winner to investigate.

We've also got:

• A cavalryman who fought in Custer's Michigan brigade--his Wolverines--the men he led in the kind of audacious charges, in that quaint mid-Victorian pursuit of glory, that would make him a twenty-three-year-old major general and then doom him 11 years after Appomattox.

• A Minnesotan who fought in the 1862 Sioux uprising. The government hanged 38 Santee Sioux warriors, cousins to the men who would rub out Custer, young men who struck back when they could no longer endure the humiliation and hunger that arrived with the "civilizing" of the prairie. They sang before the traps were sprung.

• At least four men who fought at Gettysburg; one had two-thirds of his regiment killed or wounded. Two others who fought a hundred yards apart on July 1 would wind up as Arroyo Grande farmers twenty-five years later..

• Several soldiers, both infantrymen and cavalrymen, who fought in the Overland Campaign, the last and most costly part of the war, Grant's series of sledgehammer blows against Lee in 1864-65 Virginia. It was this part of the war that was a ghastly foreshadowing to the prodigal waste of young lives in the First World War.

Before I get to the primary sources, I've got to re-read my Bruce Catton and my Shelby Foote, my Stephen Sears and my James McPherson: It's time to re-acquaint myself with a war I once knew almost by heart. And this wouldn't pretend to be a comprehensive summary of the war--that's been done, and done convincingly--but instead a series of snapshots of the roles local veterans played in winning it.

Get to work.

(*This marked the beginning of researching the book* Patriot Graves: Discovering a California Town's Civil War Heritage.)

Civil War Stories from Arroyo Grande, California

As young men, these Arroyo Grande settlers were participants in the war that both wounded and re-invented the nation. Afterward, as mature men, they came West and in a very real way, after the trauma they'd experienced, re-invented themselves. These are some of the Civil War veterans in our cemetery.

Edward S. Shaw, a farmer in Los Berros, was a participant in one of the most successful acts of insubordination in the war. At Missionary Ridge, his 74th Illinois was part of a the assault on the Confederates at the base of the ridge. Grant ordered the attackers to take the rifle pits at the base and then stop, but the 74th Illinois kept going, as did their comrades, and they swept the Confederates away. The 74th's battle flag, brand new and a gift from the women of Winnebago County, had fifteen bullet holes in it by the time it was planted atop Missionary Ridge. Three men had been killed carrying the flag up the hillside.

Joseph Brewer. Brewer farmed in Oak Park. At Gettysburg on July 2, Brewer's corps commander, Gen. Dan Sickles, would advance his men, without support, to high ground in the Peach Orchard without orders. In their now-exposed position, William Barksdale's Mississippians—Barksdale, on horseback, wore a bright red fez into combat that day, which proved fatal—fell on Brewer's regiment with a ferocity that would see seven of his regimental commanders killed in succession in a little over fifteen minutes. Brewer would get even—his 11th New Jersey would finish the war with 11-shot Henry repeating rifles used to deadly effect in the Appomattox Campaign.

Bela Clinton Ide. Ide was a blacksmith and the postmaster in Arroyo Grande, whose home—believed the oldest in town—still stands on Ide Street. On July 1, 1863, Ide's 24th Michigan, part of the famed Iron Brigade, was rushed into battle to stop the advance of Henry Heth's surging Confederates at Gettysburg. In a twenty-minute firefight, the outnumbered 24th would lose 363 of the 496 men who went into battle. At the end of his life, Ide was remembered as "the friend to every man, woman and child" he'd ever known.

George Monroe. George Monroe, an oil prospector in Santa Maria and in the Huasna Valley, heard Abraham Lincoln speak—a short speech of thanks in August 1864 to his regiment, 90-day volunteers charged with guard duty. In the 148th Ohio's case, it was guard duty at City Point, Grant's supply base, where Monroe was lucky to survive. A Confederate secret agent delivered a time bomb to a barge anchored in the James River off City Point. It turned out to be an ammunition barge, which vanished when the bomb detonated. Three soldiers in Monroe's regiment were killed among hundreds of others—most of them freedmen, black stevedores who worked the docks to keep the Army of the Potomac going in its final campaign.

Richard Merrill. Richard Merrill—his birth name was Richard Best, and his wife didn't find that out until 23 years into their marriage—was a deputy sheriff in Cambria and a school janitor in Arroyo Grande. His 130th Pennsylvania was ordered to attack the Sunken Road at Antietam and suffered appalling casualties. They were later ordered to bury the Confederate dead, stacked three and four deep, once the position had been carried. Merrill was struck with dysentery in the Chancellorsville campaign and was a sick man—"a great sufferer," according to a family history--for the rest of his life. But the children of the Arroyo Grande Grammar School

136

asked for the afternoon off the day of his funeral in 1909. They loved Mr. Merrill.

Sylvanus Ullom. Ullom was a carpenter and farmer who lived in Pozo and then Arroyo Grande. The proudest day of his life may have come at Chancellorsville, when Stonewall Jackson's corps, in a daylong march through woods so thick that they were thought impassable, burst into the open—they were preceded by terrified rabbits, foxes, and deer who dashed through the Union camp-- to fall on the extreme left of the Army of the Potomac. The Union soldiers panicked and ran for their lives—but not Ullom's 25th Ohio. They formed a defensive line and managed to fire three volleys into Jackson's men before they fell back. In those few moments, they may have saved most of the Army of the Potomac in what would prove to be Lee's greatest victory.

Henry Bakeman. The German-born Bakeman—Bakeman Lane is named for his family—owned a cattle ranch just east of Arroyo Grande. It was his Iowa regiment— their commander bellowed at them, "Come on! You wanted a chance to die for your country!"-- that overran the Confederate positions at one of Grant's first victories, at Fort Donelson. His 2nd Iowa Infantry would play decisive roles in the counterattack after the near-disaster at Shiloh and at Champion Hill, the battle that would lead to Vicksburg's fall in July 1863.

Erastus Fouch. Fouch farmed along what is today Lopez Drive, owned a local soda works, and was instrumental in the 1896 founding of Arroyo Grande Union High School. The sixteen-year-old private lost his eighteen-year-old brother in an 1862 battle with Stonewall Jackson's forces in the Shenandoah Valley. His regiment was overrun at Gettysburg on July 1 and he was made a prisoner of war. Later paroled, Fouch and his regiment would finish out their war in Florida.

Thomas Keown. Thomas Keown and his brigade comrade, James Dowell—both local farmers-- fought in the Powder River Campaign against the Lakota and Cheyenne in the summer of 1865. The campaign was a disaster. Their commander camped midway between the encampments of Red Cloud and Sitting Bull, whose warriors, according to one historian, "fell on them like angry badgers." They were later attacked by the Cheyenne Roman Nose and saw the great Lakota warrior, Crazy Horse, ride a "dare ride" within rifle shot up and down their lines, inviting the soldiers to kill him. They didn't. The expedition wound up eating their own horses to survive before they finally gave up in September.

138

Timothy Munger. Munger, an Arroyo Grande justice of the peace and city clerk, was part of a key counterattack ordered by Philip Sheridan that would lead to a Union Victory at Cedar Creek in 1864. Among the 8th Ohio's Confederate victims that day was George S. Patton, the grandfather of the famed World War II general. Munger was captured later in the war and would survive a fortunately brief time as a prisoner of war in the notorious Libby Prison, a one-time tobacco warehouse in Richmond, Virginia.

Adam Bair. Bair was a Huasna Valley rancher and an ancestor of the Tarwater and Mankins families. He somehow survived the worst fighting of the Civil War—Grant's 1864-65 Overland Campaign against Lee's Army of Northern Virginia, during which the Union Army lost more men killed than in the previous three years combined of the Civil War. Bair fought in The Wilderness, Spotsylvania Courthouse, at Cold Harbor— where Grant's men, knowing they were about to die in a frontal attack on Lee's men, pinned their names on little slips of paper to their uniforms before they went in.

Isaac Dennis Miller's 24th Iowa Infantry probably saw as much combat as any regiment in the Union Army. Miller and his comrades had fought in Grant's Vicksburg Campaign before they came to the Shenandoah Valley in 1864, where their commander was Philip Sheridan. In one of Sheridan's most dramatic victories, at Cedar Creek, Miller went down with three bullets in his right leg and shrapnel in his ankle. He refused amputation and kept his leg but walked painfully for the rest of his life. After farming in Morro Bay and Cayucos, he began farming in the Upper Arroyo Grande Valley and owned a butcher shop in town.

Dr. Charles Clark. Charles Clark was Arroyo Grande's "baby doctor." As a seventeen-year-old New Jersey cavalryman, he'd fought under the command of George Armstrong Custer. His regiment captured a vital Confederate supply train—Clark and his comrades were shocked to find it guarded by African-American troops in new gray uniforms—in the Appomattox Campaign and later participated in the battle of Sayler's Creek, three days before Lee's surrender, where the frustrated and enraged Confederates came to close quarters with their tormenters. They dropped their rifles and used knives, brass knuckles and bare fists to fight. Their energy quickly ran out: The Confederates lost 10,000 men and six generals as prisoners that day.

140

Arroyo Grande's Medal of Honor Winner

Otis W. Smith farmed in the Upper Arroyo Grande and Huasna Valleys before he retired to the Sawtelle Veterans' Home in West Los Angeles, near the UCLA campus. In November and December of 1864, he served in Gen. John Schofield's Army of the Tennessee.

Robert Hicks, in his vivid novel *The Widow of the South,* describes the windows of the homes in Franklin, Tennessee, rattling in their panes in 1864 as thousands of Confederate troops, many of them barefoot, marched into town to smash the Union army waiting for them there. This is what happened instead: The Confederates smashed themselves upon the Federals, who, because they had gotten to Franklin first, went to work with picks and shovels. They'd thrown up earthworks beyond a two-mile stretch of bare field that was punctuated only by islets of scrub not big enough to hide a dog, let alone a man.

Yet when they came into Franklin, the Confederates were ordered to cross that field and take the earthworks. This was in part because their commander's audacity had won him promotion after promotion in fighting the war that had whittled him half away. John Bell Hood's reputation for bravery grew even as he'd lost a leg and the use of an arm in validating it. At Antietam, in 1862, he'd lost even more when he sent his Texans shrieking like Comanches into the cornfield beyond the Dunker Church. They'd gone into the cornstalks and disappeared in a hail of canister fired from a Union artillery battery.

Hood was asked later where his division was. "Dead on the field," he'd replied. He accomplished the same result on November 30, 1864, at Franklin.

* * *

Otis Smith had seen dead men before—he'd enlisted in 1861, at sixteen—but never on the scale that John Bell Hood had arranged. Smith's 95th Ohio regiment came up on December 1, the day after Hood's assault, so he had seen the Confederate dead strewn in driblets across the field and packed in dense clumps against the face of the Union earthworks. Some were shapeless, torn by artillery shells, not men, but sacks of men. He may have helped burial details dig the long, shallow trenches into which the bodies, or the assembled fragments of bodies, were rolled by the dozens. *Forty Confederates buried here,* a penciled epitaph might read on a tombstone that might be nothing more than a board.

Union Army encampment at Nashville, December 1864. *Library of Congress.*

* * *

The month after the Battle of Franklin, outside Nashville, Gen. John Schofield was stalling. Perhaps it was the memory of what he and Otis Smith had seen at Franklin in the tangled mounds of Confederate dead. Now, in December, Schofield was in the same place Hood had been at Franklin. The Union general was about to lead an assault on an enemy that was well dug in.

There was one difference between Schofield's situation and Hood's. He was a subordinate officer, not in command. Maj. Gen. George Thomas was Schofield's superior, and Thomas was ordering him, in the second day of fighting at Nashville, to attack a hillside held by the entrenched Confederates. So it would be Hood's men who would be waiting for Schofield's this time, not the other way around, and they would be eager to return the favor of Franklin. Earlier that afternoon, December 16, three regiments of U.S. Colored Troops had attacked the Confederate right and were repulsed with forty percent of them dead or wounded—the Confederate officer commanding the troops that had inflicted this destruction noted the African Americans' bravery in his official report.

Now, on the Confederate left, Schofield was to duplicate that costly effort and send his men up the steep slopes of Shy's Hill. So he hesitated. He asked General Thomas for reinforcements. Thomas studied the hill for a moment and the decision was suddenly made for him: T.here were Union troops *already* attacking the entrenchments there. They were Brig. Gen. John MacArthur's men. MacArthur, an aggressive and, on December 16, an insubordinate Scot, born in a town on the River Clyde, had grown tired of waiting. Thomas ordered Schofield to follow MacArthur's lead and send in the rest of his men.

The state capitol steps at Nashville, protected by an artillery battery, 1864. Library of Congress.

Otis Smith's 95th Ohio Infantry was on the right of the impetuous Scot's attack when MacArthur let it go at 3:30 p.m. The 95th advanced silently, with fixed bayonets, and began to clamber up the hill, ironically, up hillsides so steep that they protected Smith and his comrades. The men atop Shy's Hill included a depleted Florida brigade; in fact, they could manage to field only enough troops that day to make up a regiment. Their position had been further weakened by Hood, who'd transferred troops from the hill to other points in his line. The Floridians had worked all night digging trenches, had been soaked all day by a cold rain, so they were exhausted. Suddenly, the 95th Ohio, after advancing without a cheer and without firing a shot, were in the Floridians' entrenchments, Otis Smith among them, killing the Southerners with their bayonets.

The Confederate position collapsed and Hood watched, dismayed, as his army's left dissolved. Those left behind were now surrounded by the Union brigade that included Smith. One Floridian started to tear his regimental flag into pieces to keep the victors from having it. For the 6th Florida, it was too late: during the assault, Otis Smith had seized their regimental colors.

A replica of the battle flag captured by Otis W. Smith at the Battle of Nashville. Courtesy Matthew J. Sterman.

After the capture of Shy's Hill, the rest of Hood's men followed their comrades who were retreating on the left. Hood later wrote that he had never seen a Confederate army retreat in such confusion. His army was finished. Less than a month after the rout at Nashville, Hood resigned his command, and

Otis Smith would be awarded the Medal of Honor that he never talked about, perhaps because it was tarnished.

This is why. The officer commanding the Floridians on Shy's Hill, Gen. Thomas Benton Smith, was being conducted to the rear when he was confronted by Otis Smith's regimental commander, a peacetime physician, Lt. Col. William Linn McMillen. Words were exchanged. McMillen may have been drunk. He suddenly drew his saber and began striking the disarmed Gen. Smith on the head; one blow was so deep that Smith's brain was exposed. McMillen's own men intervened to disarm their enraged commander. No charges were ever brought against him.

He was later promoted, grew cotton in Louisiana after the war, was a state senator, and won patronage jobs from two presidents as postmaster and then port inspector for New Orleans.

In 1886, his victim at Nashville, Thomas Benton Smith, was admitted to an insane asylum where he would spend most of the rest of his life, crippled by the depression that doctors said was a result of his injuries that day below Shy's Hill.

Smith was temporarily released in 1910 to attend a veterans' reunion. Out of kindness, he was allowed to conduct close-order drill with some of his old soldiers, and the moment transformed him. An observer wrote that the old general was "as full of the animation of the old days as could be imagined" as he put his little command through its paces.

Gen. Smith died on May 21, 1923, ten weeks after Medal of Honor winner Smith died at the Sawtelle Veterans' Home in Los Angeles.

John Rice and the Sioux Uprising

The yellow stone quarried from Mt. Picacho and from quarries in Los Berros, just south of Arroyo Grande, is unusually strong. A nail driven into it can't be removed. This was the building material, the same rock used for the IOOF Hall on Bridge Street and the Brisco Hotel, now a coffee house on Branch Street, that John S. Rice would select for the two-story home he built on Myrtle Street in 1894.

Rice was a transplanted Minnesotan who, as a young man, had joined the 10th Minnesota Infantry in 1862. Rice and the other young men in the brand-new regiment were probably eager to take the fight to the rebels. But Rice's Civil War career didn't work out that way. As the regiment readied to "take the cars"—the train—to the battlefields of Virginia, the Santee Sioux rebelled in Meeker County.

The John Rice home, Arroyo Grande.

The Sioux Uprising was simple to understand. They were starving to death. Their leader, Little Crow, had done everything he could to prevent war, but in the summer of 1862, their reservation, reduced in size and so hunted out, hadn't yet received its annuity payments due from the government. The payments customarily went not to the Sioux but to the local Indian agent who provided their food allotment. Theirs was a callous man who refused to advance the Santee the flour and beef that Little Crow begged from him. The agent, in the tradition of Marie Antoinette, suggested that Little Crow's people eat grass if they were hungry.

148

When hostilities finally broke out—the immediate cause was young Santee men stealing eggs from a farmer-- the agent was found dead with his mouth stuffed with grass.

What followed was five weeks of bloodshed, with the Santee attacking not only isolated farms but besieging the town of New Ulm, where 34 settlers were killed. Thousands more fled for their lives.

So Rice and the 10th Minnesota were diverted to help put the uprising down. In a punitive expedition in 1863, the 10th would take part in a pursuit of fugitive Santee that took them into North Dakota. The campaign accomplished little. It was what happened just before that expedition that would prove to be far more memorable. It was the largest mass execution in American history.

The execution of 38 Sioux men, Mankato, Minnesota, 1862. Library of Congress.

Over three hundred Santee captives were sentenced to hang by military tribunals made efficient by the absence of defense counsel. President Lincoln, as was his custom, was relatively merciful: He commuted the sentences of all but thirty-eight men, those charged with the most heinous killings.

149

On the day of the executions, Rice and the 10th Minnesota were mounted and ordered to surround the scaffold to prevent the settlers who'd descended on Mankato from taking the law into their own hands. But both the soldiers and the crowd watched quietly as the condemned men were led out of their cells. Then, in a moment that stunned the onlookers, the Santee rushed the scaffold, as if they were eager to die. They sang as hoods were placed over their heads and reached out blindly to try to hold each others' hands. The trap was sprung by a farmer whose family had been murdered. "The greater part died instantly," a reporter noted, but "some few struggled violently." One had to be hanged twice when his rope broke and sent him crashing to the ground.

The bodies were taken down after a half-hour, and Rice and the 10th were charged with burying the executed men in a sandbank on the Minnesota River. Some of the corpses were disinterred by macabre souvenir hunters; one wound up as the office skeleton for Dr. William Mayo, the father of the founders of the famed clinic.

One victim shouldn't have been there at all. A Santee fighter named Chaksa had his sentence commuted when a frontier woman, Sarah Wakefield, insisted on testifying on his behalf. It was Chaksa who had intervened during a Santee attack and saved the lives of Sarah and her family. But a mistake in paperwork confused Chaksa with another man, Chaskey-etay, who had murdered a pregnant woman. It was the Wakefield family's protector who died instead that day.

The uprising's final act was the killing of Little Crow by a Minnesota farmer. The state legislature voted him $500 and its official thanks.

John Rice left Minnesota and came to the Arroyo Grande Valley where he busied himself with local improvements, including road-building. The home he built was a happy one; one of the most memorable photographs from its time shows a wedding party gathered in the front yard. But what Rice had seen as a young soldier—the terrible deaths of thirty-eight men—happened on December 26, 1862. That had to have marked every Christmas his family celebrated in the sturdy stone house on Myrtle Street.

Why They Came, What They Left

Medal of Honor winner Otis Smith in old age. Photo courtesy Debbie Gragg.

We was on our way to Camp McLean [Ohio, near Cincinnati, where the regiment would train as a unit]. Passing swiftly from one station to another, we soon found our selves in the fond embrace of sleep on the cushioned seats of the cars.

In this excerpt from sixteen-year-old Union soldier Erastus Fouch's wartime diary, "riding the cars" seems to be a novelty and a turning point in his life. The railroad's arrival in Arroyo Grande was a turning point, as well. The Pacific Coast Railroad was instrumental in attracting a new wave of settlers to the Valley in the 1880s: Its connection to Port Harford meant that getting the crops of the Valley to market was now efficient. It was then that a mature Erastus Fouch began farming along what is today's Lopez Drive.

The railroad would play a drastically different role in another veteran's life. In the superb book about Union soldiers' postwar years, *Marching Home*, historian Brian Matthew Jordan tells the story of the veteran who commits suicide by lying down on a train tracks and leaving a liquor bottle alongside as a kind of symbolic suicide note.

So it was a troubled generation: Alcoholism was common. In the war's immediate aftermath, in the summer of 1865, only retired general Joseph Hooker could stop a drunken riot among veterans in Chicago. The police couldn't stop them, the reputedly hard-drinking Hooker did. Drug addiction was another problem: I found the story of an old soldier in Santa Monica who, in a morphine-induced stupor, knocked over a kerosene lamp and so set himself and his apartment on fire. In 1880, two-thirds of the prisoners in American penitentiaries were Civil War veterans.

There were several factors that led to sad stories like these. One of them, of course, was coming to terms, during a time in our history marked by great waves of religious revivalism, with the fact that they had taken others' lives. Seeing their friends die, of course, was harrowing. Since many young men joined along with their peers from little towns, the victims they saw drop in a hail of Confederate fire might be childhood friends. Indeed, some survivors might return home to towns empty of young men.

By the time veterans came home in 1865, Americans wanted to put the war behind them. It would take another generation for soldiers' statues to be erected around the nation. But in the war's immediate aftermath, soldiers came home and no one wanted to hear their stories. There was no way, to use a 21st century term, for them to "process" what had happened to them. In his book,

Jordan notes, too, that even small towns had changed immensely after four years of warfare. Veterans from states like Minnesota, after campaigning in Georgia or Mississippi, discovered that they couldn't stand the winters anymore.

So many of these soldiers, estranged and alienated, began moving away from home. A survey of twenty-three of the fifty-odd veterans who came to the Arroyo Grande Valley and Nipomo revealed that seven had moved twice before settling here; nine had moved three or more times. And, if it was the railroad that made farming here profitable, it was the railroad that brought many here. Union veterans, thanks in part to the railroad, were 54% more likely to move to a new state than Americans who had not served in the Civil War. What these restless, troubled men sought was a fresh start.

Most of Arroyo Grande's veterans would take up farming and they cultivated a variety of crops—pumpkins, squash, onions, potatoes, tree crops—and they proudly showed their produce at local fairs and so broadcast the fertility of Valley soil. They held out, too, in spite of devastating floods: The creek rebelled in 1911 and again in 1914, wiping out acres of produce in the ground and, in a few cases, killing Arroyo Grandeans.

They took their new home seriously. Gettysburg veteran Erastus Fouch became a leading advocate for a high school despite local farmers' determination to destroy it: The school meant ten cents' tax on every hundred dollars of assessed valuation, and it was resented. The infant school's board hired such inept teachers that students were tumbling out the windows in mid-lesson and high-tailing down Crown Hill in pursuit of worthier pursuits, like smoking or fishing. It was Fouch and the formidable teacher Clara Paulding who fought to keep the school open. Eventually, they would save it.

Bela Clinton Ide, another Gettysburg veteran, became the town's postmaster. Charles Clark would treat broken jaws, concussed skulls and knife wounds in the wild little town, but the one-time New Jersey cavalryman would become better known as the town's pediatrician. Massachusetts militia veteran Thomas Whiteley was a bootmaker and as town constable. Whiteley experienced the discomfort of being locked in a restaurant storeroom while a lynch mob launched Peter and P.J. Hemmi into the void beneath the Pacific Coast Railway Bridge. Vitalis Runels, a veteran of Sherman's March to the Sea, would build the Nipomo hotel that is today's Kaleidoscope Inn. Timothy

Munger, a veteran of the 1864 Shenandoah Valley campaign, was a justice of the peace.

This is the generation that secured the future of the little town in its beautiful valley. Like their grandsons, the veterans of World War II, what they did in peacetime was fully as remarkable as what they'd done in war.

Civil War veteran Erastus Fouch was a staunch supporter of the founding of a high school in Arroyo Grande. Here are the junior and seniors of that school in 1906. Courtesy Randy Spoeneman.

The Wall at Fredericksburg

Nothing is more illustrative of the Civil War than the experience of Lucius B. Nichols, a Confederate veteran buried in an unmarked grave in the Arroyo Grande District Cemetery. After his war, he owned a farm in Oregon, then he must've fallen on hard times: He moved several times—from Oregon to Sacramento, where his occupation is "fruit picker," and finally to Arroyo Grande, where he lived as a widower on Ide Street with his son's family until his death, at 87, in 1932.

Nichols was born in North Carolina, but he became a Georgian when his family moved there when he was a toddler. He was fifteen years old when he enlisted in the 24th Georgia Infantry in August 1861.

Within a year, Pvt. Nichols and the 24th had been bloodied badly at the Seven Days' Battles and at Crampton's Gap, during the Antietam Campaign, when the regiment lost 43% of the 292 men engaged.

In December 1862, the regiment was behind a stone wall on Marye's Heights at Fredericksburg. The 24th Georgia's position was marked by its battle flag, marked in turn by a curious addition: A gold harp was sewn into the Confederate colors. This was because so many in the regiment were Irish immigrants. Indeed, Nichols' commander at Fredericksburg was County Antrim-born. Col. Robert McMillan had been a state senator before the war and took over the regiment when his predecessor, Thomas Cobb, was killed on Marye's Heights by shell fragments.

Alfred Waud's sketch of Burnside's doomed assault on Marye's Heights, in the distance.
Library of Congress.

It was the Union commander that winter day who did most of the killing. Ambrose Burnside, who would, with great relief, surrender command of the Army of the Potomac after Fredericksburg, ordered his men to advance across open ground and take Marye's heights, where Lee's men were dug in with a commanding view of the oncoming soldiers that they would begin to kill in bunches.

Once the battle had been joined and the Union forces had begun their attack, it was Lee who provided the war with one of its famous quotes. While watching the young Northerners fall like scythed wheat, Lee turned to his subordinate, James Longstreet, and remarked that "it is well that war is so terrible. Otherwise we would grow too fond of it." The quote may be apocryphal, but it was appropriate.

It was the 24th that inflicted much of the carnage that the two Confederate generals were witnessing, but it was also one of Col. McMillan's finest moments. He behaved with great courage and was later described as walking coolly up and down the ranks of his men as they crouched behind the stone wall, counseling patience, reminding them to hold their fire until his order came. When it did come, it was at the last possible moment. The 24th stood up and fired virtually into the faces of their enemies. "Give it to them now, boys!" McMillan shouted. "Now's the time! Give it to them!"

They were killing their own kind. The unit closing in on McMillan's section of the stone wall was the Irish Brigade, made up almost entirely of the children of Famine immigrants who had settled in New York, Pennsylvania or Massachusetts. McMillan knew that. He had seen the regimental flag of the 28th Massachusetts as it approached the wall, the green battle flag with a gold harp sewn into its fabric.

The results were terrible. Every officer above the rank of captain in the 69th New York, a regiment that would win fame in World War I, was killed. The Irish Brigade was 1400 strong when they began their assault on the stone wall. All but 340 were killed or wounded in front of it.

But Nichols and the 24th would suffer their own ordeal, a prolonged one. The regiment would experience the terrible slaughter of the war's last year: The Wilderness, Spotsylvania Courthouse, Cold Harbor, Petersburg, and finally Appomattox. It was at Appomattox where the regiment's sixty survivors surrendered. Young Union officers cut pieces from their battle flag, with its gold harp sewn into the fabric, for souvenirs.

Behind the stone wall, Fredericksburg. Library of Congress.

Chapter 6. A History Teacher's Favorite (Old) Movies

The Fremont Theater, San Luis Obispo, opened in 1942. Photo by Hakkun.

We'll Always Have Paris

The Usual Suspects: Paul Heinreid, Ingrid Bergman, Claude Rains, Humphrey Bogart.
Wikimedia Commons.

It's Bastille Day today, and we'll always have Paris. Of course, I'm thinking about *Casablanca*.

It is fascinating to read about this film because so much of the cast was caught up in the events of World War II, when *Casablanca* was made. A native Berliner, Conrad Veidt, played one of the principal roles in the 1920 Expressionist masterpiece *The Cabinet of Dr. Caligari*. Veidt, who despised the Nazis, was cast as the remorseless and humorless Major Strasser and thus set the standard for a generation of *faux*-Nazi film officers. Veidt, a thoughtful, generous man, was not remotely like Strasser. He loved golf as much as he hated Hitler, but died, tragically, of a heart attack only a year after *Casablanca's* release, while playing at the Riviera Country Club.

Strasser's nemesis, the freedom fighter Victor Laszlo, was played by Paul Heinreid, an Austrian who was living in England when war broke out in 1939. The English were about to deport him as an enemy alien when Veidt—Major Strasser--spoke up for his friend and made his Hollywood career possible.

Peter Lorre was another Austrian. His character is shot ten minutes into the film. Lorre was, like Veidt, a star in German Expressionist film: He was the child-killer in the sensational and controversial 1931 film, *M*. Lorre was a Jew, and he recognized quickly the nature of Hitler's rule and fled Germany. Several of the lesser players are, like Lorre, refugees from the Third Reich: Hitler was indirectly responsible for a Golden Age in American film.

However, neither Humphrey Bogart nor the studio thought much of *Casablanca* at the time. Playing Rick, the owner of the *Café Americain*, was just another job for him. Likewise, for Warner Brothers, it was just another assembly-line feature. It was shot in a little over nine weeks, and the whole time, Bogart was extremely uncomfortable with the love scenes. He didn't consider himself a romantic lead, and his favorite part of the film must have been when he finally got a revolver in his hand. That was his moment---not, as is the case for the rest of us, the closing dialogue with Ingrid Bergman's Ilsa.

Bergman didn't think much of *Casablanca* either. She was preoccupied with snagging the role of Maria in *For Whom the Bell Tolls*. The bromide that "the camera loved her" was certainly true in *Casablanca;* director Michael Curtiz's cinematographer, Arthur Edeson, used soft focus skillfully in her closeups. The camera idealizes Ilsa, her compassion, even her indecision. We understand Rick's anguish at losing her that much more. Bergman was delighted, near the end of the filming of *Casablanca*, to hear that she had been cast as Maria, never realizing, of course, that her Ilsa would be the role that would make the bigger, more lasting, impression.

Other than Ilsa, my favorite part of the film—one of my favorite films--is the banter between Bogart's Rick and Claude Rains' corrupt Captain Renault. I am always thinking of Renault when I tell my students that wonderful things *might* happen to their essay grades if a latte magically appears at my table at Café Andreini while I'm grading them.

The script, surprisingly, is graced by some of the funniest dialogue in American film thanks to two scriptwriters in particular, the brothers Julius and Philip Epstein. The policeman, Renault, gets my favorite line:

"I'm shocked, *shocked* to find that gambling is going on in here!" (As he pockets his winnings from the roulette wheel in Rick's.)

One of Bogart's lines is a very close runner-up. Major Strasser asks Rick his nationality.

"I'm a drunkard," Bogart deadpans.

And, of course, Rick never says "Play it again, Sam." He *is* profoundly drunk in that scene, tormenting himself now that Ilsa is with another man, the noble Resistance leader, Laszlo. The more complete line is more completely painful as he orders Dooley Wilson's Sam to play "As Time Goes By," the lovers' song during their time together in Paris:

Rick: *You know what I want to hear.*
Sam: *No, I don't.*
Rick: *You played it for her, you can play it for me!*
Sam: *Well, I don't think I can remember...*
Rick: *If she can stand it, I can!* Play it!

Bogart probably never spoke more uncomfortable lines, because for once his tough guy was helpless. As Rick stares into the dark, taking a drag on his cigarette, his eyes glisten with tears.

Shakespeare in Film

I'm sorry. I cannot sit through Olivier's *Hamlet*. There's entirely too much flitting—the actor, who also directs, is like the proverbial flea on a hot stove, which makes sense, because the young prince has a habit of suddenly appearing where he's least wanted. Ophelia is the lovely Jean Simmons, who's been give the following direction, but maybe that goes with playing Ophelia:

> *Simper!*

Elizabeth and I once saw the play, perhaps Shakespeare's longest, and I was ready to personally shake off Hamlet's mortal coil about halfway into Act III.

Now Olivier's *Richard III*---that's delicious malevolence. I love that film.

Elizabeth and also I saw Tom Stoppard's *Rosencrantz and Guildenstern Are Dead* in London; I rented a little pair of opera glasses but we couldn't focus them because we were laughing so hard. We later bought standing-room-only tickets in Stratford, when we realized, to our delight, that since we were in the back, we would be the first at the bar at intermission. Knowing that, we belly-laughed through a production of *As You Like It*. That's good Shakespeare, that.

One of the best Hamlets ever was said to be John Gielgud, and Gielgud directed one of my favorite actors, Richard Burton, in the role in a 1964 film. (Edwin Booth, by the way, was said to be stellar in the role while his little brother, John Wilkes, was an overly vigorous Horatio. His swordfights tended to wound the supporting cast, the scene-shifters and the patrons in the first three rows. He was a piece of work. The creep.)

Gielgud and Margaret Leighton in a 1959 production of Much Ado About Nothing. Wikimedia.

Both Gielgud and Burton were big drinkers and did not mind imbibing before or during a performance, like the way Babe Ruth ate hot dogs during a ballgame. On a dare, Burton once drank a fifth of vodka, gave a flawless performance in *Camelot,* and then, immediately after the curtain call, passed out.

Peter O'Toole practiced the same vice, prodigiously. One of his stories, perhaps embellished, recounts an epic New York pub crawl lasting all night and into a Broadway matinee the next afternoon. The drinking buddies sat themselves down, prepared to hurl insults at the actors, when O'Toole leaped out of his seat.

"My GOD!" he cried. "I'm IN this!"

Gielgud was in his cups a wee bit in a London play where his character was to commit suicide in the final act. His final line was delivered to a butler: "A pint of port and a pistol, if you please."

Well, of course, it didn't come out that way.

"A pint of piss and a portal, if you please."

The rest was Silence.

Where's My Cheeseburger, Lana Turner?

The L.A. *Times* food critic Jonathan Gold wrote an excellent summer piece this year on great Los Angeles hamburgers. It made me think about my strange affection for a city I largely dislike unless it's about 1946 outside and the Red Cars are running. I'm a San Francisco kind of guy, with the exception of the Dodgers, and that has more to do with Vin Scully than with any loyalty to the Southland. But there is no film *noir* like Los Angeles *noir*; I watched *Double Indemnity* one more time recently on late-night television, and the list of good *noir* films set in Los Angeles is amazing. Here are just a few favorites, many of them made, in tribute, years after *film noir* became a victim of Technicolor, among other things:

1. *Chinatown*. Not only a solid hard-boiled detective film, in the detective novelist Raymond Chandler's tradition, but it deftly sketches the water wars that made Los Angeles and its orange groves, which were the attraction that lured my mother's family from the Minnesota prairie. J.J. Geddes, I think, is one of the most memorable characters in American film, and John Huston's cameo, both jovial and deeply sinister, is stunning.

Putty in her hands: MacMurray and Stanwyck in Double Indemnity. Paramount Pictures.

2. *Double Indemnity*. The murder plot flows seamlessly to the point when the plotters dump the body of Barbara Stanwyck's husband on the railroad tracks. Then she and Fred MacMurray can't get her car to start in order to leave the murder scene. Then the seams start to unravel, and it's a lovely thing to

watch. Doom can be interesting. In a perverse way, it's even kind of fun, including, earlier in the film, in the implicit comedy of Stanwyck-MacMurray plot-hatching in the aisles of the local grocery store: The two are interrupted by little ladies asking the lanky MacMurray's help in reaching the canned goods.

3. *True Confessions*. John Gregory Dunne's screenplay about two brothers: One, Robert Duvall, an L.A. homicide detective, and the other, Robert DeNiro, a politically ambitious monsignor, is deeply moving. Duvall must solve the mystery of a priest found dead in a prostitute's bed, and he has to tear down the wall DeNiro's character has constructed to protect his church and his career. This is a wonderful story about redemption, and how redemptive personal destruction can be.

4. *The Big Sleep*. Bogart and Bacall star in a plot so arcane that even the scriptwriters couldn't figure it out. Bogie's Philip Marlowe builds on the fast-talking Sam Spade we'd first seen in San Francisco, in *The Maltese Falcon*. His ability to shift character, posing, for example, as a dirty-minded bookworm in one scene, foreshadows James Garner's television detective, the delightful Jim Rockford. Bacall is smoky, alluring, mysterious, dangerous, and Bacall.

5. *L.A. Confidential*. A superb ensemble cast– the now-disgraced Kevin Spacey, Guy Pearce, Russell Crowe, Kim Basinger as a call girl, a Veronica Lake look-alike. You've got your fast-talkers, con men, like Spacey, but you've also got your straight arrows, like Pearce and the emotionally wounded Crowe. All three, it will turn out, are decent men at their core in a department so corrupt that even they, despite their own casual infidelities to the law, must finally take a stand. Again, a wonderfully redemptive story crowned by a harrowing shootout scene.

6. *The Big Lebowski*. I'm a little dense, but by the third or fourth viewing, I realized that this was a wonderful tribute to and parody of the Chandleresque formula, with Jeff Bridges as the bowler/stoner who becomes, accidentally, a kind of soft-boiled detective and the incomparable John Goodman as Walter, his manic, explosive and completely inept partner. Includes femmes fatale, slipped Mickeys (in Lebowski's White Russian), a couple of Falcon-like talismans (a toe, Lebowski's rug), and a flock of Nihilists.

What makes these films even more compelling is, of course, real tragedy. Human wreckage has always surrounded the film industry and examples

168

include Elizabeth Short's grisly 1947 murder, when she became immortalized as "The Black Dahlia;" the implosion of film comedian Fatty Arbuckle's career when he was charged with the 1921 murder of aspiring actress Virginia Rappe; the suicide of actress Peg Entwistle, who leaped to her death in 1932 from the Hollywood sign; the mysterious 1924 death of producer Thomas Ince, "father of the Western," after a visit to William Randolph Hearst's yacht, *Oneida*. Here, Hearst's mistress, Marion Davies, played hostess, as she did at San Simeon. What ended Ince's life? Was it a heart attack or a bullet intended for another guest, Charlie Chaplin, Davies' putative lover?

The classic *noir* films entangle us in L.A.'s dark *Day of the Locust* allure, in its pretension and deception. This is a place where nobody is who you think they are. It's a place where, as Chandler wrote, the Red Wind--the Santa Anas--can lead even the most dutiful Valley housewife to contemplate her husband's back while he happily eats his hamburger. She's absently squeezing the handle of the kitchen knife she'd used to slice his tomato.

By the way, speaking of hamburgers, some purists might note that I've left out *The Postman Always Rings Twice.* There are several problems in this film that would take up several pages. Let's leave at this one: While John Garfield and Lana Turner are plotting their coverup inside the home behind their little hamburger café, they seem to take *hours*. Maybe they're trying to figure out the plot, although it's considerably simpler than the one Bogey and Bacall had to deal with. In the meantime—and here's my complaint—dozens of customers are outside waiting. And waiting.

Where's my cheeseburger, Lana Turner?

Damn You, Hitchcock!

James Stewart, as Scottie, is in a tight spot. Wikimedia.

I really should not read essays about films. The one I read yesterday has messed with my head, because, citing the British Film Institute, it put Hitchcock's *Vertigo* (1958) at the top of the all-time greatest films list, bumping *Citizen Kane* from the top spot.

I have never doubted *Kane* to be a great movie, but it would never be my #1. It is stylistically and technically stunning, but it's cold at the heart. My picks, if I were in charge of things—which would be a mistake—at least for American films, would be *Casablanca* or *The Searchers* or Coppola's *The Godfather Part II*, for the incredible history it retells while leaping from one part of the twentieth century to another. And I've never seen a more arresting appearance than Robert DeNiro's as the young Don Corleone. I was, I think, pinned to my movie-chair seat.

But in *Vertigo,* James Stewart is the lead—Scottie, the washed-up San Francisco Police Department detective—and if I immediately connected with DeNiro, I was repelled by Stewart. He'd betrayed me: This was the James Stewart of *Mr. Smith Goes to Washington,* with Jean Arthur, one of my favorite actresses, of *The Philadelphia Story* and *It's A Wonderful Life.* This was the war hero. This was the man, a Robert Taft Republican, whose best friend was Henry Fonda, a Henry Wallace Democrat.

And in *Vertigo,* he is—to borrow Keenan Wynn's pronunciation from *Dr. Strangelove*—a damned pree-vert. He's a stalker, obsessed with Kim Novak's Judy because she looks so much like a lost love, done away with in the second reel, Kim Novak's Madeline, who fell from a church tower to her death (supposedly) because Scottie, afraid of heights, failed to save her.

Ironically, Scottie *had* saved Madeline earlier in the film, when she, apparently despondent, jumps into the Bay near Fort Point. He brings her home (his apartment was on Lombard Street) and she awakes wrapped in his robe. In 1958, this was explosive stuff. Scottie had seen her nude, a precondition to getting her dry. My mother would not have let me see this film.

Then he loses her anyway, with her going off that church tower at San Juan Bautista. It turns out that she was murdered. Are you confused yet? So was I.

To be even more confusing, a critic has written that Hitchcock was fascinated by the San Francisco writer Ambrose Bierce, famed for the short story "Occurrence at Owl Creek Bridge," in which a Union Army detail hangs a Confederate saboteur. The rope breaks, the condemned man escapes and after a harrowing journey, returns home to his loving wife and family and...

...Realizes that he's imagined the whole thing. He's back at the bridge, swinging slightly after the drop, thoroughly dead.

The smart-aleck proposed that the same thing happened to James Stewart's Scottie. In the opening scene, Scottie the detective and a uniformed SFPD officer are chasing a suspect across rooftops. Scottie slips and is hanging by his fingertips from a rain gutter when the uniformed officer, trying to help him, falls to his death.

The scene ends. The next time we meet Scottie he's on disability retirement because of the trauma of that moment on the rooftop. But Mr. Smart-Aleck argues that Scottie died up there, too. After all, no one was around to rescue him and his grip was slipping, so everything that follows, for the next two hours, is just a dream, like the condemned man's dream in "Owl Creek Bridge."

I'm not buying it.

Scottie tries to win over a dubious Judy. Wikimedia.

But again, it's James Stewart who bothers me even more than that critic's essay. Stewart's Scottie loses Madeline, then finds a girl walking on a San Francisco street: It's Judy, also played by Kim Novak. Judy reminds him immediately of Madeline. I'm not sure why. Judy is no Madeline: She is coarse, with eyebrows layered thicker than Van Gogh pigment. She lives in a cheap walkup apartment bathed in sinister green light from a nearby neon sign. She's from Salina, Kansas. Yet Scottie somehow intuits the refinement that he'd seen in both Madeline and her early California ancestor, Carlotta, whose portrait figures early on in the film.

So Scottie spends the greater part of the film's second half trying to remake Judy into Madeline in a creepy Pygmalion way. She dyes her hair for him, She wears the same gray suit Madeline favored, after an excruciating scene at a fashion house in which model after model fails to meet Scottie's requirement for the *exact* gray suit. The pair even dine at the same steakhouse—Ernie's, an actual City restaurant where Scottie first saw Madeline, so they fall in love on the pretense that she's not Judy: She's Madeline. Which, by the way, she *is*.

Yes, it's weird.

But, for me, it's resonant because location filming, in 1957, would've been about the same time I first saw San Francisco, as a little boy. There was a storm, with lightning flitting atop the skyscrapers, something I'll never forget. So the film that repels me so is at the same time set in a place that's so familiar to me and has enchanted me ever since those lightning flashes. It James Stewart that's unfamiliar.

But I think that's exactly why it's a great film. It was panned, like other great films, on its debut. Hitchcock would blame his casting of Stewart. The director, in hindsight, thought the actor too old, at fifty, to have been Kim Novak's love interest. Of course, as I get older, I disagree. Beyond that, I've decided that *Vertigo* deserves to be watched several times. If it still leaves you as disoriented as Stewart's Scottie was, then I think its greatness has been confirmed.

It's a Wonderful Story

I just read a wonderful story. It goes something like this:

It was James Stewart's first film since coming home from World War II. He was struggling. He was agitated and angry. There was good reason for his moodiness.

After seeing so many young airmen die as their bombers plunged to earth or blew into fragments, Army Air Force Col. Stewart was emotionally shattered. He'd been rotated home after twenty-five B-24 bomber combat missions, not the requisite thirty-five, because he was suffering from what was then called "combat fatigue." It was a tribute to his close friend Henry Fonda, who'd been caring for him since his return to Hollywood, that Stewart was attempting to make a movie at all.

It wasn't working out. Movie acting now seemed so frivolous and trite that Stewart couldn't bear the guilt he felt at taking it up again. He told some friends he was ready to quit this new film, go home, and run his dad's hardware store. Indiana, Pennsylvania, was where he could live a real life. Nothing about Hollywood was real.

He talked about his feelings with an older actor, Lionel Barrymore.

You're thinking of yourself, Barrymore told Stewart, not about the ability you have to make others happy. After this terrible war, they need you now more than they ever did. You must understand that.

Stewart understood. He finished the film, *It's a Wonderful Life.*

Barrymore, the veteran actor who straightened Stewart out, played the banker Potter, one of the most memorable villains--an American Scrooge--in film history.

Barrymore's Potter, too, helped to save director Frank Capra's film from unforgivable sentimentality, but the real revelation was the intensity and authenticity of Stewart's portrayal of the despondent George Bailey, a character struggling with the meaning of his life and at one point determined to end it.

So what you see on the screen is James Stewart's struggle, as well as George Bailey's. Both men found themselves again.

An uneasy-looking Col. Stewart is awarded the Croix du Guerre, *1944.* U.S. Air Force.

175

GWTW

The lead story in the January 13, 1939, San Luis Obispo *Telegram-Tribune* was sensational. Five convicts attempted an escape from Alcatraz and two of them were killed in the process. One of the survivors was a former FBI Public Enemy Number One, Alvin "Creepy" Karpis, killer, kidnaper, bank robber. Not only was he captured, but Karpis would win the dubious distinction of being the inmate who did the most time on The Rock: Twenty-six years. Karpis spent so much of his life in prisons that many years later a youthful inmate asked him for a guitar lesson. It was Charles Manson.

But next to the Karpis story, and given equal play, was another stunner: David O. Selznick announced that the British actress Vivien Leigh would be cast as Scarlett O'Hara in the forthcoming production of Margaret Mitchell's *Gone with the Wind.*

It had taken two years to find Scarlett in a process that, thanks to Selznick- MGM publicists, became an obsession with Americans. Four hundred actresses tried out; nineteen took screen tests, many of which are online today, and finally Leigh beat out Paulette Goddard for the role, in part because Goddard was, as the term went then, living in sin with Charlie Chaplin.

There had been little doubt about Rhett Butler. That role was Clark Gable's almost from the beginning.

Production began with the burning of Atlanta scene, a $25,000 exercise in arson on studio back lots. Three directors and several marathon script re-writes later, the film opened in Atlanta in December.

Couple Number One: Rhett and Scarlett at the charity ball...

Gone with the Wind would finally make its way to our part of California in March 1940. This is when Hollywood had a decisive impact on the future of my family. My parents married in Taft in September 1940, and their courtship was smoothed by one of the most extraordinary years in American film history. A series of $1.50 investments (at 75¢ each; Cokes were a nickel) on my father's part meant that the young couple would've seen not only *GWTW*, but they also had the chance to see *The Wizard of Oz, Stagecoach, Mr. Smith Goes to Washington, Ninotchka, Goodbye Mr. Chips, Destry Rides Again, Gunga Din, Dark Victory* and *Young Mr. Lincoln.*

And that's not the complete list.

So it's not an exaggeration to say that Hollywood made us four Gregory kids—Roberta, Bruce, Jim and Sally-- possible.

Gone with the Wind had an impact that is remarkable even today. It played in San Luis Obispo at the now-defunct Elmo Theater and farther south at the Santa Maria Theater. Both theaters added, thanks to the film's length, a 10 a.m. matinee, the first morning shows in their history. The Santa Maria *Times* devoted quarter-page ads to the film's premier and newspapers in both Santa Maria and San Luis Obispo featured large studio stills at the top of their news columns; the most popular showed Gable gathering Leigh in his arms.

The film even found its way into the little snippets of what were once called "The Society Pages."

--Mr. and Mrs. Roy Sherwin drove to Santa Barbara during the week to see "Gone with the Wind."

--Mr. and Mrs. Nicholas Marquart were in town [San Luis Obispo] from the Josephine District [near Templeton] Wednesday to see "Gone with the Wind."

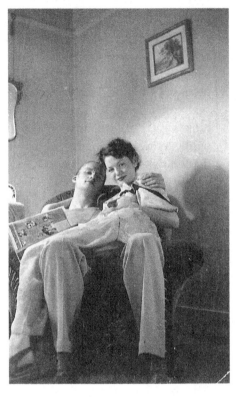

...Couple Number Two: Patricia and Robert Gregory shortly after their marriage, 1940.

In Bakersfield, probably where my parents saw the film, Pastor B.B. Baird of the First Christian Church took advantage of the film's arrival to announce an evening service and sermon entitled "Not Gone with the Wind."

In San Luis Obispo, Brown's Jewelers ran a display ad to confide in the *Telegram-Tribune's* readers that

'Scarlett' of today would choose CLARENCE BROWN for Fine Diamonds.

The ad featured Leigh, as Scarlett, in a still that unfortunately showed her in widow's black during her all-too-brief mourning for Charles Hamilton, the soldier who died of measles. Perhaps she was wearing a Clarence Brown diamond when she shocked Atlanta society by dancing, in her widow's reeds, with Rhett at a charity ball.

The sensation over the film's arrival was only heightened because of its incredibly short run. It showed for only a week locally, so reserved tickets were recommended. They were $1.10, not the 75¢ matinee price for those willing to endure what had to be lines that snaked around the block. The display ads in local newspapers warned moviegoers urgently that *"Gone with the Wind* will not be shown anywhere except at advanced prices at least until 1941. ONE WEEK ONLY."

America, and the Central Coast, of course, would be dramatically different by the time the film returned. Hancock Field in Santa Maria, the site for the primary flight training for thousands of Army Air Forces cadets, would by then be operating at its height. At Camp San Luis Obispo, the 40th Infantry Division comprised a city the size of San Luis Obispo just a few miles north of San Luis Obispo; it would be the 40th's soldiers who would be summoned back to the camp by the wailing of "Ferdinand," the city's fire siren, on December 7.

In the meantime, Clark Gable had returned to the Central Coast, but this time in the flesh. The exterior scenes for *Strange Cargo*, starring Gable and Joan Crawford, were shot at Pismo Beach. The actor lodged at The Pismo Beach Hotel on Pomeroy. He took a quick break from shooting one day to play a pickup softball game on the beach with girls — they had to have been thrilled-- from San Luis Obispo High School. But Gable's life, too, would never be the same after December 7. He lost his wife, Carole Lombard, in a plane crash during a January 1942 war bond drive; in 1943, the myth had it, he sought death in the five combat missions he flew as a gunner in the 351st Bomb Group.

But in March 1940, all of that was in the future. Moviegoers lost themselves in the technicolor fantasy of Twelve Oaks and Tara and in the lives of Scarlett and Rhett. Hollywood, in an extraordinary year, had created a dream world on the eve of a national nightmare, in World War II, that would last nearly four years. Neither America nor Hollywood would be the same afterward.

...And One Movie That's Not So Old...

Good filmmakers know what to leave out of a story. I don't want to know if Rick slept with Ilsa that night. Not seeing the Great White in *Jaws* or the Comanches early on in *The Searchers* made both films even more terrifying.

And Sofia Coppola knew what to leave out in her script for *Lost in Translation,* which she directed, including the ending that we knew, if we were honest with ourselves, was the ending we really wanted.

Coppola has too much integrity for that, and it's integrity that makes Murray and his character, Bob Harris, admirable. It seems so implausible that a young woman might fall in love with him, with his Ichabod Crane-like arms and legs that are an insult to Japanese interior design. But there's a kind of heroism to Bob Harris that gradually emerges.

Steinbeck wrote about opening a book and letting the stories crawl in by themselves, and Coppola knows how to do that, too. The episodic and seemingly inchoate structure of the film reflects the reality experienced by two vaguely lost souls traveling in a strange land.

And Japan seems, to us, such a strange land. It is frenetic and crass and as fake as karaoke and it is also impossibly beautiful and the Japanese themselves impossibly graceful. My favorite moments are some of the briefest--Murray's tee shot with Fuji, so beautiful, anchoring but not obscuring the meaning of the scene, of a man alone. We then we see Johansson's Charlotte, alone. The serenity and sensory delight of her walk in a Kyoto park is shattered by an interruption: A traditional, exquisite wedding party.

Charlotte is so beautiful, but is the only beautiful thing alive in that park without roots, without *belonging,* and she knows it. She is ready to commit herself and to dedicate her life, but there are no roots and there is no soil. Her ache for permanence is heartbreaking.

Bob Harris's life, for a Hollywood celebrity, seems mundane. Long-distance conversations with his wife about floor covering seem to take on the weight of the Versailles Peace Conference. He is not in love, but he is dedicated to his marriage and he is committed to his family. While duty may be a poor substitute for love, it is profound bravery, and there is no substitute for that. In the end, Bob is brave enough to say goodbye to Charlotte.

This is what makes the film so sublime and so bittersweet. You know that in the very last moments of his life, Harris will return to that final embrace on a Tokyo street. Letting go of Charlotte then will be even harder than it was the first time. But that's exactly what he will do.

A Meditation on Glamor

Grace Kelly in that Rear Window *ensemble,
designed by Edith Head. Her tomb in Monaco is
strewn with rose petals, as it should be.* Wikimedia.

I reached into the mailbox and there, amid the Neptune Society cremation offers and the AARP supplemental insurance ads ("You're old! You need it!") was this month's *Vanity Fair*.

On its cover was the sometime *Sports Illustrated* swimsuit model Kate Upton, who would go on to bigger things—Super Bowl ads where she was covered by strategically-placed fruit—and there she was, walking right out of the *Vanity Fair* cover, with all her equipment deployed.

Bogart and Bacall in The Big Sleep. *Pixabay.*

Glamorous? The extravagantly voluptuous Ms. Upton *would* be if I were 14 or if it was, say, 1959. I'm not. It isn't. You may remember that the Sixties followed 1959, almost inevitably.

And it was my generation, the Sixties kids, that tore down all the taboos— *The Graduate, Midnight Cowboy*, assassinations on a regular basis. We grew up in an era bracketed by Fess Parker and Madonna Ciccone. In the years between, excess became both obligatory in popular culture, including the portrayal of sexuality, so it became kind of boring, too.

By contrast, I miss subtlety, and that was something that was a counterpoint, in the 40s and 50s, to the Kate Uptons of those decades. I miss Grace Kelly—my students and I visited her grave in Monaco; it was appropriately strewn with rose petals-- and Audrey Hepburn. I miss Lauren Bacall—all of them, by the way, from the generation before mine and, it increasingly appears, from an alternate universe, too.

And I miss mystery. Smokey-eyed stuff (but sans the smoke, thank you), wordplay, humor, intelligence, warmth, all those things, thank God, that you can still see on Turner Classic Movies.

Hepburn in Breakfast at Tiffany's. *Wikimedia Commons.*

It doesn't even matter that all those things I miss might never have really existed in what we call "real life."

They're still there, in the movies, and so they'll be there forever.

When Lauren Bacall arched one eyebrow in *To Have and Have Not*, even though I was only in my pre-teens when I first saw the film (and Bacall was only nineteen when she made it), I was puddles. There's something to be said about an actress who projects such confidence and self-awareness. The something to be said is called "everything."

184

Chapter 7. Teaching

Crossing Brooklyn Ferry

I have been thinking all day about Walt Whitman's "Crossing Brooklyn Ferry." And I am not a Whitman guy. I am a Dickinson guy--"a narrow fellow in the grass;" "the nerves sit ceremonious, like tombs;" "...rowing in Eden..." I have always liked her economy, and there is nothing I've ever written that wasn't better when written with fewer words.

With Whitman's great verbal expanse, I suspect that he would come over to your house, drink your imported beer, eat the meatiest ribs off the barbecue, hold the center of attention at the dinner table for four hours, this Niagara of verbiage, then leave singing sea shanties with the wicker basket full of tollhouse cookies that Emily had baked clamped firmly under one arm.

Whitman. Library of Congress.

But I always loved teaching this poem. Sooner or later, you realize, as you navigate your way through his hallooing and disgusting jubilance, his ecstatic self-regard, you realize...

...Who knows, for all the distance, but I am as good as looking at you now...?

...He's reading his poem *with* you, right over your shoulder. It is the damnedest thing. He's smiling, too, the old coot, under those cotton-candy whiskers. It is a miraculous, timeless poem, and he knows it.

I think that's why I loved teaching. Teaching has a chance at timelessness, too. The results of what you teach you see fitfully but they flicker and disappear. The consequences of *how* you teach may come years later, may even come beyond your own lifetime. They may appear, as a small causative, in someone you've taught who decides to do something courageous and decent--it might even be something immensely unpopular precisely *because* it's courageous and decent.

I was thinking today of Eileen Taylor's defense of our Japanese-American neighbors when they returned to our home, to our valley, justifiably fearful (Iso Kobara heard gunshots in the night) in 1944-1945. A grocer told Iso's mother, Kimi, never to come in his store again.

It is not upon you alone the dark patches fall,
The dark threw its patches down upon me also

Eileen heard about this incident. She was the president of the Arroyo Grande Women's Club. She decided, I think, to read the membership the riot act at the next meeting--we'll never really know, because, like Lincoln's legendary Cooper Union speech in 1860, we've lost the notes. She must have spoken about their obligation, as women, as mothers, as neighbors, to open their arms and their hearts to people who needed them and who had earned their compassion.

Kimi Kobara remembered in an interview many years later that the atmosphere improved immediately after that Women's Club meeting. Because Eileen spoke up, this happened: Many years later, I had the great privilege of teaching both Eileen Taylor's great-grandchildren and Kimi Kobara's.

So an event that happened before I was born--time avails not, as Whitman writes in the poem--became an important part of my life. The lives of Eileen and Kimi, two women I never met, became entwined with my life.

You furnish your parts toward eternity,
Great or small, you furnish your parts toward the soul.

And my teaching--how I taught my Taylors and Kobaras-- was a product of people they had never met, either. My teaching was shaped by the good teachers I'd had, and there were many, and it was shaped by my mother and father. If you were a student of mine, and knew me, then you know them. You also know Arroyo Grande High School speech teacher Sara Steigerwalt, Cal Poly Journalism professor Jim Hayes and history professor Dan Krieger, University of Missouri History professors Richard Bienvenu and David Thelen.

That's why I so enjoy this poem. It's life-affirming, and lives lived 150 years ago are just as important today as they were then.

Even better, they are just as much *alive*. They are right beside us, like Whitman standing at the rail of the Brooklyn Ferry, these old lives that give life.

What is it then between us?
What is the count of the scores or hundreds of years between us?
Whatever it is, it avails not—distance avails not, and place avails not...

The Valentine on My Desk

Last week, a student left a Valentine on my teacher's desk at Arroyo Grande High School.

It read: "Thank you for believing in me."

She was born in Guerrero, a Mexican state I know from my college studies of the revolutionary Emiliano Zapata, who was born in nearby Morelos, south of Mexico City.

Zapata's life, ended by assassination in 1919, galvanized peasants who wanted a little land to farm. He fought rapacious sugar planters who monopolized the land and guarded it with Maxim guns. The planters, in fact, wanted to expand their holdings, threatening to plant cane even in the naves of every parish church in Morelos and Guerrero.

My life is ordinary. I'm no Zapata. I am a bespectacled and aging teacher who has been inspired in watching this girl discover the power she has inside herself.

Her family's first language is Spanish, but she is mastering the arcane details of Advanced Placement European History, with its Hapsburgs and Bourbons, Calvinists and Anabaptists, Girondins and Jacobins, Bolsheviks and Spartacists.

She is getting an "A" in one of the most difficult classes we offer, and she has just turned sixteen. I want to see her in a UC when her time with us is done. That's when her time will begin.

Going to be a Teacher?

I always wanted to be among those teachers who seem to command the fondest memories and the greatest respect, and in my high school experience, in the school where I teach today, those were Sara Steigerwalt, my speech teacher, and Carol Hirons, my journalism teacher. They generate fond and respectful memories, and I was terrified of both.

I also loved them.

I tried to terrify *my* students early on in my teaching career, but something unexpected happened: My stomach began to hurt so badly that I would actually have to stop and catch my breath. I couldn't sustain it.

So I went back to being myself. And, as much as I'd like to, mostly to salve my male ego, I can't be a tough guy. It saved my pride a little when I came to realize that I deal with children, not calves at branding time.

That doesn't mean I'm not demanding. I expect a lot from my kids, and I hold them to those expectations. And my most demanding demands are for civility and effort.

But I fail, every year, the basic Jesuit rule about teaching: Don't smile until Christmas. This is because if I couldn't be funny when

I prepare for a lesson on the Franco-Prussian War.

I teach-—I was my high school's Class Comedian, in 1970-—I would almost certainly die. Sometimes, especially when I'm watching students write an essay or take a test, when they're not watching me, they make me so happy that I can't help but smile.

I once took one of those education classes, and they're *dreadful* things, education classes, when we observed a not-very-competent teacher on videotape. The prof asked for feedback. Mine was that the teacher didn't seem to like kids much. The professor looked as if I were the Village Idiot he'd caught stealing his prize hen, which was still in my arms. "Who said," he asked, both rhetorically and icily, "that it's necessary to *like* kids?"

I later taught two of his children. They were brilliant students and gentle, selfless human beings. I liked them. I loved them, in fact. I came to realize that my professor must have been going through a hard time. When I met him again many years later at Parent Conference Night-—I didn't bring up our previous acquaintance-—he was a changed man. He was much happier and he was, most deservedly, a proud father. He had done a beautiful job with them, and the gift he gave me in those children trivialized that bitter moment years before in his classroom.

I need to point out that I am not a saint, plaster or otherwise, either. I've screwed up in the classroom in ways that still make me flinch, years later. I've gotten angry; I've absolutely and flamboyantly lost my temper, and reamed a class with all the in-your-faceness that a Parris Island D.I. could summon.

I once completely mishandled a situation involving a young man throwing the F-bomb at a young woman sixty feet away. I was furious. He was suspended. it wasn't until much later that I realized that the young woman had probably provoked him. She was fluttering her eyelashes in mock innocence. What he said was completely inappropriate, but the chances were that she completely deserved it.

This is the one part I love about getting older: I don't get angry so much anymore. At my students, anyway. When I *do* get angry in the classroom, it's more likely that I'm *pretending* to be angry. I've learned to pick my spots: those talks, at the right moment, can be marvelous motivators, and it's fine with me if I'm the only person in the room who knows I'm delivering a monologue in the Globe Theater of my mind, usually as either Henry V or Richard III.

But if I forget, and if I *do* get angry enough to embarrass a student, here is what I've learned to do:

Apologize.

Within earshot of that student's friends.

Here's why: Teaching is about human relationships, and a student you've humiliated isn't going to be in relationship with you. He's going to shut down, he's not going to learn, and you've failed him. If kids see an adult fail, it's essential for them to see that adult accept responsibility for the failure.

The basketball player Charles Barkley was absolutely right when he said once that it wasn't his job to be a role model. But it is for teachers.

That goes for my behavior outside the classroom, as well. If I want to buy something from the lunch cart, I made this a cardinal rule: Never cut in front of the kids. Wait your turn with them instead. Inside the classroom, I will never ask a student to do an assignment I haven't done myself.

I've also gradually come to realize that "classroom management" isn't about disciplining kids: It's about disciplining yourself. It means thinking out your lesson—my role model in lesson design is Filippo Brunelleschi, the jeweler who designed the *duomo* of the Florence cathedral and engineered the incredible machinery that made its construction possible. It's means you make your objectives clear, you know how to change the subject or the learning style at least three times in a class period, and you know your students–the last is as much intuition as it is science–and, most of all, it means what comes easiest for me: Being excited about what you're teaching and, for that matter, about the honor of being a teacher.

It is amazing how something so unmeasurable—those educational theorists adore the term "data-driven," and they're easy to visualize with tape measures, calipers, and thermometers, always measuring, and meanwhile an eighth-grade girl has tied their shoelaces together, is also so marvelously effective.

But it also takes a tremendous amount of hard work. My easy workdays are ten hours. We don't, despite the popular belief, go home at three. School is why we're scribbling in our weekly plan books at our kids' soccer games, or why I'm grading essays at the local coffeehouse while my peers are stopping by for an espresso before they go on a bike into one of our beautiful coastal valleys, or sipping a cappuccino with the *New York Times Book Review*. That's not how teachers spend their weekends.

And while I love kids, they can take a toll: I'm also a raging introvert, and all those surging emotions and all the needs and all the questions that young people have can wear me out. Sometimes, on my prep period, I have to turn out the classroom lights and put my forehead down on my desk and just let the exhaustion take over for a little while. That moment comes to every teacher. It's a price, we've decided, that's worth paying.

Fortunately, I am not so absorbed in my own noble suffering that I'm not willing to share some outrageously cheap stunts. in the name of classroom management, that might illuminate the young teachers who will replace me:

• Not getting an answer to a question you've asked? Threaten to hold your breath until you die, in which case it will all be their fault, and will have to live with that for the rest of their lives! Somebody will raise her hand.

- I will sometimes lie down on the floor and pretend to take a nap, and ask them to wake me up when they want to re-engage in the class discussion.

- It's useful to have a few stage tricks, too. Sometimes I will have to chew out a kid, but we'll go outside to do it, get our signals straight again, and then I will hit a locker (darn it, they are gone now) with my fist and we'll re-enter the classroom with the kid rubbing his arm and wincing. When they laugh, it's because the joke is ours—mine and the kid who got into trouble—and we've turned the tables on something that could have been hurtful.

- I hate them in the classroom, but sometimes cell phones are quite useful, especially if you have a parent's cell number. It's a marvelous thing to call a student to the door who's frittering away a chance to study for an exam, hand him your cell phone, and whisper:

"It's your Mom."

By the way, I once asked a parent, and my anger was not well disguised, who was texting during my Back to School Night presentation to turn the phone off. He did.

Another time, I got so frustrated with a class that I left the room and walked out in seeming cold fury. Then I ran around to the other side of the building, where there's a bank of windows, and crawled under the lowest ones and brought my face up, glowering, very, very slowly, as if I were a periscope. When they started laughing, I got them back.

I've gotten the kind of angry teachers can get with a kid that's such a bad anger that it keeps you up all night. We lose a lot of sleep worrying about you, American students. Here's what I finally learned to do: I go to the records office, find the student's folder, and look at the first-grade school photo. That little, little boy, whose hair has been combed so carefully, is your student, too.

At the same time, my humanitarian tendencies are tempered by an occasional snappy line:

When they're supposed to be doing quiet seated work:

"I can hear voices, and the last time I checked, I wasn't Joan of Arc."

Two boys were sending eye signals when they were supposed to be reading. Some teachers would immediately launch an all-out nuclear strike. I waited for a few minutes, then took them outside.

"Gentlemen," I said. "I've been teaching for a long time, and can always tell the kind of guys who are going to give me trouble, the kind of guys I'm going to butt heads with."

Pause. The pause is the most important part. I learned to pause from the sportscaster I so admire, Vin Scully.

"And you aren't those guys."

And then you describe the behavior, and why it's a problem, and they get it.

I'm a firm believer in the philosophy of catching them when they're good. When a student gets a good grade on a difficult test, or she tries to answer a difficult question, or when he is kind to another student, they know I am proud of them. And when I pass that student's desk and give him or her just the briefest pat on the shoulder, they know what I'm saying: You matter, you did your best, your behavior is admirable, and I admire you, too.

When it comes to behavior, I am, ironically, the worst note-passer—now antiquated, true, in the cell phone age-- in my own class. A 15-year-old honors student last week told me she was having a panic attack and left the classroom in tears. Later I passed her a note: *I've had them, too. So have Lincoln, Adele, Johnny Depp and John Steinbeck. We're not weirdos. We're humans, you and me.*

King Charles I and Mike the Wonder Chicken

This song was part of a lesson plan that included the 1649 execution of King Charles I of England. The scholarship that underlay this lesson was supported by an unimpeachable source: A "Ripley's Believe it or Not" strip in the Sunday funnies in 1960. Old Ripley alleged that the king muttered a line from the Lord's Prayer ("*Thy will be done…*") *after* his head had been separated from the rest of him. Kids love beheading stories. Me, too, so this led to yet another beheading story, which inspired the song.

According the artist Van Dyck, Charles evidently had three heads, a luxury not found in Fruita, Colorado. The Royal Collection Trust via Wikimedia Commons.

Mike was a gentleman chicken executed for dinner in 1945 in Fruita, Colorado. Unfortunately, or not, the executioner, Farmer Olsen, aimed a little high (his mother-in-law was coming over, and she liked the neck) and Mike not only survived beheading, but he walked around the yard in evident good spirits afterward. It seems that Olsen missed the brain stem, and, beyond that, I can assure you from personal experience, chickens don't have that much more intellectual capital to invest. Mike would live pretty happily for several months. Olsen fed him with a little eye-dropper and the two traveled together to county fairs and university veterinary schools. Sadly, on one such trip, Mike expired. So we would sing this song, as a class, every year, when we studied the English Civil War and Charles I's demise. By the way, the king's nemesis, Oliver Cromwell, was beheaded as well, but that was *after he'd already died.* They had to exhume him to execute him. So much for British reserve.

But that's all water under London Bridge.

This is for Mike the Wonder Chicken. We love you, little buddy.

To the tune of "Puff, the Magic Dragon."

Mike, the Wonder Chicken

Mike, the Wonder Chicken
Did not have a head
No one had in-formed him,
He really should be dead.

Mike, the Wonder Chicken
Was known far and wide,
For in the town of Fru-ita
He sur-vived Chickencide.

Mike, the Wonder Chicken
Was a friendly chap
He pecked alongside barnyard pals
Who ig-nored his mishap.
(Slow and mournful)

Then, one night in a mo-tel…
Mike began to choke…
Farmer Olsen tried to help…
But…poor…Mike….finally…croaked!

Mr. Adams, 1956

We live close by Margaret Harloe Elementary School in Arroyo Grande, and a former student there, Andrew Harp, shared this vivid memory.

Harloe opened Sept, '55. Before that, we attended Orchard Street. Leila Adams' father headed up the Harloe admin. He was in a wheelchair, but pitched our baseball games. He would field a grounder, underhand the ball backward to second base, and get a force-out. At World Series time, TV's would appear, all teaching stopped, and we watched the games. Witnessed Don Larsen's '56 perfect game in my Harloe classroom. It was great to be a kid back then in AG!

This intrigued me, for many reasons, but chiefly for the warmth of the way Mr. Harp remembers Mr. Adams and his school and how "it was great to be a kid back then." Here's the point: In 21st Century American education, warmth has no metric. Having a great childhood can't be measured on a standardized test

I like metrics, used modestly. Here's one: I found a photograph of the first pitch Don Larsen threw, with Yogi Berra behind the place, at Yankee Stadium in a game that would last just a little over two hours. The stadium clock indicated that it was 1 p.m. What *this* tells me is that Mr. Adams stopped instruction at 10 a.m. here in Arroyo Grande so his students could watch a baseball game that lasted into lunchtime. Granted, they watched one of the most famous games in history, but they watched it during "instructional time," and in the late morning, some of the most fruitful instructional time in a child's day. That's a fertile field that Mr. Adams failed to plant.

Do you know what would happen to him if he did that *today?*

Wrong. That's not how education works. He would be transferred, probably to an obscure assistant superintendent's position that sounded good, paid a little more, but was essentially a career dead end: In the military, the equivalent might be the third time a lieutenant colonel is passed over for promotion. Removing someone like Mr. Adams from his principalship, however, would be a tragedy.

Schools today are, obviously, different, and I do not think they are better. Mr. Adams would've been transferred today because schools and curricula are so tightly wired that two hours wasted watching the Series would mean defeat and ruination at the hands of a kid in Singapore whose score on the international PISA test is 12 points higher than the score of a kid in Arroyo Grande, California. No matter that the higher-scoring student might grow up unable to change a tire, approach a girl at lunch for a movie date, or write a newspaper lead.

But the Singapore kid would win in the only world that matters to educational theorists today: Metrics Land.

Mind you, I'm not advocating we substitute *Spongebob Squarepants* reruns for prime mathematics instruction time. Far from it.

But, honestly: What do you remember most about your education? I can still diagram a sentence, I never pretended to be able to solve a quadratic equation, but here are the things I remember:

• My sixth grade teacher, Mr. Burns, taking me aside one day and telling me I was a wonderful writer (I thought he was referring to my penmanship) and, at the end of the year, giving a me a thesaurus that read *Someday I expect to read great things by you.*

• My speech teacher, a tiny woman who was, like Mr. Adams, in a wheelchair, Sara Steigerwalt, was a complete autocrat and she terrified me. One day she called me to her desk. "Mr. Gregory," she said quietly. "I don't feel well. I need your help." I called her sister, we got her home–I think I wheeled her out to Betty's car–and from that moment on, I would literally have given my life for her, even if my speechmaking would never reach the heroic levels I wanted so much to reach for her.

• My senior year, I was writing and directing the class play in the gym and basking in my own glory when my journalism teacher, Carol Hirons, stormed in and all but dragged me by the ear back to the classroom, where I had a Page Three of the school newspaper to put to bed. I had "forgotten." I will never forget that moment.

I think that the lessons that stick come from relationships between teachers and children. In those moments where "teaching" is left behind and replaced by something much more enduring: "Mentoring."

And just how was Mr. Adams "mentoring" by parking a flickery black-and-white TV in the Harloe cafeteria? I can't answer that precisely, so I won't really try. But what Mr. Harp remembers so vividly and so beautifully *does* mean something: He knew he was a part of a community bonded by a shared experience that is now a shared memory. He knew who that community's leader was because Mr. Adams modeled leadership, from his wheelchair, with such grace.

I think what America has lost isn't an edge in math and science. What's been lost, instead, is a sense of common purpose—just look at Congress—and there's no better metaphor for that than third graders, if just for a few hours, holding their breaths together, waiting expectantly for a base hit that will never come.

We Interrupt This Chapter for a Dog Story

The Facebook thing is pure evil, I know, but it's fun to follow your students through their lives—college, careers, marriage, kids of their own. You get to meet their dogs, too.

Ashley was a student of both Elizabeth and mine when we taught at Mission Prep. She belongs to a Wheaten Terrier with a lovely name from history: Isadora. Tillie is the name of the Wheaten who owns my sister, Sally.

They are lovely dogs--eager, frolicky, and more affectionate than your typical terrier, a prickly but adorable lot. Wheatens are charmers and even more charming because they aren't pretentious about it. Their main business is going about being a dog.

Isadora has a tumor in her lung and so her days are numbered. When I learned this, there was a deep and profound hurt inside. I have a hard time with death.

The worst, of course, was my Mom's. She was and will always be the most formative person in my life. Mom's spirituality was profound, but my own spiritual life has been influenced both by her and by dogs. I've been around dogs all my life, beginning with a Scottish Terrier and a Cocker Spaniel in my first memories, on Sunset Drive in Arroyo Grande. The dogs who complete my life today are Mollie and Brigid, our Irish Setters, and Wilson, our Basset.

Mollie will leave us soon. I notice this more because the grizzling of her muzzle and the gradual slowing of her gait, her struggles to climb onto the sofa or our bed, make her aging so obvious. (At sixty-seven, I secretly identify with her, especially when I go to the gym and watch, out of the corner of one eye, twentysomethings doing workouts I could never hope to do.)

Every time a dog leaves us, when we hold their heads in our hands and talk softly to them, we aren't quite sure whether the last moments we spend together are understood. I think the animals somehow know what is happening. They understand the earnestness of our words when we tell them how much we love them. We are part of their passage and they need, just as all of us will someday need, a little company as they cross that fearful space that leads to the other side.

Mr. Wilson.

In a lifetime of dogs, I have loved each a little differently and they have loved me with no discrimination whatsoever. They are entirely unselfish in love, if not in food or rawhide treats. We don't encounter that kind of love very much in life--the "unconditional" kind, to use a trite adjective--and that's what makes losing an animal one of the most painful moments in any human's life.

Brigid, with her ball, and Mollie.

It's supposed to hurt because they love us the way God does, without stipulation, without judgment, without reservation, and so when they leave us they leave an immense empty space behind.

Here's just one small example of the grace dogs bring into our lives. I spend, and have spent, much of my life criticizing myself, condemning myself, and finding fault with myself. But every morning there is a miracle: Brigid is so transparently happy--and wiggly--to see me again after a night's sleep that she gives me enough confidence to start another day. There is something in me that she finds invaluable and joyful. I think God must see that something, as well.

I think, too, that God understands that dogs and their humans need to be together. Ashley's dog, Isadora, has a bond with her that can't be broken. Heaven, I suspect, is a place for happy mornings where we will see each other once again, and forever.

Most Inspirational. Ever.

The Jim Hayes look. Translation: Re-write. Photo by Wayne Nicholls,
Courtesy the San Luis Obispo *Tribune*

Jim Hayes taught me journalism at Cal Poly and was on the copy desk when I was a *Telegram-Tribune* reporter. Jim was the kind of editor who brings to mind the Tsukiji fish market in Tokyo. He treated your brilliant copy as if it were a tuna, not quite fresh enough, that you'd plopped down in front of his stall. He would study your fish with a look of slight disdain and scowly concentration. You watched him, apprehensive. While you watched, he set about fileting your beautiful fish. He did that with several of my stories--at least one because I'd used the pronoun no journalist can ever use: *I.* When I got my copy back, there were about two sentences still standing. It was a Hayes Filet. A tiny one. And I got the *look,* the one you see in the photograph.

Of course, he was right. The rewrite was infinitely better, because it wasn't about *me.* Reporters don't belong in the stories they write. If you want to write like that, then "failed novelist" is probably the best job description for you. Or, in my case, "retired history teacher."

Jim struck terror into a couple of generations of both Poly journalism students and professional reporters. But if you paid attention to him and to what he wrote on your copy, this is what happened: You became a better writer.

If you got to know Jim a little better, you became a better person.

The gruffness in him never went away. But neither did the wisdom and neither, if you had the audacity to look at him closely, did the man's immense humanity. Jim was himself a skilled observer of humanity—he had a sixth sense about people that was incredibly accurate-- and a superb writer. His teaching was so good, though, that the Los Angeles *Times* made him their writing coach. He has made some of the best reporters in journalism better. He was able to do that because he loved writing, he loved teaching and most of all—this finally dawned on me in our own relationship, but I'm a little dense— he loved his students.

He is now in hospice care with a brain tumor, and his Facebook page has been flooded—post after post, page after page–with tributes from former students. As he faces this terrible fight, all the devotion this ostensibly scary man has invested in others is coming back to him in waves. Here is a tribute I wrote for him:

* * *

One of my first students was named a young woman enrolled in Poly's journalism program. I was just a student, too, but Jim made me her writing coach. Here's what happened: She would go into a broadcast career to anchor at the local NBC affiliate, KSBY, and not because of me, but because she was bright, hard-working, and incredibly positive; she actually *could* light up a room—newsroom or otherwise. As it turned out, she was a far better reporter than I was. All she'd needed was something I would discover over and over in the young women I would teach over thirty years in the classroom: Confidence in herself. I was heartbroken when that first student, Missie, died young, of cancer, but our newswriting tutorials so many years before had been the first hint I'd ever had that I might have a gift for teaching.

Jim knew that before I did.

* * *

Jim died in June.

To the Girl on the Lawn at Cal

This year AVID students--kids whose family backgrounds do not include a college experience-- invited me to go on the northern college tour, and I was honored. I had never visited Cal until a few years ago with another AVID group. I did go to Stanford. For a week. I won a teachers' fellowship in 2004 and got to study the Great Depression and New Deal with David Kennedy, whose book on the subject won the Pulitzer Prize for History. I tried not to look too adoringly at him while he taught us. It was difficult, because not only was he brilliant, but he was a real human being– engaging, witty, and you could tell he loved the history of the time because he so admired the Americans who had lived it.

But on the AVID trips, I quickly learned to love Stanford's rival, Cal, even though I had to fight the impulse, so common to my generation, to run off and occupy the administration building, Sproule Hall, and demand that we leave Vietnam.

My mother in high school.

The other thing I thought, with a little sadness, was that my Mom-- Patricia Margaret Keefe--should've been here. She grew up poor, a child of the Great Depression. She was a human footnote in the immense body of Kennedy's scholarship. Her father, my Irish-American grandfather, deserted the family in the mid-1920s, so my grandmother worked long hours as a waitress in a Taft, California, coffee shop. This meant that my mother, as a little girl, spent a lot of time alone. Those years left their mark on her. We had a can cupboard longer than the cupboards in the back of my classroom, hers full of food we'd never eat, because the thought of going hungry must have terrified her. That fear marked her generation.

Despite her childhood, she's there in the 1938 yearbook, the Taft Union High School *Derrick,* and she's is in CSF, GAA, she is class secretary and class vice president. She'd made her mark. Still, going to college, for the daughter of a waitress from an isolated outpost on the oil frontier, must have been out of the question.

Earl Denton, the first superintendent of the Lucia Mar school district and a family friend, said that my mother, whose education ended with her graduation from Taft Union High School, was one of the most brilliant people he'd ever met. I remember her devouring the works of the Jesuit theologian and anthropologist Pierre Teilhard de Chardin, who argued that evolution was no contradiction of faith; in fact, it was a divinely-inspired process. She--as I would years later with books like Eugene Genovese's masterful history of

American slavery, *Roll, Jordan, Roll*--wrote almost as much in the margins of Teilhard's books as he had written in the text.

When I was very little, we played school. She even rang a hand bell when "recess" was over. It had been my grandmother's—Dora Gregory, her mother-in-law, had been a schoolmarm in the Ozark foothills. My first day of formal education was in the first grade in a two-room school, Branch Elementary, in the Upper Arroyo Grande Valley. I remember realizing, with a little shock of pleasure, that I could read the names of my classmates as our teacher, Mrs. Brown, wrote them on the blackboard.

My mother and I hadn't been "playing" school at all. She just made it seem that way.

So, many, many years later, on that visit to Cal, while the AVID kids explored, I had the briefest and loveliest mental image of her, about 1938 or 1939--blouse, pleated skirt, saddle shoes, bobby socks, with her books and notebook spread out on one of those lush, verdant lawns, studying between classes. My mother was a beautiful woman, but the most beautiful thing about her may have been her mind.

And I think that's why I enjoy these particular trips, with this particular group of kids. It's my way of repaying Mom. One of them might take her place, studying in the sunlight on the lawn at a place like Memorial Glade. She would love that idea.

And she would love these kids because she would understand them completely. Despite my ne'er-do-well grandfather, I believe completely that my mother's empathy and her love for the written word had deep genetic and psychological roots in Ireland's County Wicklow.

So she would love without hesitation the AVIDS who show the incredible desire, the hunger, to improve themselves that she'd had, and who extend themselves to help their classmates. She believed that all of us are intricately and intimately connected, and that this connection requires us to be responsible to and accountable for each other.

The young person who understands these things is close to my mother's heart.

Room 306, Year 27 of Teaching

Goodbye, Room
Yet one more time.
The year's gone (Zoom!)
And now you're all clean.
What do you do all summer
Bereft of your teens?
No offense, but you're a bore,
Empty like this,
No kids at your door,
(No furtive Doritos
All crunched on your floor.)
I've been here in summer—
It's so cold and dark

There are squirrels outside
But you're empty and stark
With no kids at all—
        But
They'll come back this fall;
They'll be all of fifteen, while
I'm in full grampage, getting small
        er every year.
I'm still full of stories--
While I forget names now.
I still look for glories
In the pages of books,
And when their hands go up
In teenagers' looks.

Chapter 8. The Food Chapter

I make another exuberant batch of enchiladas.

Sopa, Sushi, Lumpias and Tamales: Life is Good

There was a time that is gone forever when mothers would look at me accusingly. I would think I had done something wrong. I hadn't. "You're too skinny." I miss those words. Once our neighbor, Mary Gularte, said those exact words to me. She sat me down at her kitchen table on a cold morning in the tiny house where she raised her brood of Gularte boys and girls. Mary served me a big bowl of *sopa*, or Portuguese stew, aromatic and dense, and I was never so happy to follow orders as I was that day with her. I didn't have to eat the rest of the day.

Another food stands out: The sushi I had, long before it was fashionable, at Ben Dohi's house, across from the high school—tuna and sticky rice wrapped in *nori*, strips of seaweed, a huge task for his wife and her Yamaguchi sisters to prepare, so it was reserved for traditional Japanese holidays like the Fourth of July and Labor Day. It was sweet and savory, chewy and delicate, and sometimes while Ben and the men watched sports in the living room and digested, I would hang out with the Yamaguchi sisters in the kitchen, both because they were hilarious and because I was closer to seconds.

Lumpias were another treat, and I am reasonably sure that I could eat them until I needed transport to the emergency room. These are Filipino egg rolls, crunchy and filled with vegetables and pork. An association of Filipino women sold them during the annual Arroyo Grande Harvest Festival, the big community celebration. It was a courtesy, after a bit of cooling once you'd bought them, to eat the first one in front of their booth. It gave them a chance to watch your face, to watch the way your eyes closed and then the smile began as you took that first bite of lumpia. It made them happy because they were moms, too.

And then there's Mrs. Flores. Her son Rogelio was one of my best friends in high school until he went astray in life and became a judge. I will not hold that against him, because his mother introduced me to *nopales* (cactus) as a side dish. Not only were *nopales* delicious, you could feel all those good green vitamins surging through your bloodstream. Wait. That may have been Mrs. Flores' *salsa*. And I thought I knew tamales—the best ones come from a nice lady in a pickup who knocks on your door without demanding a religious conversion-- until my friend and the best man at our wedding, Robert Rosales, introduced me to his grandmother's (*abuela's*) dessert tacos. They are a sweet Christmas treat in Mexican-American homes, and the challenge is to let them dissolve as slowly as humanly possible in your mouth to extract the last doughy sweetness from them: Someday, if I have one on Christmas, I am shooting for December 28. And someday I want my stocking filled with them, please.

In the 21st Century, Arroyo Grande is seeing increasing numbers of immigrants from the Middle East and South Asia, and their children are a joy to teach. The 20th century belongs to the waves of people, immigrants and their children, who came from the Azores, from Japan, from the Philippines and from Mexico. All of them, thank goodness, have brought their food here, too.

Chickens of the Sea

Despite the fact that I can swim just far enough to get to the edge of the pool and beg for a lifeguard and that I'm *still* incensed that the Monterey Bay Aquarium refused to let us bring home just one measly penguin from our last visit (We have a bathtub, thank you. We are civilized people. They were sending a pair to *Dallas,* for cryin' out loud.), I retain a lifelong passion for the sea and, more specifically, for seafood. Fortunately, I was raised in Arroyo Grande and the sea is conveniently located just a short distance past Orcutt Burger.

Here are some of the highlights of a lifetime of love for *frutti di mare* (Italian for "Watch this guy's face when we serve him *this!*")

1. **Squid-ink pasta**

WHERE: Venice, Italy

WITH: My wife, Elizabeth Jane Bruce Gregory, our sons, and 48 of our closest teenaged friends, while leading a trip to Europe.

COMMENTS: I'm glad I can't read Italian, because I never would've ordered it from the menu which was, incredibly, *in* Italian. The pasta is black. When Tony Soprano went to Italy, the Jersey-bred Paulie Walnuts was so offended at the looks of *his* pasta that he sent it back to the kitchen. I couldn't do that. My honor was at stake. Then I closed my eyes and inserted a forkful into my mouth. My taste buds did little can-cans of delight. A fortunate flavor juncture of delicate, salty ocean and mushroomy earth, but it turns your lips and tongue black and your sons, returning from the pizza place, point at you and laugh. Even more than usual.

2. **Paella**

WHERE: (The Late, Great) Old Vienna Cafe, Shell Beach

WITH: My wife.

COMMENTS: What is this "saffron" stuff and why is it more expensive than gold leaf? And why are dishes so much tastier when they're so vast that they need to be wheeled out to the dining room? This was wonderful restaurant, but I still feel badly about the wonderful and warm owners, the Reithofer family. We were role-playing "Sink the Lusitania" in my history class, and their daughter, Heidi, was at the periscope, when I said: 'Okay, Heidi, you're the dirty German U-boat commander.' To which she replied: 'Mr. Gregory. I'm German.'

3. **Bucket o' Mussels.** Yo, ho. Repeat. Bucket o' Mussels. Or, for you French speakers, *Moules marinièrs.*

WHERE: Honfleur, France. Henry Tudor sailed from here to slay Richard III.

WITH: My friends, my English teaching partner, Amber Derbidge, her husband, Nephi , and 24 teenagers we were leading on another trip to Europe. This is not as bad as it sounds.

COMMENTS: Yummy, yummy, yummy, I've got love in my tummy. Nephi and I had a bucket each with fresh bread as soft as cotton candy, just enough garlic to singe the napkins, and just enough butter–about two cows' worth–so that we could *slide* on our tummies back to the tour bus.

Why must fried food be so delicious?

4. Sand dabs

WHERE: (The Late) Pezzulo's Ristorante, Shell Beach

WITH: My wife. We used to go out a lot, before the term "Mortgage-backed securities" appeared in the nation's vocabulary in 2008.

COMMENTS: A little dabs will do ya. Heavenly: Firm and fleshy, yet they melt meekly in your mouth. A fish only a mother dab could love, though. They can't decide whether they're sideways or not, or, like the subjects in a Cubist painting, where exactly to place their eyeballs. This represents a total lack of commitment I do not normally countenance in vertebrates.

5. Crab Cakes

WHERE: Fisherman's Wharf, San Francisco

WITH: My wife, Elizabeth

COMMENTS: Why didn't I have these when we were in Maryland? Not to worry: We went to Camden Yards in Baltimore and saw a little marker that celebrated a Ken Griffey Jr. home run that had landed somewhere in Virginia. I took a photo of the great infielder Cal Ripken Jr, then in his last season, with no film in the camera. I did the same when I once took a picture of Elizabeth and David Crosby of Crosby, Stills and Nash in Santa Ynez. If I'd worked for Matthew Brady, we'd have only crude drawings on the lids from boxes of hardtack to document the Civil War. Anyway, the crab cakes were wonderful, and San Francisco is spectacular, especially the bearded lady who rides the Muni down Market Street.

6. Toro (Fatty tuna) sushi

WHERE: Mr. Ben Dohi's house, Arroyo Grande 1969

WITH: A delightful gathering of Dohis and Yamaguchis–including future Olympic Ice Skating Champion Kristi. She was an adorable baby. *Hey! I didn't drop you, Kristi! Where are my royalties?*

COMMENTS: Delicious, and a the kind of food where texture matters as much as taste. But, something worries me: Do the other tuna call the Toro "fatty" to their faces? And do they let them join in any Tuna Games?

7. Deep fried abalone steak

WHERE: Bob's Seafood, Morro Bay, 1965

WITH: Mom & Dad

COMMENTS: This was when the abalone were so thick that cowboys would herd them down the Los Osos Valley to market. You may remember that an important rail center in the Old West was Abalone, Kansas. Best served with cole slaw, fries, and about a quart of Tartar Sauce. Dad always liked to do takeout, though, and drive up by Morro Rock and see *just how close* he could drive the '61 Dodge Polara wagon, which weighed slightly more than the Space Shuttle, to the edge without plunging into the Bay and having us all wash up, dead, broken, but nicely salted, on the shore of Midway Island. The meal was followed by a Dad nap and outside the car, there were surly-looking seagulls looking at our lunch scraps with penetrating stares. They would gather gradually but menacingly in ever-larger groups. I think they were washed-up actors on the long downward slide after stardom-come-early in Hitchcock's *The Birds.*

8. Tuna Sandwich

WHERE: Branch Elementary School, Arroyo Grande

WITH: Branch Elementary School

COMMENTS: Putting a lot of frills–tomatoes, avocado, capers, truffles–on a tuna sandwich is an abomination and will not be tolerated. Classic tuna sandwiches should be on whole wheat, toasted, mixed with a little mayo—and not too much!-- and pickle relish, and the sandwich must be sliced diagonally. If you are of dubious moral character, potato chips slipped inside the sandwich just before you eat it provide a nice textural addition to the iceberg lettuce already there. I had tuna sandwiches every Friday between 1958 and 1966. Afterward, I sat on the sandwich's wax-paper wrapping to go down the playground slide faster.

I am reasonably sure American middle-class certainties like these—tuna on Friday, *Bonanza* on Sunday--is why we did not all turn into communists at this time in Cold War history. You may thank my Mom. And Ben Cartwright.

I Hate Walnuts

The wind's freshening and I think it's about to storm, which made me think of how much I hate walnuts.

I hate them with the heat of a thousand white-hot suns.

Black walnuts were a big deal in Arroyo Grande—the fields of row crops across the high school and down to the creek, to the Fred Grieb Bridge, were once all walnut trees. Walnut trees had us flanked: There even more to the south of the campus and there were menacing arrays of them on Allen Street, just lurking there in an otherwise pleasant neighborhood. What followed was wonderful.

The Good Lord set the husk fly to our valley, and their larvae are rapacious walnut-eaters. They killed walnut farming here and then my friend Joe Loomis cut the trees down for firewood, which was only one of several thousand good deeds Joe did in his lifetime.

Before that blessed event, when it was about to rain this time of year, we ran like RAF pilots on alert during the Battle of Britain to cover the drying frames with plastic tarp so that the walnuts we'd harvested wouldn't get wet and mildew.

But I *wanted* them to. I wanted them to die soggy mildewy deaths.

Here is why: When black walnuts are green, they are as dense as cannonballs and with a sharp pointy nasty tip. They leave a spectacular welt when someone, including, possibly, an older brother, throws them at you, but I am not intimating anything here.

Harvesting walnuts is stoop labor. You squat all day and fill buckets and your back hurts. Then you shake the tree—or poke it; a belt-shaker, strapped around the trunk like a girdle, is expensive, so we were pokers—and the result of that is that you are pelted by doomed walnuts falling on your head.

Everybody at Branch School knew who had walnut trees because you came to school with your nails a vile greenish-black from separating the nut from the hull. Your hands weren't clean again until Christmas, which is when our teachers compounded our misery by assigning roles for the Christmas Play. I was the Littlest Angel (a classic example of miscasting), the father in "A Night Before Christmas" and Scrooge in *A Christmas Carol*. Here, let me prove it. This is from 1965:

If I had my way, every fool who went about with a 'Merry Christmas' on his lips would be boiled in his own pudding and buried with a stake of holly through his heart!

225

And we had to sing Christmas Carols. I still have 'em all down. At Christmas Mass, I feel superior because I don't need to consult the Missal until we get to the third verse of "O Come All Ye Faithful." Then I fake it.

I don't care how many Christmas plays I had to endure—eight—walnuts were far, far worse.

Sometimes you could sell them in little paper bags to those foolish enough to buy them. I didn't like eating them, though, because they make your palate burn.

I had one exception in this business of walnut consumption

For the walnuts you kept, you got to whack them with a little hammer to get the nut out—the inside of a walnut looks amazingly like a human brain—for Mom's sublime chocolate-chip cookies.

It felt good to whack them. You were getting even with the little rascals.

Then, the best part: Mom let you clean the cookie-dough bowl. When I was much, much older, someone invented chocolate chip cookie dough ice cream. Sir or Madam, whoever you are: You deserve the Nobel Prize for Ice Cream.

However, if you are a walnut, I still despise you. I'm sorry. It is what it is.

My Grandmother's Mashed Potatoes

I made tonight's dinner—oven-fried chicken and mashed potatoes—thinking of my grandmother, Dora Gregory. Her fried chicken, although I only had it a few times, was divine. It was what I'd call Border State Fried rather than Southern Fried—no batter, but the pieces sprinkled with top-secret seasonings and then coated in flour.

I remember that family gatherings at her house in Taft would include an array of salads--macaroni and fruit, I think, and one made with hominy, and vegetable casseroles, with green beans a favorite, liberally flavored with bacon, sweet potatoes laced with butter and brown sugar, baked beans flavored with molasses—it's a wonder I'm not dead yet.

There would also have been sliced ham. Her ham deserves a whole separate essay. Her husband, my grandfather John, raised hogs; slaughtering, curing and smoking happened in winter and whole families would participate, moving from one neighbor's Ozark Plateau farm to another until all the hams were hung. It would've been a dreadful time of year to be a hog.

Of course, Grandmother's crowning glory, and even the fried chicken took a little bit of a back seat, was mashed potatoes, fluffy as clouds. The chicken cracklings and their lubricant were turned, through some kind of alchemy, into flour gravy ladled over the potatoes, ready with a

Dora Wilson Gregory about 1910

little crater in their midst. But I thought that since her mashed potatoes were so good on their own that the gravy was better used over biscuits.

I like to think that my grandmother would have loved my mashed potatoes. Even their blessed little lumps.

Kale as a Communist Plot

I was innocently walking the dogs, with Mr. Basset investigating a poop and Ms. Setter looking hopefully for ducks, when a produce truck pulled over so the driver could check his load.

On the two flatbed trailers were high stacks of harvest lugs, marked OCEANO. This made me a little proud, knowing that local produce was bound for exotic places like Ketchikan, Tonto and Versailles (Missouri).

As we passed, I looked closer at the labels.

One stack was marked *cilantro*, not something cultivated around here when I was growing up, but I let it go, because cilantro goes on tacos, a dish as American as George Washington's mother's Sunday calash bonnet.

Another stack was marked *escarole*. I admit this led to a thread of suspicion in my mind, "escarole" being one of the French words that may or may not refer to snails. I then remembered that "escarole" is a kind of lettuce, so I guess this is an improvement over the three more common varieties grown here historically, "iceberg," "Romaine" and "That's not lettuce, stupid. It's cabbage."

It was the third stack that was the deadliest. It, too read OCEANO, and then, in much smaller letters

Flowering Kale.

I am glad I've taken relatively good care of my teeth, because if I'd been wearing dentures, I'd have spit them out to shatter on the sidewalk.

Let me be clear on my feelings about kale: It is the source of all evil in the world today, along with its unholy twin, quinoa (SEE: "Llama Food"). My wife has tried to introduce it into my diet, putting it in smoothies that are never smooth because there are always little crunchy chunks of kale in them, all bitter green nastiness.

Once I'd learned to hide my wife's smoothies in the washing machine, I quickly and logically came to the conclusion that this New Age wonder food is nothing of the kind. I am a child of the Cold War, so here is my quick and logical conclusion:

Only communism could have produced a vegetable this loathsome.

It is patently obvious that Red agronomists, modeling themselves on *The Manchurian Candidate's* Laurence Harvey, but with American accents, have hyped this aberrant vegetable on public radio and in the health magazines at the checkout counter. They've made kale key to our national diet, where it's ranked as good as or even better than the foods that have made us free men and women.

Including chicken-fried steak and nachos.

And I foolishly thought that we had *defeated* communism.

After all, Americans beat them to the moon, unless, of course, all of that *was* videotaped on a sound stage in Burbank. Compared to them, we have many more nuclear plants that have not blown up. We all watched happy and deserving Berliners tear down that damned Wall with sledgehammers and then return for many nights to beat on the fragments with smaller hammers. It was wonderful.

But was it all just an illusion? Have the communists slipped us the Red Mickey, although, technically, it's green? And it's not just that it's "kale"—it's "flowering" kale. It *grows.*

Subversion via vegetable is nothing new. After all, aliens tried that in the 1956 film *Invasion of the Body Snatchers.* They grew mindless, robotic human replicants in vegetable pods. The vegetables eventually replaced the red-blooded American population of a town called Santa Mira, California.

I am glad I brought this movie up.

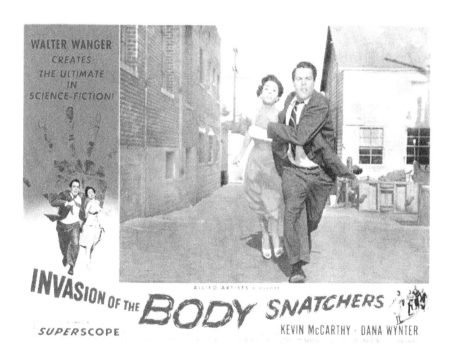

Run all you want, kids. You're toast. At least you're not kale.
Wikimedia Commons.

231

The good people of Santa Maria were relatively defenseless. In fact, in *Body Snatchers,* tranquilizers, so merrily prescribed to American women in the 1950s, seemed to be the only way to deal with the alien invasion. At several points in the plot, Dr. Bennell (Kevin McCarthy), slipped his nurse, Becky (Dana Wynter), a tranquilizer or nine when the ever-growing poddage threatened to unhinge her.

"*HERE!*" Dr. Bennell would shout, in a tone only a 1950s male who drove a thickly-chromed Pontiac Bonneville could summon, shoving a fistful Becky's way: "*TAKE SOME OF THESE!*"

I think he ran out of them, because she'd turned into Becky-Pod by the end of the film and Dr. Bennell was raving incoherently and playing tag with the cars on the freeway before they caught him and locked him away.

If this film is any indicator—and I am sure that it is—your Armageddon survival kit should now include dehydrated water, thousand-calorie survival bars, a brace of Glock 9 mm Parabellum pistols AND about 5,000 units of 10-mg. industrial grade Librium along with some cheap red wine. We need to heed Dr. Bennell's advice.

The alternative is something resembling Podhood. "Flowering Kale" is merely the first wave. Don't say you haven't been warned.

Missouri-Fried Everything

This child was NOT raised on a vegetarian diet. This is my Baby Dad. The 100th anniversary of his birth will be July 31, 2018, so we are wondering what we should eat to celebrate his memory. Since he grew up on the Ozark Plateau, some of the potential dishes:

- Chicken-fried steak. I haven't had chicken-fried steak in thirty-five years. The last time I tried it, it was so good that I barely noticed that my arteries were slamming shut like Walmart doors at closing time Black Friday.

- Ham-hocks and Lima beans. Nope. Lima beans are the only

vegetable I find more disturbing than kale. Their interiors have the texture of beach sand and taste about the same. Lima beans deserve to be extinct, like Dodo birds and Whigs.

• Squirrel stew. Not bad. A little peppery when Dad made it, about as bony as a lake trout, but darker and more mysterious in flavor. Not for me: The squirrels around here, I assume, are all rabid and homicidal.

• Missouri fried chicken. Not as batter-y as Southern Fried chicken. Roll it in either corn meal or flour, after you've dusted it with Secret Spices, fry, inhale. Grandma Gregory's Missouri fried drumsticks were especially divine. I ate them when I was little and would wave a denuded drumstick like a baton to express my happiness.

• A full-out ham dinner, with accompaniments, but it requires a table at least twelve feet long. And an immensity of hams. Fruit salad, potato salad, hot German potato salad, Jell-O salad, macaroni salad, mounds of deviled eggs, cinnamoned yams grown in the Old Confederacy but invaded by melting Yankee marshmallows, biscuits smeared generously with butter melted with honey, string-bean casserole, those mashed potatoes that remind you of fluffy clouds--if we could somehow get butter up there--and so many pies that another table is required just for them: Sweet potato pie, pumpkin pie, Dutch apple pie, chocolate pie, lemon meringue pie, peach pie and, most of all, pecan pie, with the "can" in "pecan" pronounced the way you'd pronounce it in the term "tin can." (Also, the emphasis is emphatic on the first syllable in the words "July" and "insurance" and you go to see a movie at the "thee-AY-ter.")

In defense of the Ozark Plateau, a meal like this Meal of Many Hams is intended to reinforce ideals like family and community, and it's eaten in several shifts that are interspersed with funny stories, family stories, local scandals, livestock inspection--Ozarkers love horses, and love commenting on them, as much as County Wicklow Irish do--neighborhood walks to work the food off where the neighbors wave from the front porch. Afterward, for folks my age, there are pleasant naps in recliners while the kids from all over the neighborhood scream at Badminton to the Death on the back lawn, because yards in the Border States are immense and fenceless.

But here's the winner in the Celebrate Dad food competition:

- *Biscuits and gravy,* with a creamy gravy studded with nougats du pork and sided by fried eggs and bacon or ham. Or bacon *and* ham. Again, the Ozark Plateau is no place to be a hog. Or a catfish. Biscuits, to be measured with calipers, must be at least two inches thick and also must be able to float effortlessly just before serving. In my hometown, Arroyo Grande, CJ's and Francisco's Country Kitchen both serve up biscuits and gravy like that.

I think that's the meal I'll go for. Don't tell my cardiologist. Dr. Tackett's from Kentucky, where they eat *exactly* the same things I love so dearly. Nevertheless, I suspect that my doctor eats kale. She might occasionally and accidentally smell bacon if she's out for breakfast and it's served on a table at the opposite end of the restaurant. But she will ignore that wonderful smell, I'm sure. She is a much stronger person than I could ever hope to be.

Biscuits and gravy, with the required nougats du pork. *The only possible problem with this photograph might be the conservatism with which the gravy was applied.* Pixabay.

Chapter 9. Desert Years

Butte Camp, part of the Gila River Internment Camp. National Archives.

Pearl Harbor and Arroyo Grande

Just before eight o'clock on December 7, 1941, a bomb's concussion on battleship *Arizona's* stern blew the lifeless body of Navy bandsman Jack Scruggs into Pearl Harbor. A little more than five minutes later, the second, fatal, bomb penetrated the teak deck, killing a second sailor, Wayne Morgan, and over 1100 of his shipmates when it detonated the forward powder magazines. Scruggs and Morgan had grown up in Arroyo Grande.

As fuel oil leaks from ships on Battleship Row, two bomb hits can be seen on Arizona's *stern. This is the moment of Jack Scruggs's death.* National Archives.

Park Service divers can still see, just behind portholes, December 7 air trapped in pockets inside *Arizona's* submerged compartments. A clock recovered from the chaplain's cabin was frozen at just past 8:05 a.m., the moment the ship blew up.

Nothing else can be frozen in time. History is remorseless and it demands change. The war changed Arroyo Grande forever.

Residents here heard the first bulletin at about 11:30 a.m., as they were preparing for Sunday lunch, the big meal of the day for churchgoers like Juzo Ikeda's family. Like many of the town's Japanese-American residents, the Ikedas were Methodists. They were also baseball fans. Juzo's sons had played for local businessman Vard Loomis's club team, the Arroyo Grande Growers, and for Cal Poly.

Juzo was technically not "Japanese-American." He was not permitted citizenship. The Supreme Court maintained that this honor was never intended for nonwhite immigrants.

The court couldn't deny citizenship to Juzo's sons, born Americans, or to the sons and daughters of families like the Kobaras, the Hayashis, the Fuchiwakis, the Nakamuras.

These young people played varsity sports at the high school on Crown Hill, served in student government or on The *Hi-Chatter,* the school newspaper, joined the Latin Club or the Stamp Collecting Club, founded by cousins John Loomis and Gordon Bennett, known for committing occasional acts of anarchy as little boys (John's mother grew so frustrated that she once tied him to a tree. Gordon freed him.) and known even more for being good and loyal friends.

Many young Nisei men would respond to the humiliation of internment by fighting for the nation that had imprisoned them. Sgt. George Nakamura won a Bronze Star and a battlefield commission for rescuing a downed flier in China. Pfc. Sadami Fujita won his Bronze Star posthumously. He was killed as the 442nd fought to reach the "Lost Battalion" in France in 1944, when nearly a thousand Nisei GI's were killed or wounded in relieving 230 young Texans pinned down in dense woodland that had been splintered by German shellfire.

When Sgt. Hilo Fuchiwaki first came home at war's end, he went to the movies in Pismo Beach. He was still in uniform, but a patron spat on him anyway. When the Kobara family came home from the Gila River camp, they could hear gunshots in the night as they slept, for protection, in an interior hallway of their farmhouse.

The Silveira family, like so many Arroyo Grande farm families, had watched over Mr. Kobara's farm and farm equipment while they were interned. That was more typical of locals' behavior than anonymous men firing shotguns in the dark.

But what had happened to families like the Kobaras, beginning in April 1942, had been so painful that less than half of the prewar Japanese-American population came back to Arroyo Grande after the internment camps closed.

Wayne Morgan never came home; *Arizona* is his tomb. Nine miles away, Sadami Fujita is buried in Oahu's Punchbowl, in the National Memorial Cemetery of the Pacific.

Arizona, twisted grotesquely at her mooring, burned for two days after the attack. The scar that this terrible fire left behind, even here, seems invisible only because it is so deep.

War Heroes Here at Home

Clarence Burrell, a Stanford graduate, was a teacher and administrator in Arroyo Grande schools from 1929 until 1952. He was also instrumental in founding the Santa Lucia Boy Scouts Council.

At the high school, then on Crown Hill, he was principal and baseball coach; before that, he'd been principal of the grammar school and after that, he was the superintendent of Arroyo Grande City Schools.

It was Burrell who'd convinced the school board to take in migrant teens from the Nipomo camps so that they had a chance to attend a real high school in 1939.

Burrell was very close to local Japanese-American families. The Fuchiwaki daughters babysat his children; one was a secretary at the high school. After Pearl Harbor, when the internment rumors began mounting, Burrell ordered the teaching staff to accelerate the curriculum for the Nisei seniors in the Class of 1942 so that they could graduate on time.

Burrell and those young people ran out of time. The buses that gathered in the high school parking lot at the end of April took his students and their families away to the temporary relocation center at the Tulare County Fairgrounds, where they would sleep in livestock stalls.

Clarence Burrell

While the majority of Arroyo Grande residents were outraged by what had happened to their neighbors, there were those who were outraged instead at one of Burrell's faculty members, Arroyo Grande Union High School English teacher Gladys Loomis, and at her husband, Vard.

The Loomises were putting up Kaz Ikeda in their home after his friends and neighbors had been taken to Tulare. Kaz was caring for his father, Juzo, who was in the hospital in critical condition after a farm accident. So Kaz looked after his Dad and he babysat the Loomis children. He'd been a standout baseball player, by the way, at Cal Poly. Vard Loomis had pitched for Stanford, and Kaz had played catcher on Loomis's club team, the Arroyo Grande Growers. Gladys had been the Nisei team's "Mom" when they were on the road playing tournaments.

The Loomis family also owned the most important farm supply business in Arroyo Grande at the base of Crown Hill.

"Get rid of that Jap," some of the E.C. Loomis and Son customers grumbled.

Today, Kaz Ikeda's image, a tribute to his postwar contributions to his community, anchors a mural in downtown Arroyo Grande. Kaz paid another tribute when he named his younger son Vard.

But in June 1942, six weeks after the buses had left what is today the Paulding Middle School parking lot for the Tulare fairgrounds, Clarence Burrell made what was, in that fearful time, a controversial decision. He drove to Tulare with a box of diplomas so that he could, in a little ceremony, personally confer them on his students, on the Nisei members of the Class of '42.

Their banishment had done nothing to lessen his devotion to them or his respect for their families.

Meanwhile, Burrell continued with the business of being an educator. When our Japanese-American neighbors began coming home from the camps in 1944-45-- fewer than half of them ever came back--he was there to welcome their children back to school.

It seems like a small thing, but there's another incident revelatory of Burrell's character. His career in Arroyo Grande ended when he became the superintendent of schools in San Leandro. In June 1960, a brutal heat wave hit the Bay Area, so classrooms were sweltering and students were suffering. Burrell found out that the thermometer in one of his high school classrooms read 111º. His district was the only one to cancel classes the following day.

Today, San Leandro's high school football games are played in stadium that was completely renovated in 2013. It seats 2,500, features a state of the art all-turf field and a composite track.

The only thing the beautiful new stadium kept from the old stadium was its name: Burrell Field.

"We Cannot Condemn:" Executive Order 9066

From a letter to a University of Oregon alumni magazine that ran an article on the internment of World War II:

In 1942, U.S. Marines were battling the Japanese in the Guadalcanal jungles. American aircraft carriers were sunk by Japanese warplanes. So many ships were sunk in the Solomon Islands 'slot' that it was nicknamed Iron Bottom Sound. The fighting was a match of equals that could have gone either way. The American public was frightened of a West Coast invasion. We cannot condemn 1942 policy using our 2013 mores and sensibilities. The prospect of a ready-made collaborationist population, following a Japanese invasion, impelled the internments of Japanese Americans.

The Mochida family waits for transport to an assembly center. Hayward, California, 1942. Photo by Dorothea Lange. National Archives.

This, of course, condones the irrational.

The letter accurately cites how badly as the early war would go in the Pacific. But this was what was going on in the war against Germany:

In 1941, German U-boats were already attacking American warships: the destroyers *Greer* and *Kearny* came under fire; a torpedo sank the *Reuben James* and claimed 115 of her 159-man crew in October, five weeks *before* Pearl Harbor.

German U-boats sank 82 American ships in all waters in December 1941 alone. In 1942, they sank 121 American ships off the East Coast and 42 along the Gulf Coast. Americans on holiday, from Coney Island to Miami, could see our ships glowing at night as they burned, with their crews, just offshore. We were, in fact, bleeding ships—the U-boats claimed 500 American ships in all during 1942—and that meant that English children were beginning to go hungry: They were allowed one small egg every four weeks.

In 1941-1942, Japanese submarines sank a total of four ships off the West Coast.

The war in the European theater was not going well, either. While the United States would join the ground war against Germany with Operation Torch in November 1942, American forces were routed by the *Afrika Korps* in Tunisia's Kasserine Pass three months later. The Anglo-Canadian Dieppe raid in August 1942 was a disaster. On the Eastern Front, a German army group was making rapid headway in a drive to the Caucasus oilfields.

By then, 120,000 Japanese-Americans had been interned under Executive Order 9066. Fewer that 14,000 German-Americans and Italian-Americans were interned during World War II.

Despite claims to the contrary that I've heard many times, not a single incident of espionage occurred among the Japanese population along the Pacific Coast. There was one act of sabotage. From the National Park Service:

When told to leave his home and go to an assembly center, one farmer asked for an extension to harvest his strawberry crop. His request was denied, so he plowed under the strawberry field. He was then arrested for sabotage, on the grounds that strawberries were a necessary commodity for the war effort.

Lessons from Coach Sab's Generation

Coach Saburo Ikeda's Little League team, about 1965. Photo courtesy Marty Childers.

I had the good fortune to speak to Mrs. Ainsworth's class at St. Patrick's School about the 1942 evacuation and internment, in the Arizona desert, of our Japanese neighbors.

It was a wonderful chance to talk to young people about important things like honor and character, courage and loyalty, and, most of all, friendship, all of these the qualities that local families like the Loomises and many others— the Taylors, the Phelans, the Silveiras, the Bennetts, to name just a few— exemplified in 1942. They seem in short supply today. But in the World War II years, these were the businessmen and the farmers who shepherded, throughout the internment years, their Japanese neighbors' fields and homes, their sheds and the expensive irrigation pipe stacked inside, their trucks and their tractors. But after they'd been taken from Arroyo Grande in April 1942, the Japanese families lost other, more personal, property--love seats and dining-room sets, rocking chairs and bedsteads, maple dressers and black-lacquered hutches imported from Japan decades before Pearl Harbor--all of these disappeared, stolen or broken up by cowards armed with hatchets.

In August, the internees went to the Gila River camp, where they lived in barracks with cardboard-thin walls that carried them, unwilling, into the deepest secrets of the families on the other side of the wall. This is where they shook their shoes in the morning to let the scorpions out and where outfielders let fly balls to left drop because of the rattlesnakes waiting for them there.

Young people especially hated the camps. By 1944, an entire generation was missing from Gila River. The young women got out for jobs or college in Denver or Chicago or St. Louis. The young men got out to college, as well, got out to top sugar beets in Utah or they got out by joining the Army. Some of them would die in the Apennines in Italy or in the Vosges Mountains in France, where the Germans had learned to fire their artillery into the treetops to impale the Nisei GIs below with jagged splinters.

Despite the tragedy visited on local Japanese-Americans, I was struck most by something Haruo Hayashi, the patriarch of a prominent farm family, once told me. He'd trained with the 442nd Regimental Combat Team at Camp Shelby, Mississippi, and he never got over the black GIs standing outside the camp gym for USO shows that the white and Nisei GI's watched inside. He couldn't understand Jim Crow, couldn't understand something so shameful.

Haruo's family, of course, was behind barbed wire.

In late 1944, the first Japanese-American families began to come home from the camps.

It was then that Mr. Wilkinson, in his meat market and grocery on Branch Street, proved to be just as generous as he'd been in 1942, extending credit to the people returning from the desert just as he had in the days before they were taken away.

The town blacksmith, Mr. Schnyder, repaired the Kobara family's water pump on Christmas Day 1945 because there are no holidays with crops in the ground. He understood that and he understood, too, that the Kobaras were his friends, not just his customers.

In the years after the war, the Japanese families who returned to the Valley demonstrated the same kind of friendship and generosity that their neighbors had in the war years. One way they expressed it was in coaching baseball to more than two generations of Little Leaguers.

Sab Ikeda's 1965 Little League teams was so well-coached that its players knew always to take out the lead runner, knew how to lay down a bunt, knew how to grip a curveball. His kids, now in their sixties, still remember all those lessons from Coach. What they remember even more was the constant smile on Coach's face as he taught them.

When Sab's brother, Kaz Ikeda, died in 2013—he was a gifted catcher for Vard Loomis's prewar club team, the Arroyo Grande Growers, and for Cal Poly--the mourners gathered at the Arroyo Grande Cemetery sang the valedictory hymn: "Take Me out to the Ball Game." It was, of course, the perfect choice.

So the families, including the Ikedas, who did come home from the desert not only picked up their lives where they'd left them, but they began, from the moment they came home, to devote those lives to the community that had been stolen from them in April 1942.

How painful were the war years? The people who were taken to Gila River refused to talk about the desert with their children, who wanted desperately to hear the stories of what their parents and grandparents had endured. But the Nisei didn't want the subject brought up.

In their public lives, their generosity was open and seemingly effortless. They never stopped giving to their neighbors—in youth sports, in service clubs, in countless volunteer hours, in the Methodist Church, in homes where their refrigerators were always open to two generations of ravenous teenaged boys.

But Gila River remained, both submerged and sharply painful, until they began to approach the ends of their lives.

This is when they began, hesitantly, to open up to historians and to young history students. They began to tell the stories of their lives. Despite the wounds visited on them during this terrible war--which included both German shellfire and a spike in coronary disease rates among those who'd lived in the internment camps--they decided, in those stories, to give us the most precious gifts of all. In the telling, they remind us honor and character, courage and loyalty, and, most of all, they remind us of friendship.

The American Girl

When I retired from teaching last year, it was time. I hadn't lost my love for young people, or for teaching, but I couldn't think of a better graduating class for my goodbyes than the Arroyo Grande High Class of 2015.

One of my very favorites is named Leila. The smile you see on her face is a constant: she radiates the kind of warmth and openness that captures others, but there is nothing calculated in the capturing. Leila's smile comes from Leila's heart. At the end-of-the-year senior assembly, she gifted me with a farewell bouquet. She was fighting tears, and seeing her struggle to master her feelings was an even greater gift. It's good to know the love you've spent means something to someone so important.

I have rarely read a college letter that brought *me* to tears, but Leila's did. One part told of her family's trip to Egypt, to visit her grandmother. I saw photos of the woman and she has a kind of Leila-ness about herself, as well. You wonder if there are applications you can send for to become her adoptive grandson. Her health has not been good. She had to have surgery, and the passage I remember is when Leila volunteered to change the dressing on her wound. Her grandmother apologized for its appearance, but Leila did not hesitate and did not flinch, and I don't think anything so clinical has been done with such gentleness and compassion.

Leila.

We have common heroes: Doctors without Borders. I immediately thought of her while listening to an NPR story about a doctor who'd lost 19 of the first 20 patients he'd treated for Ebola in West Africa. It was heart-breaking, but this doctor was a man of spiritual depth. "Curing disease isn't the most important thing a doctor does," he said. "The most important thing a doctor can do is to enter into another's pain." Leila has that kind of empathy.

The experience with her grandmother only reinforced Leila's dream to become a person who can make a difference. She'll study engineering at Cal Poly State University.

I will come to the obvious part. Leila is an observant Muslim, and as captivating and welcoming as her smile is, there are those--some have been in the news lately--who are blind to kindness because it's so threatening to the comfort they find in hating. Leila can take care of herself--she gets those reservoirs of strength from the deep wells her family has made for her--but she also is the kind of student who can evoke every paternal instinct a male teacher has. You want to protect her from the blind and the bigoted who also have the unpleasant tendency to be loud.

The comfort is knowing that those people do not matter and have no enduring impact, unless you count, of course, the agonizing depth of the pain God feels when they broadcast their hatred.

I gained a lot of wisdom by talking to Haruo Hayashi in researching the book about Arroyo Grande during World War II.

After Pearl Harbor, Haruo , then in high school, and his community went through the kind of bigotry that I fear so much. But, while the bigots were loud and threatening, they do not matter to him 75 years later. They were small people whose names he's lost. He clearly remembers the name of a tough classmate, Milton Guggia, who told him in December 1941 he would personally beat the living crap out of any kid who called Haruo a "Jap."

Milton Guggia. That's a real American name.

As is Leila's. She's the girl who went to proms, who served in ASB, who played powderpuff football, who participated every year in Mock Trial, who played in the school band. Haruo played in the school band, too. And you can see him in a yearbook photo with the 1941 AGUHS Lettermen's Club--his bad eyesight ruled out sports, but he managed for every team and earned his spot, with all the jocks, right next to Coach Max Belko, a former USC All-American. Southern Cal football legend Howard Jones called Belko "the finest example of a man I've ever coached." The kid from Gary, Indiana, like Haruo, the son of immigrants—Belko's parents were Russian Jews—became the kind of big, boisterous and indestructible coach whom students idolize.

He was destructible, it turned out. Belko, a Marine lieutenant, died on the beach at Guam in 1944. He told the Marine who came to his aid that he knew he was dying.

But there, and forever, in the old yearbook, are Max Belko and Haruo Hayashi, shoulder to shoulder: two real Americans. Leila—and Leila's marvelous family, so much like Haruo's—are no different. Their fidelity to each other, their quiet insistence on hard work and service to others, and the openness of their daughter's heart--all of these have been blessings in my life. They are, I think, the kind of Americans we would all wish to be.

The Finest Man I Finally Met

Don Gullickson, top row, right, with the South County Historical Society.

Don Gullickson of Arroyo Grande has passed away at 91. There are many reasons this is a big deal.

I knew Don, but only slightly. I talked to him three or four times, found him intelligent, articulate and very funny. I wished I had talked to him more and listened to him even more than that. I'd heard about him for years but met him very late in his life, and I wish I'd met him far sooner than that.

He told me a little about bootlegging days, when he was just a little fellow. His Dad, Ole, was among a group of hunters, including the local pharmacist and other luminaries, who liked to secure a supply of powerful beverages before they went up north to hunt deer.

I am not, mind you, advocating the combination of powerful beverages and 30.06 rifles. That was their deal.

They bought their bootleg booze from a supplier in Shell Beach. Don, when I talked to him, couldn't grab his name, but he was Greek.

So was Alex, the owner of the famous Alex's BBQ and known to be a modest bootlegger.

Ole and his friends would always take Don along with them when they made their booze purchases, sometimes right on the beach. Their reasoning was that no deputy sheriff would be suspicious of a bunch of guys with a five-year-old tagging along.

They were right.

Ten years later, Don was a member of a kind of Four Musketeers: Himself, John Loomis, Gordon Bennett and Haruo Hayashi. Maybe "Boococks" is a better term than "Musketeers." That's what their little circle, the founders, among other things, of the Arroyo Grande Union High School Stamp Club, called themselves.

After Pearl Harbor, Don, John and Gordon stood by all their Nisei friends, but they stayed especially close to Haruo, a young man who seemed to bring that kind of loyalty out in people. When he was a little boy, Haruo had learned English from a kind little girl, his classmate at the old grammar school on Traffic Way, where the Ford agency is today.

At the end of April 1942, the buses came to take Haruo Hayashi and his family away, along with the Kobaras, the Fukuharas, the Fuchiwakis, the Ikedas (except for Kaz, who stayed after to care for his father, his back broken after a team of farm horses ran away with him), and so many more. A line of high-school classmates, teenaged girls—twenty-five of the fifty-eight members of the Class of 1942 were Nisei—walked up the hill together to where some of the girls would board the buses. They were holding hands. They were sobbing.

And so this was the day that Executive Order 9066 broke up the Four Musketeers.

Three of them would fight in the Pacific. John, the Marine, fought on Peleliu and in the last terrible campaign on Okinawa. He didn't know it, but his cousin Gordon Bennett at one point was just offshore, on a fleet oiler like the ones the painfully young *kamikaze* pilots excitedly mistook for heavy cruisers or battleships before they went in for their dives. Don was a swabbie, too.

Haruo joined the 442nd Regimental Combat Team, but he was so young that the war in Europe ended before he had his chance to fight. He was a heavy machine-gun instructor when word came that he could go home.

When he did, he found that the Phelans and Taylors had taken care of his father's land and his farm equipment. He lived with the Bennetts during the period of transition—not always peaceful—until he could take up farming again.

John, Gordon and Don all came home, too. The Boococks were together again, and they remained that way for seventy years.

I think there can be no finer compliment to a man like Don Gullickson than to call him a true friend to his friends.

He was an Arroyo Grande boy, you see.

Chapter 10. War Stories

The German Major

Once World War II in Europe had ended in the spring of 1945, Europeans went hungry–the Continent's infrastructure had been obliterated by ground combat and by the Allied air campaign. The footage of German kids eating out of garbage cans in 1945, in the long months before the Marshall Plan, always stunned my students. In the meantime, thousands of POW's in our care died of hunger or of opportunistic diseases because civilians got first priority for food, and there never was enough.

Nearing the end: 11th Armored tanks on the autobahn, March 31, 1945. U.S. Army Photo.

It was then that a *Wehrmacht*, or German Army, major, who outranked my father, then a U.S. Army captain on occupation duty, somehow latched onto him and became his personal body servant for a few weeks: The German officer cooked for him, cleaned his quarters, washed and pressed his uniforms, the works.

He did that because Dad was a Quartermaster officer and so had access to food. The young German officer wanted to live: His pride meant nothing when compared to his determination to see the wife and children he wanted in his arms again. My father, once his enemy, was the man who could keep him alive.

Later, in the fall of 1945, he would begin the long walk home along roads still choked with refugees and gaunt, tired soldiers. Dad never learned what happened to him but hoped, in talking about him years later, that the German major had lived a long and happy life. What started as a relationship of expedience had begun to edge into a friendship.

The tough American soldiers of Easy Company—the "Band of Brothers"—liked the English, for the most part, loved the Dutch, but, like my father, felt most at home with Germans.

The grandfathers of these GI's fought a war in the face of another great evil, in slavery, eighty years before. But there was a lull in one Civil War campaign that gave a Union army band, its vast audience in bivouac, time enough for a concert. Confederates on a nearby hillside were listening.

One of them called "Yank! Play one of ours!" So the band played "Dixie," and at the song's conclusion, both sides erupted, thousands cheering, tossing their caps in the air. They embraced a vivid moment when they were at peace together, before the close-quarters murder so characteristic of that war—and, sadly, so necessary for its resolution—resumed.

Similarly, the German major' reached across the divide to make peace with the American captain. For both men, the time for soldiering was over; it was time for them to be fathers again.

Lt. Robert W. Gregory, 1944.

The Amazing McChesneys of Corbett Canyon

The reason I write books is to disabuse us of the notion that, because we're from a rural California county, we're not all that important to the great events of American and world history. This is not so.

The McChesney family of Corbett Canyon--I was taught by a relative, Eva Fahey, at Branch School, went to Arroyo Grande High with another, Leroy McChesney III, and finally, taught a third, Kathryn, who is quietly and incandescently brilliant--is a perfect example of what I'm talking about.

Before World War II, the family owned the Royal Oaks Dairy The McChesney children would lay out milk cans on a trestle for the Pacific Coast Railway and, magically, have it return to them as ice cream from the Golden

State Creamery in San Luis Obispo. Dairy cows, however, were far from their chief interest.

One son, Leroy McChesney Jr., tall and rangy, would take breaks from the milk barn to, in borrowing Whitman's phrase, "stare in perfect wonder" at the vultures drifting effortlessly overhead. He caught the flying bug early.

And the first time he may have caught it might've been when he was eight, in 1922, when a wrong-way biplane from Santa Maria landed in a pasture alongside the McChesney farm. The pilot had mistaken the pasture for his landing strip in Santa Maria, which was most likely *another* pasture just a bit farther south.

Jess McChesney, top right, and his B-24 crew. Photo courtesy Michael McChesney.

The proof that Leroy had become hooked on flying came long after he'd earned a pilot's license, once he'd married and started a family. He began building a full-scale glider, for whatever reason, in the living room. It grew.

The kids had to dodge the fuselage to make their way to the kitchen for Golden State ice cream in the freezer. Eventually Leroy's project migrated outside, but his love for flying remained such a constant in the family that, years later, after he'd suffered a heart attack, his wife, Grace, took up flying. She reasoned that she'd have to land the damned plane. Truth be told, she, a member of the "99's," a women's flying group, may have been the better pilot.

But, unlike Leroy, she didn't get the country airport, McChesney Field, named for her. It was Leroy's boundless energy as an advocate for fellow fliers and as a member of several state and national aviation boards that got that well-deserved honor.

His little brother, Jess, caught the bug, too. And he was a war hero. So was the more famous son of another dairy family, the Edna Valley Righettis, who gave us P-51 pilot Elwyn, an enormously gifted flier and leader, lost in Germany in 1945.

Jess flew his thirty-five B-24 combat missions in the Fifteenth Air Force out of Italy. He was a pilot whose career was book-ended by crash landings on both his first and final bomb missions, which wended their way over the Alps and into Austria, Germany, and Hungary, where civilians lynched downed aircrews. On both those book-end missions, the latter a belly-flop on a British airfield, the big bomber he piloted had been shot to pieces.

One of his gunners tried to contact the family many, many years later, and learned, over the phone, that Jess had died. He was devastated.

"I would fly to the gates of hell with that man," he said simply over the long-distance connection.

Jess's career did not end with the end of World War II. He would win his fifth Air Medal in "Operation Vittles," which we know better as the 1948-49 Berlin Airlift, when Stalin, determined to drive the western Allies out of Berlin, deep inside East Germany, closed the borders to ground traffic.

That meant that German children were going to starve. So in one of the most heroic episodes in our history, veteran World War II pilots whose wartime planes had been holed by German flak or by fighters--who'd once unleashed terror on Germany, including on German children--turned instead to airlifting fuel and food and medicine to Germans and especially to children. That's when Jess Milo McChesney was activated from the Reserves and flew the 100 missions that would add a fifth Air Medal to his Distinguished Flying Cross.

We tend to downplay the Berlin Airlift in favor of the "Memphis Belles" of World War II but, truth be told, what Jess did in 1948-49 was nearly as dangerous. The relief flights were so relentless and so constant--one of the biggest cities in the world had to be supplied completely by air--that exhausted pilots made mistakes that killed them and their aircrews, or exhausted airframes failed and plunged, in pieces, into Berlin suburbs. These were enormously courageous and compassionate young men.

Of course, the most famous of Jess's comrades was Gail Halverson, *Der Schockoladen Flieger,* who tied handkerchiefs to Hershey Bars and dropped them, in their little parachutes, to the children of Berlin on his approach to the airfield at Templehof.

Halverson did this because he loved children. I remember watching a story on CBS News about the fiftieth anniversary of Halverson's chocolate campaign, on the occasion of his return visit to Germany. When he landed in Berlin, he was immediately surrounded by a mass of adoring and middle-aged German *hausfraus,* who had never and would never forget Gail Halverson.

And Jess Milo McChesney, far less famous than Halverson but just as brave and just as bound by duty and by compassion, is just as important to American history. Similarly, a city as prominent as Berlin has an unexpected link to a largely unknown place--Corbett Canyon, California.

Boys and their Dogs

One of the most wonderful discoveries I made while researching the book *Central Coast Aviators in World War II* was learning how much young American fliers loved their dogs. In the records of the American Air Museum in Britain, the best resource for the American Eighth Air Force, lovingly and meticulously kept by our historian friends across the sea, a dog's nationality is officially listed as "British."

I was reminded, too, of how young these men were–the average age of a B-17 or B-24 pilot was twenty-two. There were waist gunners as young as sixteen. When you are that young, you have reason to live.

You want to get home. After twelve or fourteen hours in the air, where breathing and urinating and speaking in unpressurized cabins at 25,000 feet, where the temperature is twenty degrees below zero, are all encumbered. The discomfort is broken up by moments of unimaginable terror when you watch your friends' airplanes break up in the air or you stop breathing to listen to anti-aircraft shrapnel—called "flak," from a German word too serpentine to pronounce—hit your own plane. Flak sounds like dense hail on a tin roof. Some of it will sever throttle cables or hydraulic lines, or, far worse, some of it will kill friends far closer than the ones you watch falling so slowly beyond the Plexiglas window. There is nothing you can do about flak.

You want it to be over. You want to get home to the one friend who will still be there for you.

Even Army Air Forces generals became attached to their overseas friends. This is Brig. Gen. Ira Eaker and his pup. U.S. Air Force.

The historian for one bomb group, the 92nd, provided me with my favorite find and she told me that the ground crews remembered this very clearly. At mission's end, a pilot's dog would become suddenly happy and excited. The animal, of course, had heard the B-17s returning before the ground crews had. But what the dog recognized was the individual pitch of his or her human's B-17 engines. He was coming home, now, twelve hours after he'd left. I don't know that there's a love greater than this.

Outward bound B-17 from the 303rd Bomb Group. Clair Abbott Tyler of Morro Bay, a co-pilot in this group, was killed in action near Lorient in 1943. U.S. Air Force.

Making Friends, Living and Dead

I wish I could write fiction. I have neither the talent nor the patience: I would put protagonists, antagonists and all those minor characters and plot-advancers in front of a firing squad before I got to Chapter Five.

End of book.

This is not a bad thing. A well-trained firing squad would save both me and my potential readers substantial agony and would be no loss to the literary canon.

The good news—I think— is that I was a history major, and that devotion to a college major with such a dismal financial future stuck through thirty years of teaching the teenagers that I still miss three years after my retirement. What being a history major meant, additionally, is that I am hopelessly addicted to historical research. That's a pursuit, for writers of both history nonfiction and fiction, that is as infuriating and tedious as it is rewarding and fascinating.

For the book *Central Coast Aviators in World War II*, that meant four hours of research inside a World War II database of every American military aircraft built during World War II, in this case to match a B-17's serial number with the name the pilot had given his B-17 once he'd been assigned to it. Was it "Flaming Mayme?" or "Flaming Maybe?" I decided on the latter. That particular B-17 collided with Mr. Skiddaw in the Lake District in September 1943, killing every airman aboard.

One of the passengers on "Maybe," who was just hitching a ride for a weekend pass to Edinburgh—my father's favorite city during his World War II stint in the United Kingdom—was from my home town, Arroyo Grande.

A memorial cross marks the site of the crash that killed Hank Ballagh in 1943. Courtesy aircrashsites.co.uk

His name was Hank Ballagh. He was the Class Valedictorian, 1937, of the high school I attended and where I later taught. He graduated from Cal with

270

an engineering degree, did his training as a B-17 co-pilot in Florida, fell in love and married Frances Marie Hogan there, in Broward County, and the two became the parents of a little girl who was just beginning to walk when "Flaming Maybe" ran into dirty weather with a pilot, new to flying on instruments, who flew the bomber into the face of Mr. Skiddaw.

This happened three weeks before Hank's first combat mission. He might well have been killed on one of those. His B-17 was a "Pathfinder," with a radar bulb in place of the ball turret underneath, designated to locate the aim point for the bombers following. As the first in over the target, the Pathfinders would be the first planes downed. But Hank didn't die taking the war to the enemy. He died in a terrible accident, as did about half the eighteen San Luis Obispo County fliers killed during the war.

His wedding band—*Hank-Fran 7-17-42*, the inscription inside read—was returned to Frances Marie Hogan Ballagh, who lived on Cornwall Avenue in Arroyo Grande, in 1949. (The wristwatch of San Luis Obispo ball-turret gunner Donal Laird, killed on his very first B-17 mission in 1945, was returned to his family in 2015.) Hank and Frances's little girl, Enid, had by then pressed her small handprints into the fresh concrete of a sidewalk, dedicated to her father's memory, just outside of Hank's Methodist church on Branch Street in Arroyo Grande.

The sidewalk is gone now. My job is to make sure, in some small way, that Hank Ballagh's memory isn't. The problem is, even for a research addict like me, is how attached the writer becomes to characters who lie wholly and thankfully outside his invention.

Second Lt. Clarence Abbott Tyler of Morro Bay had a little girl, too. He married a local schoolteacher, a Renetzky, who was descended from an old-time *ranchero* family, the Danas. Alex Madonna, he of the Inn, was the best man at their wedding. Two years later, in March 1943, cannon rounds from a Focke-Wulf 190 obliterated him in his co-pilot's seat and so from his toddler's memory on a B-17 mission over Lorient.

Nick Covell's fifth-grade class toured the local newspaper offices of the San Luis Obispo Telegram-Tribune and plugged their ears in the din of the press room. He attended Patsy Berkemeyer's birthday party, and the Berkemeyers were bakers, so the cake must've been terrific. He went to Cal Poly and the steer he exhibited at the Los Angeles County Fair won a ribbon. The B-29 he piloted was on fire when it was spotted going down over the Kawasaki District of Tokyo in the spring of 1945.

In researching an earlier book, I met Mess Steward Felix Estibal, essentially a U.S. Navy servant–his was a rating reserved for Filipino- and African-Americans—who provided me with a touching and hilarious letter home (the boatswain's mate was "the leather-lunged whistle-blower"), written from his destroyer in the South Pacific, which I found published in an early 1943 edition of the local weekly, the Arroyo Grande *Herald-Recorder*.

Three hours later, I found the article that listed him as "Missing in Action" after a Japanese Long Lance torpedo had blown the bow off his little fighting ship, USS *Walke*. Some of *Walke's* sailors survived the sinking, I found out later, only to be killed by the concussion of the ship's depth charges as they exploded while tumbling to the seabed of Ironbottom Sound near Guadalcanal. Felix Estibal's body was never recovered. Reading the bare-bones little 1943 newspaper article about Felix's death so soon after reading such a warm and life-affirming letter did what it should have done. It devastated me.

So that's the problem with writing historical nonfiction. You make friends or you adopt surrogate sons—ironically, mine are from my father's generation—and sometimes you lose them.

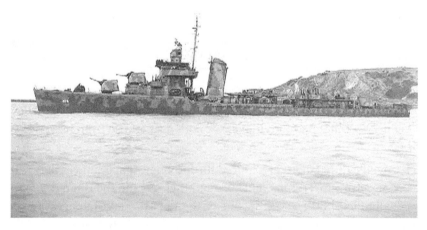

After a refit at Mare Island, USS Walke (DD416) *leaves San Francisco for the last time.* U.S. Naval Institute.

For the book *Aviators*, I made friends that I will never forget, and luckily, many will be with us for a long time to come. Lucy May Maxwell, young enough to be my daughter—or, I fear, my granddaughter—is a British researcher with the Imperial War Museums and its Duxford branch, the American Air Museum in Britain, which has more information on the American air war in Europe than any three comparable American organizations. Lucy was invaluable to me in tracking down photographs, identifying planes and fliers, and she reminded me, no matter how strained it becomes, of the "special relationship" between the United States and Britain share.

The sources for *Aviators* included MACRs (Missing Aircrew Reports), the aforementioned endless lists of aircraft serial numbers, mission reports from websites dedicated to bomb groups in England, Italy and South Pacific—some included strike photos, aircrew lists, and even formation diagrams for bomb squadron missions–four local museums and their staffs, *The New England Journal of Medicine* (for the tropical diseases Pacific fliers had to endure),

aviation archaeology groups who locate and memorialize crash sites around the United Kingdom and Hawaii, training and personnel manuals from the 303rd Bomb Group, part of the Eighth Air Force, genealogical websites like ancestry.com and genealogybank.com (the latter is invaluable for its newspapers), video interviews of local fliers that are now part of a Library of Congress collection, and, best of all, interviews with two 94-year-old Army Air Forces veterans.

Al Findley Jr., a B-24 radioman, was shot down twice. The first time was over a newly-liberated French town, Epernay, whose residents were so taken with their crash-landed American guests (they put them up in warm straw or even feather-beds and the wine, as the saying goes, flowed) that one became pen-pals with Al's mother in

Findley's POW portrait. Courtesy Al Findley, Jr.

Oklahoma. Al's squadron commander finally had to buzz Epernay to drop a canister that contained the sad order for the aircrew to get their sorry rear ends back to base. There was a war on.

The second time Findley was shot down was over Germany, and that was an ordeal made terrifying by getting strafed, twice, by American fighter planes. Thankfully, Findley not only survived but became a lifelong Air Force sergeant—a Command Master Sergeant—who, after his retirement, opened a little antique shop in England with his wife. He later moved to Los Osos. Seventy years after his wartime service, Sgt. Findley drives to a retirement home outside Morro Bay every Sunday and takes his World War II friends out to breakfast.

The author and Al Findley, Jr., Estrella Warbirds Museum, Paso Robles, 2018.

The other nonagenarian I got to meet was John Sim Stuart, a longtime Cal Poly architecture professor and, in the war, a P-47 Thunderbolt pilot who flew out of his Ie Shima base on August 9, 1945, to witness the blood-red flash and then the mushroom cloud of the Nagasaki bomb.

A year before that mission, Stuart was a flight instructor with his two closest friends at an Army Air Forces base in Pierre, South Dakota, when he met a young woman named Mary at the Hopscotch Inn (The Hopscotch Inn was in another time zone, which meant an extra hour of beers for Stuart and his two friends, a kind of Army Air Forces version of the Three Musketeers). John and Mary met at the Hopscotch every night for the next week. They decided it made no sense to wait to get married, so they didn't.

A few months later, at a party on an isolated little base in Texas, one of Stuart's flight-instructor friends, one of the musketeers, told Mary quietly and earnestly that he was certain that her new husband would survive the war. He wasn't as sure about the others–and he was one of them. He was right, of course. John made it. The other two—one, after an engine failure over the East China Sea, the other in a fiery crash at the edge of Hickam Field on Oahu—didn't.

But seventy-three years after that first meeting at the Hopscotch Inn, John and Mary Stuart are still married.

John Sim Stuart as a cadet trainee in the Army Air Forces. Courtesy the Stuart family.

Meeting at Colleville-sur-Mer

The American Cemetery at Colleville-sur-Mer, just above Omaha Beach, 2010.

It has been more than seventy years since 160,000 Allied troops landed along fifteen miles of Norman coastline to begin the campaign to liberate Western Europe.

Many of them made it only to the bluffs above Omaha Beach, to the American Cemetery at Colleville-sur-Mer, the emotional anchor for the film *Saving Private Ryan.*

Others who are buried here died later in that summer of 1944. Among them were three San Luis Obispo County soldiers. In 2010, Arroyo Grande High school students found their graves on a trip to the battlefields of Northern Europe.

AGHS students Ryan, Marisol and Katy walk along Omaha Beach. It was a beautiful day.

On the day the students, traveling with my English teaching partner, Amber Derbidge, and me, visited Omaha Beach, there were young men in tiny sailboats, the sails bright oranges and reds, celebratory of life. It's as if time and the sea have washed away the violence of June 6, 1944.

Understanding that day comes only when the visitor looks up at the bluffs beyond the beach.

They are so steep and offered the Germans such a complete field of fire that no American below should have survived. It's no wonder that Omaha, assigned to two American infantry divisions, was by far the deadliest of the five invasion beaches—2,400 of the 4,000 Allied soldiers killed that day died here.

A German bunker remains on the bluffs above Omaha Beach.

The balance wavered on Omaha. The invasion came close to failure. It didn't. The men who delivered the victory still occupy the high ground, in the American Cemetery.

It was there that our students found the grave of one San Luis Obispo County soldier, Pvt. Domingo Martinez: Plot C, Row 13, Grave 38. He'd enlisted, as many local young men had, in Los Angeles.

He'd been a farm worker. I grew up in the Upper Arroyo Grande Valley and learned my first Spanish from farm workers, braceros, and so Martinez was special to me. He was born and grew up in New Mexico, and he was 25— the same age as my older son--when he died.

Another group of students found the grave of an artillery officer from San Luis Obispo, Second Lieutenant Claude Newlin. Ironically, Newlin's unit, the 216th Field Artillery Battalion, attached to the 35th Infantry Division, had spent a year training in his hometown, at Camp San Luis Obispo.

A P-38 like Langston's, with its D-Day recognition stripes. U.S. Air Force.

Newlin had survived some of the most vicious fighting of the campaign, near St. Lo, only to die just hours before the 35th broke out of Normandy to join Gen. George Patton's breath-taking race across France to Metz and the German frontier.

Domingo Martinez, meanwhile, fought as a rifleman in the 313th Regiment, 79th Infantry Division. The 79th was part of the assault on Cherbourg, a deep-water port that the Allies were desperate to secure after D-Day: the original beachheads couldn't sustain the flow of supplies needed to maintain the armies fighting in France.

While the 79th fought in the streets of Cherbourg-- street fighting is something a soldier very quickly learns to hate-- another San Luis Obispo County serviceman died in the skies above the city.

279

On June 22, Second Lieutenant Jack Langston was flying his P-38 fighter in a low-level attack with his 367th Fighter Squadron, when the Germans demonstrated the power of Cherbourg's anti-aircraft defenses. Langston's last flight was almost a suicide mission: He and four others in the 367th were killed in the attack, which accomplished little.

He, too, is memorialized, on a wall dedicated to the missing in action.

Once Cherbourg had been secured, Martinez's 79th Division shifted from street fighting to a drive through the farms and villages of the Cotentin Peninsula.

American commanders gave the 79th far too much ground to cover and the Germans, who had the advantage of fighting defensively, in the *bocage,* the Norman hedgerows, chewed them up. The hedgerows enclosed fields farmed since Agincourt and were a hopscotch of natural fortresses—roots and compacted earth had formed walls, built up over centuries—and the GIs had to assault them, one by one.

Hedgerow country, Cotentin Peninsula. National Archives.

German soldiers could take the Americans in enfilade from both the front and the flanks when they entered a field. The famed 88-mm field gun and the heavy machine gun, the MG 42, with a rate of fire so rapid that a burst sounded like canvas ripping, annihilated entire rifle squads.

The hedgerows that hid these formidable weapons were so dense that the GIs could not see who was killing them so efficiently and so easily. It had to be terrifying.

Each division would work its own solution to hedgerow fighting, including welding teeth, using steel salvaged from German beach obstacles, onto the front hulls of Sherman tanks so they could punch through the hedges and deliver the suppressing fire that saved so many foot soldiers' lives.

The American soldier was a superb improviser, and here, it was necessary. Tactical planning, once GIs got off the beaches and into the Norman peninsula, was virtually nonexistent. Staff officers' thinking had stopped where the sand ran out.

Pvt. Martinez's war ended on July 12, , in fighting near a town called Bolleville. He was struck in the head and chest by shell fragments from one of the 88-mm cannons.

Years later, teens who grew up 5,500 miles away from Bolleville found the young man they'd lost before they were born. They were happy that they'd found Domingo Martinez-- their GI, their dogface, their neighbor, their friend.

Afterward, the students wandered through the rows to touch the cool marble of the crosses and Stars of

David. They were so young, and the soldiers at Colleville-sur-Mer will always be young, and the power of this place is such that what was happening was clear, even to us adults. The two generations were speaking together without the encumbrance of words.

World War II Voices from Arroyo Grande

Arrival in America

I remembered his brother, a naval officer, from his photograph, and I found a man who resembled him. I thought that this was the man I was about to marry. From the deck I fixed my eyes on him, even though I had never met him. That is why it is called a 'picture bride.'

When my new husband got up at 4 a.m. every morning to get Mr. Tomooka's horses ready for the field, I realized how hard farm life was.

I wondered what I had gotten into. I wondered every morning, and I cried every night.

Kimi Kobara, arriving in Seattle to marry Shigechika Kobara, an Arroyo Grande Valley farmer. The Kobaras, interned at the Gila River camp during World War II, would be married for over thirty years. They were the parents of two daughters and a son.

Pearl Harbor

Along with all of the young men, Jack registered for the draft. He was not looking forward to serving in the Army, and wanting to further his musical education, applied to the Navy School of Music. He was accepted and looked forward to what he thought would be two years at the school and four years in the Navy. Jack arrived at the school in December 1940 and was sent to Norfolk. After boot camp he reported to the school to start his training of different musical subjects as well as private lessons on the piano and trombone. He played in the band and dance band. He soon sent home for his accordion and played that quite a bit, since all the pianos were being taken off the ships.

Pauline Scruggs, on her brother, Jack Scruggs, an Arroyo Grande sailor and bandsman who was one of the first killed on USS Arizona.

I was in the ward room [sic] eating breakfast about 0755 when a short signal on the ship's air raid alarm was made. I immediately went to the phone and called the officer of the deck to sound general quarters and then shortly thereafter ran up to the starboard side of the quarterdeck to see if he had received word. On coming out of the wardroom hatch on the port side, I saw a Japanese plane go by, the machine guns firing, at an altitude of about 100 feet. As I was running forward on the starboard side of the quarterdeck, approximately by the starboard gangway, I was apparently knocked out by the blast of a bomb, which I learned later had struck the face plate of No. 4 turret on the starboard side and had glanced off and gone through the deck just forward on the captain's hatch, penetrating the decks and exploding on the third deck.

Lt. Commander Samuel Fuquoa, describing the moment of Jack Scruggs's death as the Arizona *ship's band assembled for the Colors Ceremony and the playing of the National Anthem.*

The Japanese have attacked Pearl Harbor Hawaii by air, President Roosevelt has just announced. The attack also was made on all military and naval activities on the principle island of Oahu...

CBS News Bulletin, 11:30 a.m. PST.

We were completely shocked. It was beyond our understanding. Bewildered! We went home and turned on the radio to hear more. Still could not make any sense of it. After Pearl Harbor, rumor mills had a heyday about it. All kinds of wild rumors about everything: a large farmhouse off Halcyon near the highway had a basement full of guns! Another house had a secret room full of short-wave radios and they were in constant contact with Tokyo...on and on. It seemed like someone was trying to turn us against our neighbors. Most of us couldn't buy it. We had grown up with them.

Will Tarwater, Arroyo Grande Union High School student in 1941-42.

Haru, if anybody calls you a "Jap," I will personally beat the crap out of him.

Milton Guggia, to Arroyo Grande Union High School classmate Haruo Hayashi.

Three letters to Mutual of Omaha broadcaster John B. Hughes, one of the first to call for the removal of Japanese and Japanese-Americans from the West Coast, January 1942.

Today's [broadcast] really came close to home. We live near this small town where nearly one half are Japs. They farm all the best land and pay outrageous prices per acre, such as $45 or $50, and live in a shack to do it. Besides [they] own the theatre, half the garages and just about run this town...really, this is no country for such people.

From Guadalupe, California

...We want to congratulate you on the stand you are taking towards the Japs. We wish there were more like you. We have lived in and around San Luis Obispo all our lives and have seen enough of the Japs to know that our races can never mix.

From San Luis Obispo, California

I have talked to many people around the Arroyo Grande Valley...and the Japs farm two thirds of the best valley land and own 10% of it now, and every one of them are of the same opinion that now is the time to put the screws to the Japs before it is too late.

From Arroyo Grande, California

Internment

Relocation of the Japanese from the West Coast in 1941 created a catastrophe, which cannot be ignored or left untold because it is a fact of history.... crops were left in the field as the farmers were rounded up with their families and shipped to internment camps.

...During the absence of the Japanese farmers from the West Coast some families had their property burglarized and destroyed. The families that farmed in the Arroyo Grande Valley were very fortunate and their losses were minimal because they had good friends in the valley that looked after their farmland and their possessions. Peter Bachino, John Enos, Vard Loomis, Cyril Phelan, Joe Silveira, Ed Taylor and Ernest Vollmer were among those who stepped forward, in the face of pressure from their own community, to help their Japanese friends.

History of the Pismo-Oceano Vegetable Exchange

After a small flurry of opposition had been stirred up by some of the citizens of Parkville, Mo, and overruled by the trustees of Park College, a

Presbyterian school in the city, Abraham Dohi, honor graduate of the Arroyo Grande Union High School, Arthur Kamitsuka, A.G. yell leader, and six other evacuees were enrolled as students at the college.

Arroyo Grande Herald-Recorder, *September 1942*

They made one main diamond in the camp. I lived in Canal, in an offset corner, and it was quite a walk to practice. (The center was divided into two camps, Butte and Canal, which were 3½ miles apart, with the baseball diamond located in Butte.) In the relocation camp, I formed the "A" team (varsity) which was composed of all the youth from the area that I knew from Santa Barbara to San Luis Obispo. I got the best players. When we started to practice, our pitcher's mother passed away and then the next thing you know our catcher's mother passed away, then our third baseman's mother passed away, and then somebody else died. Most of the Japanese families were Buddhist, and when a mother or father passes away, there are 49 days of services. So, I ran out of players. Around that time my father said to me, "I know that I'm going to die sooner or later. If I die, you don't have to wait."

Kaz Ikeda, in a 2010 interview. Kaz's father, Juzo, died in the Canal Camp Hospital at Gila River, Arizona, as a result of injuries inflicted by a runaway team of farm horses in late 1941. What Ikeda describes here are deaths from Valley Fever, a fungal infection common to the Arizona desert and to California's San Joaquin Valley.

The War in Europe

We had bombed the target and had started back when fire broke out in the cockpit so furiously I though the plane would blow up any minute. Flares were blowing up and shells were going off.

The pilot, Jim Lamb, gave the order to bail out and then the intercommunicating phone went out. Our engineer and bombardier (Cliff) and navigator (Charley) bailed out over German territory.

At that time Jim's parachute caught fire as did an extra one we carried. Mine was burnt but not seriously. With his chute gone, Jim couldn't jump. I decided to stay with the ship while Jim put out the fire. He succeeded in getting it under control, but his hands were so badly burnt that he couldn't do anything the rest of the trip.

He held the ship level while I finished putting the fire out…Somebody handed a fire extinguisher through a hole the fire had burnt, and so I looked back and everybody was there (in the tail) for which I thanked God. Nobody…had bailed out. They had not heard the order.

…I had dived the ship immediately after the fire so that nobody would pass out it the oxygen was cut off. Suddenly we started to get an awful lot of flak (anti-aircraft fire from the ground) so I had to hurry back to the cockpit to do some evasive action which worked okay, incidentally. I had one of the boys get the maps…and had the radio operator get fixes so I plotted a course for home with as little flak as possible. The radio operator did a fine job so we came out on course and landed OK. All this was above the clouds, so I think I can qualify for navigator now as well as pilot…

…Your prayers are standing by me. I was praying up there and all the rest of the men were praying, too…

Lots of love,

Elliott

Daniel Elliot Whitlock won the Silver Star for bringing his B-17 home to Snetterton Heath airfield, Norfolk. His parents owned the Commercial Company Market, now Mason Bar and Grill.

Right now I'd rather see Arroyo Creek than the Tiber River, Mt. Lassen rather than Vesuvius, and the grammar school porch would appeal to me a lot more than Mussolini's balcony — and I'll take a ride through the Huasna any day in preference to the Appian Way.

Arroyo Grande GI Homer Edgecombe, writing from Italy

Well, I went through the commando course last week. You have probably read about it in the magazines and papers. Boy! I'm telling you they do everything but kill you, and sometimes they do that, but it's surely good training. It teaches a man to stay down low, or else get hit like a couple of them did when I went through at the same time I did. One of them got hit through the shoulder and one got his heel knocked off.

SSgt Frank Gularte, writing from Camp Hood, Texas. Gularte would be killed by a sniper on the German frontier on 28 November 1944. His first child, Frank Jr., was born five days later.

I just saw one of the swellest sights. You will never believe it when I tell you. It was fresh green peas in a field…if you had been where we were and as long as we were, you would know why we thought so much of seeing a field of vegetables. We saw many wonderful sights…. We saw country that reminded me of the Cuyama, some places reminded me of the scenery between San Simeon and Monterey. For the past few months we have seen nothing but country like that at Devils' Den, except there is more wind and sand here.

There are some places where deer would thrive. Hillsides of brush, lots of oaks, creeks and water holes. They have big trout like the rainbows at home in the water holes, and doves, and I found a treasure: a nest of quail eggs.

Arroyo Grande GI William Carnes, writing from North Africa

You can tell the editor of the Herald-Recorder that I would like very much to get the paper. The first chance you get, I wish you would take out a subscription for me…I would also like for you…[to] send me some of those flashlights that you can get down at Don's [Variety Store]. You can have Fritz do that for you. Also stick in a few candy bars.

Pvt. Francis Fink, from "somewhere in France"

We were in Naples the morning after Vesuvius erupted. That was a great sight, to see that smoke curling up into the air to great heights. I shouldn't say curling. I should say billowing. It was fully 20,000 to 25,0000 feet in the sky…The night scene was the magnificent and gorgeous one. The red hot molten lava was flowing down the sides in all directions and boiling over the top of the crater. The whole mountain was an orange-red outline…

PFC Kenneth Juler, Italy

We have been talking French to the natives. We don't get along so good, but I guess it will be alright in time. The first Frenchman to whom I said "Bonjour!" ("good morning" in French) answered me in good English. Did we laugh!...Dottie and I were talking this A.M. to a Frenchman who gave us some onions which we made into sandwiches with crackers and cheese. He also gave us a big bouquet of roses.

2nd Lt. Virginia Campondonico, U.S. Army nurse

While I was on my furlough, I got to see the King and Queen and their daughter. They don't look any different than anybody else. I also got a chance to see the Scotsmen marching down the street playing the bagpipes. They were dressed in kilts...I surely had a good time.

Pvt. Herman Petker, convalescing in a British hospital from trench foot

The Pacific War

The censor says I can't say much,
Can't talk of so and so and such and such.
Can't even saying we're having weather,
Or you'd put two and two together.
Can't say where I am or what.
Can't tell you if, or why, or but.
Can't tell you what we do, or don't.
But I can send my love to you
Without restrictions. Which I do.

Pfc. Orval Wrong, from a New Guinea Hospital

Dear Pan:

I hear the boatswain's mate passing a rumor that mail will leave in the near future, so I will include a brief report on myself. I am filled with good intentions to write you more often, but am fuller of good excuses.

During the rare occasions when the weather is bad, I don't write on account of the bad weather. When it is fair, the hot sun enhances my natural inclinations to be lazy and sleepy. My eight hours a day on watch add the finishing touches. I watch mostly for the little men who aren't there, but the Captain insists that they may be there any time. Anyway when [the members of the crew of his ship, the *Walke,* her named struck out by the censor] see them then they won't be there long.

Notwithstanding all this I frequently get out my papers and pen and drape my elbows over a mess table in a threatening manner. I think of you and wonder what you're doing. I reflect that this is a big wet ocean, and that we've been at sea so long that the salt is caking in my hair, that this business about mermaids is a lot of baloney, that seeing the world would be nicer if it wasn't all water, that mail and Christmas come with about the same frequency, and that the war will over in six months to 10 years.

I day dream about shore liberty in a good old U.S.A. port where there are a hundred pretty girls to one sailor, nothing costs over a dime, and me with three months' pay on the books. Oh Boy!

About that time my literary efforts are interrupted by that leather-lunged whistle blower, the Boatswains' Mate, yelling that it's time for drill, battle stations, chow, target practice, movies, inspection, field day, air bedding, sweep down, peel spuds, scrub decks, fuel ship, carry stores, dump garbage, darken ship, pump bilges, blow tubes, pipe down, relieve the watch, or what have you.

Whereupon I sheath my pen and go to work, eat or sleep, as the case may be, without having written a word to you. It may be just as well, as the censor would probably have cropped them out anyway.

…While I can't exactly say I'm having a good time and wish you were here, I hope you are well and wish I was there. In the meantime, don't worry about me as I can take good care of myself and the other guys and I'm doing all right. At least I'm well and O.K.

Say Hello to all of your friends and the most to you.

FELIX

Mess attendant 3rd Class Felix Estibal, writing to Javier Pantaleon of the Waller Seed Company, October 1942. Estibal was killed in action shortly after he wrote this letter.

USS *Donald S. Runels*. U.S. Navy

Mrs. Donald S. Runels, widow of Nipomo's first World War II casualty, is in Texas with her eldest son, Donald, aged 10. Tomorrow, August 7, she will launch a destroyer escort christened for her late husband, Ensign Donald S. Runels, who was killed in action on the *Northampton* when it was sunk in the South Pacific December 8, 1942.

Arroyo Grande Herald-Recorder, *August 1943. When the Japanese torpedo struck Runels' ship,* Northampton, *the explosion was so violent that the bridge crew on the nearby light cruiser* Honolulu *burst into tears.*

Three tractors of Company B landed on the left side of Red Beach Two. When the men tried to disembark from the first two tractors, only nine of the twenty-four men actually reached the beach...Private First Class Murray's Casualty Card indicates that he died of gunshot wounds to the head and chest on 20 November 1943. Private First Class Murray was reported buried in East Division Cemetery…Row A, Grave 6. Based on PFC Murray's recorded circumstances of death and the indication that he was initially buried at this location, it seems likely that PFC Murray did make it to the beach before being killed.

Official description of the death of Marine PFC George Murray, of Oceano, on Tarawa, 1943. His body was finally recovered, identified, and returned to Arroyo Grande in 2017, thanks to a mission to bring him home—one that took years-- on the part of Oceano historian Linda Austin.

The black cabriolet, with its top down, pulled up close to our commanding officer, LTCOL Piper, who presented us to the Commander-In-Chief. I was in the front rank within 20 feet from the auto and could hear their voices. The auto was driven so close to the commanding officer that he hardly needed to move to reach the side of the vehicle.

A Marine describes FDR's visit to Camp Lejeune, December 1944. The driver of the car was Sgt. Thelma Murray, USMC, sister of the Marine lost on Tarawa.

I got it in the right side in June, and had malaria three times and jungle rot. This is a nice place to have them all.

Pvt. Charles Faux, writing from India

This will be the bloodiest fight in Marine Corps history. We'll catch seven kinds of hell on the beaches, and that will be just the beginning. The fighting will be fierce, and the casualties will be awful, but my Marines will take the damned island.

Gen. Holland Smith, Marine commander, on the eve of Iwo Jima

FROM COMMANDANT MARINE CORPS

TO   Mr and Mrs Antonio Brown (parents)

Rt #1 Box 662

Arroyo Grande, California

DEEPLY REGRET TO INFORM YOU THAT YOUR

SON **PRIVATE LOUIS BROWN**

WAS KILLED IN ACTION

1 MARCH 1945 AT **IWO JIMA VOLCANO ISLANDS**

IN THE PERFORMANCE OF HIS DUTY AND IN THE SERVICE
OF HIS COUNTRY. WHEN INFORMATION IS RECEIVED
REGARDING BURIAL YOU WILL BE NOTIFIED. TO PREVENT
POSSIBLE AID TO OUR ENEMIES DO NOT DIVULGE THE
NAME OF HIS SHIP OR STATION. PLEASE ACCEPT MY
HEARTFELT SYMPATHY. LETTER FOLLOWS.

5 APRIL 1945

AA VANDERGIFT LIEUT GENERAL USMC

COMMANDANT OF THE MARINE CORPS

*The telegram notifying Mr. and Mrs. Antonio Brown of their son's
death. The Browns farmed in Corbett Canyon. Louis was two days away
from turning twenty-one when he was killed on Hill 362A on Iwo Jima.*

I have been able to get around and see most of the island. There is quite
a bit of game here, but we are not allowed to hunt, as there are so many
fellows there would soon be nothing left: besides, there's the risk of shooting
each other where there are so many of us.

There are a lot of deer here. Only last night about sundown as I was coming in from work, there was a great big buck standing right in the middle of the road. He was plenty fat, but also plenty slow. A deer that slow around Arroyo Grande wouldn't last five minutes.

US Army Staff Sgt. Bob Little, writing from Guam

In Marysville we were…at Camp Beale. And one night, four of us wanted to go into town 'cause we learned there was a Chinese restaurant there. We wanted some rice, you know, Chinese food! We hadn't had any in a long time. And we just sat around, no service. So the Sergeant called over the waiter and the waiter called the manager. The manager said, "I'm sorry, Sir. We can't serve Asians." Now this was a Chinese restaurant and I guess we were startled when we heard that…And he explained that, "Hey, I'm sorry we can't serve you. There's a city ordinance that we can't serve Asians." And here we were soldiers, you know…Colonel Offley made a stand. He went to the city fathers and told them, "Hey, you serve my people, they are American soldiers, or I'll declare Martial Law on you."

A member of the First Filipino Infantry Regiment, formed at Camp San Luis Obispo, describing his commander, Lt. Col Robert Offley. There were no further incidents in Marysville. Several South County Filipino men joined the First Regiment.

We are back three miles from the front licking our wounds now, and waiting for I don't know what. Maybe we go back and maybe we don't. I guess I've seen most of this island so far— enough, anyway. Shuri Castle was a rich joint and Naha used to be quite a town…I had my picture taken the other day with a couple of fellows by "Division." I don't know if it will get in the papers or not. I sure didn't look like much that day.

USMC Pvt. John Loomis, writing from Okinawa.

The End of the War

The State Board of Equalization has requested all sellers of alcoholic beverages, whether retail or in bulk, to suspend the sale of such beverages for 24 hours after the announcement of cessation of hostilities in Europe.

Arroyo Grande Herald-Recorder, *October 6, 1944*

The official announcement that the German Army had surrendered unconditionally...and that Tuesday, May 8, would be officially observed throughout the nation as V-E Day, was greeted by Arroyo Grandeans with quiet satisfaction and determination to gird for the finish fight to bring complete and final victory in the Pacific as soon as possible...There was little public demonstration, but nearly all businesses were closed...The town area was bright with American flags flown from flagstaffs set in the sidewalk and a Sunday calm of rededication pervaded the city.

Arroyo Grande Herald-Recorder, *May 11, 1945*

The ringing of church bells, followed closely by the blowing of the blackout horn and the fire siren at 4 o'clock Tuesday afternoon ushered final victory into Arroyo Grande and announced the end of the world's worst war, a war which called to the colors between 750 and 1,000 men and women from the southern third of S.L.O. County, and took the lives of at least 30 of them...The blowing of motor car horns, the firing of a few residual firecrackers, the display of large American flags along the sidewalk, and children racing up and down the street determined to celebrate but not knowing just how to do it—these were the visible signs of public rejoicing at the hard-won victory.

Arroyo Grande Herald-Recorder, *August 17, 1945*

In conformity with the announcement of President Roosevelt, acting as commander in chief of the Army, the Western Defense command has issued a proclamation, a copy of which was sent to the Herald-Recorder, stating that citizens of Japanese ancestry are to be allowed to return to the Western states, beginning at midnight on January 2, 1945.

Arroyo Grande Herald-Recorder, *December 29, 1944*

The S. Kobara family was the first family to return home in 1945. They opened their home to help friends resettle in the Arroyo Grande Valley. The families that had returned had farms to come back to but very little capital with which to farm and businesses willing to extend credit were almost nonexistent. Once again, it was the same families, along with Jack Schnyder, the village blacksmith, and Wilkinson's Meat Market, who helped their Japanese friends by extending them credit when no one else would. The trouble families had returning to the valley was compounded by the hate some people openly displayed. Families could not sleep in their beds at night and had to sleep on the floor because a few people vented their anger by shooting into the homes at night.

History of the Pismo-Oceano Vegetable Exchange

Right away, he said that we didn't have much time, that they were looking for someone to marry, and it's gonna be quick, because we have to go back. After about a month's time, I found out he had already talked to my grandmother and grandfather, and my uncle and aunt. He told me he didn't have any more time to stay in the Philippines, and he wanted to... well, *marry* me.

Oh, we were so shocked when we came here. We thought we would come here and live in a big two-story, three-story house. But they worked at the farm, and we were shocked! We said, "This is where they live? I thought you lived in some three-story house? It's all muddy and farmy."

We had to clean and scrub because, well, they're single, and they worked long days, early to late, they have no time to clean the house.

Evelyn Betita, remembering her marriage to Perfecto, an Arroyo Grande farmer. The immigration of Filipinas was almost completely prohibited before the war; Filipino men outnumbered women 100 to 1 in many places in California. The War Brides Act made it possible for Perfecto to bring his new wife home

Al Spierling's Thirteenth
Combat Mission

For the two years before D-day, the Americans in England who had been carrying much of the nation's fight to Nazi Germany were the airmen of the Eighth Air Force. They made up forty-nine bomb groups and twenty-two fighter groups, and their bases were seventy-one airfields concentrated in East Anglia, from Norfolk south to Essex, in places that must have sounded quaintly medieval to American ears: Bury St. Edmunds, Knettishall, Little

Staughton, Matching Green, Molesworth, Snailsworth, Snetterton Heath and Thorpe Abbots.

Unfortunately, Army food followed them across the Atlantic. Bill Mauldin, the great editorial cartoonist who created the imaginary Willie and Joe, his comrades in the Italian campaign, once remarked, without malice, that his mother was the worst cook in the world. Then he encountered army food, which was infinitely worse. At least airmen understood that they were fed better than men like Mauldin, dogfaces, who commonly used GI powdered lemonade to wash their socks. Still, even in the AAF, the green-hued powdered eggs, along with the ubiquitous Spam, were breakfast standards, and creamed chipped beef on toast—referred to as "shit on a shingle"—remained what seemed to be, to the military, a perverse culinary masterpiece. Radioman/gunner Albert Lee Findley Jr. of Los Osos found little relief off base. "English food took some getting used to," he admittted tactfully. (Many years after the war, Findley and his wife would live in England as the proprietors of an antique shop.) One vegetable, brussels sprouts, was as common to English fare as Spam was to American mess halls, and at war's end, many English-based GIs swore they would never eat them again.

Al Spierling beside his gun turret, 1944. Courtesy the Spierling family.

There were other features of English culture that the Americans found more to their liking. Airmen immediately found pubs near their bases, and the attraction was powerful. Historian Donald Miller writes of the 1943 arrival of an AAF engineer battalion, charged with laying out an airstrip outside the village of

299

Debach, near the North Sea. Their discovery of what English called "the local," this one called the Dog, resulted in the Yanks buying so many rounds "for the house" —the last round, just before closing time, was for forty-seven drinks— that the next day, a doleful little sign was posted outside the Dog: "No beer." It was, Miller notes, the first time the pub had been closed in 450 years.

The Americans, of course, also found young English women to their liking as well. The War Department discouraged what were called "special relationships" and made it nearly impossible, thanks to a bureaucratic maze, for the best-intentioned American soldier to marry, but of course, the War Department failed. Special relationships were as common as visits to the local pub. Al Spierling of Arroyo Grande, a B-17 crewman, lost a little of his youthful idealism—Spierling was a thoughful young man who made a special trip to York to explore the setting for Brönte's *Wuthering Heights*—when he learned that a gunner he knew, a married man, had taken up with an English girl. He was a little shocked. "For a twenty-year-old," he said, "I learned a lot."

* * *

Al Spierling's "epitaph" in his 1940 Bucks County, Pennsylvania high school yearbook was revelatory:

> *Over a motor he will often pose,*
> *Experimenting, Tormenting,*
> *On thru life he goes.*

After the nation went to war in 1941, the Army Air Forces battery of aptitude tests quickly uncovered the young Pennsylvanian's gift for mechanics. He would go to engineering school in Amarillo, Texas, and would emerge as a flight engineer and top turret gunner in the Eighth Air Force, 457th Bomb Group, stationed at RAF Glatton in East Anglia, in early 1944.

TSgt Spierling would soon find out that bomber crews had to deal with the harshest of elements: The oxygen supply, of course, was critical at missions flown in unpressurized cabins at twenty-five thousand feet. Masks were donned once the aircraft reached ten thousand feet, and it was the bombardier's responsibility to do "oxygen checks" —to check in, via intercom, with each crew member every five minutes. But the cold—some temperatures at forty below zero—impinged on breathing, as well; any moisture inside the oxygen mask froze, blocking the air supply, something a crew member might not notice until one of his comrades lost consciousness. (Urine froze as well, so the "relief tube" provided each bomber crew frequently proved useless; veterans used buckets or just relieved themselves inside their clothing.)

Clothing was crucial to survival as well; skin exposed only momentarily at altitude was subject to frostbite, so airmen dressed in layers, described in a 1997 U.S. Air Force paper:

In the spring of 1943, a typical combat dress for a B-17 gunner consisted of: heavy woolen underwear, two pairs of lined wool socks, a modified F-1 electric suit [itself unreliable—if one element went out on the suit, like 1950s Christmas lights, the entire suit failed], RAF designed electric gloves and socks, standard A-6 boots, and A-4 coveralls with a B-5 helmet. Additionally, some men wore a leather A-2 jacket over the coveralls. If an electric suit was not worn, the standard protective garb was the heavy fleece-lined B-6 jacket and A-5 trousers in its place. Clearly, all this clothing was a lot to wear and maintain and became cumbersome while trying to perform even the simplest task.

Discomfort was compounded by terror. It was German ground fire, or flak, from the German word *Fliegerabwehrkanone*, or "antiaircraft cannon," that provoked the most fear among American fliers. The twenty-pound enemy shells, fired from ground batteries that were dense around key targets, exploded in angry black puffs that sent steel fragments slicing through wings, fuselage and crewmen. On one mission, shards of flak sliced the oxygen lines necessary to survival at twenty-five thousand feet; the waist gunners and tail gunner in Spierling's ship kept passing out—symptomatic of anoxia—until he could repair the system..

Spierling kept a log of his missions. They included bombing oil facilities at Hamburg and at Ruhland and another, infamous site: the ball-bearing factory complex at Schweinfurt, where, in October 1943, the Eighth Air Force had lost sixty bombers. The fighters came up again came up again as they had then, this time after the 457th Bomb Group's B-17s. But by the time of Spierling's missions in 1944, the bombers had as escorts the powerful, nimble P-51 Mustangs, with wing tanks giving them the range earlier fighters didn't have, and Spierling watched, amazed, as four Mustangs sped toward a formation of more than thirty Messerschmitt 109s and broke them up. The German fighters reappeared on the 457th's homeward leg—"We got bounced," Spierling remembered—but the Mustangs reappeared, too, and the B-17 crewmen watched what turned into the airborne equivalent of a barroom brawl. Spierling never forgot the German pilot he saw crawling out of the cockpit of his doomed FW-190. The Luftwaffe flier was wearing a yellow flying scarf that flew straight out, and his parachute was on fire. The young American watched the beginning of the young German's fall to earth.

Flak bursts bracket a B-17 on its bomb run. Museum of the United States Air Force.

Another memorable mission was the unlucky thirteenth, over Berlin in the summer of 1944. As the squadron began its bomb run, turbulence caused the B-17 above Spierling's to drop so close to Spierling's ship that day, "Georgia Peach," that he could count, watching transfixed from his top turret, the rivets on its bomb bay doors. The other ship crumpled "Georgia Peach's" tailfin, then it dropped its bombload. Somehow, the bombs missed and "Peach" kept flying. But more trouble came with the trip home.

A German 88-mm anti-aircraft shellburst perforated the fuselage next to Spierling and just behind the pilots' seats. It left a gaping hole. Spierling was okay. The plane was not. Flak from the exploding shell had severed the throttle cables to both engines, Number One and Number Two, on the left wing. "Peach" began descending from the 22,000 feet typical of the squadron's missions; she was rapidly hemorrhaging altitude when she approached the edge of the Continent and the North Sea.

When the B-17 was 1000 feet above the water, the pilot, 1st Lt. William Clarkson, yelled *"Al! Get me some power! NOW!"*

The damaged Georgia Peach *limps home on Al Spierling's thirteenth mission.* Courtesy the Imperial War Museum, London.

As soon as Lt. Clarkson bellowed for more power, Spierling understood what had happened. He said many years later that this was because of eighteen weeks of training, at Amarillo. But it was his intuition--he had an inborn and uncanny mechanical gift--led to what happened next. He crawled into the bombardier's station. wiggled beneath the pilots' seats and found the two severed cables. He gave them a yank. The B-17 was now 200 feet above the water and the kind of water landing—the North Sea's surface was no more forgiving than concrete-- that often proved fatal to American aircrews.

The engines re-started.

"Peach" made it home safely. Spierling, a smoker then, emerged from the airplane and couldn't get the cellophane off his pack of cigarettes because his hands were shaking so badly. He would win a Distinguished Flying Cross. He had just turned twenty-one. He had twenty-two more missions to fly.

Spierling would survive them to come home, get a bachelor's degree at UC Santa Barbara, start a family, get his master's degree at Cal Poly, and become a longtime fixture at Arroyo Grande High School as the auto shop teacher. Spierling wasn't "just" a shop teacher. He would become the real founder of the excellent vocational education program at Arroyo Grande High School and would prove to be a gifted administrator.

After retirement, he worked as a docent at the Paulding History House in Arroyo Grande and was a go-to problem solver in his part-time job at Miner's Hardware. But his passion was teaching students about engines. His students loved him, loved his integrity, his patience, and his knowledge, and so they caught Mr. Spierling's passion. Many of them say that he was their favorite teacher in high school.

San Luis Obispo County and The Wall

Sometimes, as arid as they may seem, statistics can reveal history in a poignant way. This essay isn't about Cliometrics, which is a much more sophisticated discipline that uses statistical analysis to understand history. It's based, instead, on a small but very precious sampling, from the young men whose names are recorded on The Wall, the national Vietnam War Memorial.

34 total dead, San Luis Obispo County, Vietnam War (1965-1972)

National average, Vietnam war dead, per 100,000 population: 28.5

California average per 100,000 population: 27.9

San Luis Obispo County average per 100,000 population: 32*

Deaths by municipality:

San Luis Obispo:	9
Arroyo Grande:	4
Atascadero:	8
Grover City (Beach):	4
Morro Bay:	2**
Oceano:	2
Paso Robles:	4
Pismo Beach:	1

Deaths by year:

1965	1
1966	1
1967	6
1968	11
1969	9
1970	3

1971	2
1972	1

Average Age at Death: 22.4

Average Age, Vietnam soldier: 22

21 most frequent age for SLO County servicemen killed [Two were 18, one was 19; the oldest was 31]

Service Branch

Army	24
Marine Corps	8
Air Force	1
Navy	1

[Three were officers; 31 were enlisted men]

Cause of death:

Explosive device	3
Helicopter crash	4
Aircraft Crash	1
Accident "other"	3
Accident, friendly fire	1
Grenade	8***
Artillery/mortar/rocket	6
Unknown	3
Small arms fire	3
Illness	2

*County Population, 1970 Census: 106,403. Our average is higher than either the state or national averages. One supposition is that military service, in rural America during the 1960s, was seen as a way to serve America and a way to advance in life. This was still very much a rural county in 1965, when the war began to accelerate and long before it became so divisive.

**The two Morro Bay soldiers were killed within four days of each other in April 1968, when Tet was still convulsing South Vietnam; the impact on such a small town had to be devastating.

***This statistic is shocking. It meant that those casualties were the result of extremely close combat.

Belleau Wood, 2018

At the Aisne-Marne American Cemetery near the Belleau Wood battlefield. U.S. Marine Corps.

I used to show a short but harrowing film clip to my AP European history students every year when we studied the First World War. It depicted the opening, re-enacted by modern Marines, of the U.S. Marine Corps attack on German machine-gun positions in Belleau Wood in the summer of 1918–unbelievably, one hundred years ago.

That was when one Marine top sergeant encouraged the men behind him by bellowing: "Come on, you sons of bitches! Do you want to live forever?"

The Marines were under-equipped: Their helmets are Army knock-offs of British helmets, and the light machine guns they used were French Chaucats. Our troops went into the Meuse-Argonne in French trucks driven by French colonials, from a nation that would someday be called Vietnam. Our tanks were French Renaults. Our airplanes were obsolete Nieuports.

The Americans were under-trained, too. Pershing was still enamored of a tactical doctrine that called on the audacity of the individual soldier and the lethality of the bayonet, lessons the Europeans had unlearned by 1915. When they'd first gone into action, the Americans had died in parade-ground rows; they were babies to war.

Modern-day Marines from Quantico re-enact the assault at Belleau Wood, 2009. U.S. Marine Corps.

But this ignorance saved the Marines—who died by the bushel-load, too—because the survivors kept advancing anyway. The Germans remembered them coming toward them in Belleau Wood: They were smoking cigarettes and firing from the hip.

The Germans, themselves disciplined and courageous soldiers, finally could take no more of this madness. They broke and ran.

It was one of the clearest and most decisive turning points in history. The year before, the Bolsheviks had begun to pull Russia out of the war. The French Army had mutinied. The British had little blood left to spill: Whole towns and schools and factories were emptied of the young men killed together in the "Pals Battalions" they'd joined together.

And then the Americans brought themselves, their innocence and their daring to Belleau Wood. A few months later, they brought influenza, too, and so the war collapsed in November 1918.

In November 2018, the president canceled a planned visit to the battlefield and its cemetery. It was raining.

Chapter 11. Good Men, Fictional and Otherwise

Ben Hogan and Eddie Nowak

Number One Son got me not one, but TWO books about golfer Ben Hogan. The photograph shows his one-iron to the green to win the 1950 U.S. Open on the 72nd hole of the championship.

Hogan was a great athlete, but he was not a warm human being. He loved golf. He loved his wife, Valerie, and there it ends. The year before this shot, he'd thrown his body instinctively in front of Valerie's as their car, on the road to another tournament, crashed head-on into a bus that had emerged suddenly from a dense Texas ground-fog.

The impact nearly crushed Hogan. He walked with a limp for the rest of his life. But he'd saved Valerie's life, and his own, in that moment. Had he not loved her so much, had he not thrown himself in front of her, the steering column would have impaled him.

So the next year, limping, he won the U.S. Open with this one-iron, with a club so difficult to hit that no golfer carries it anymore. His shot was golf's equivalent to breaking the sound barrier, to landing an Olympic triple-axel triple-toe, to climbing Everest, to baking a weightless soufflé.

His talent was relatively modest compared to that of his contemporaries, naturals like Sam Snead, Byron Nelson and Jimmy Demaret. But he had an engineer's mind. He rationalized the elusiveness of the golf swing and broke it down into component parts in a way that made sense to him. In so doing, he practiced , it's said, until his hands bled. Despite that, he wasn't a drudge. He loved to practice, loved the moment when the impact of the clubhead on the ball created a perfect one-iron–his described a gentle fade–in a way that only *seemed* to be effortless.

Shagging balls for Hogan wasn't effortless, because he could be merciless with the young boys who shagged for him in practice: He grew so accurate that he hit them repeatedly, and it hurt. He didn't notice. He was focused on the impact as much or more than the shot's destination. His cigarette glowed furiously between shots. Impatient, he motioned his shagger to move backward ten yards, out of the line of fire, while he changed clubs and started to hit him repeatedly with a six-iron rather than a seven.

Once a knot of overbearing Kern County oilmen begged Hogan, playing an exhibition in Bakersfield, to give them lessons. He would be paid handsomely. He looked at them narrowly through his cigarette smoke, and flat turned them down. He was angry. Didn't they know what he knew? They already had the best teaching pro in America, a stubby little guy named Eddie Nowak.

Nowak, many years later, would teach me how to play at Black Lake, in Nipomo. Hogan was right: Nowak was one of the best teachers I've ever had, and one of the toughest. The discipline and the work ethic he taught me has lasted me all the days of my life, one in which golf has been mostly absent. Eddie didn't just teach me golf. He taught me how hard you have to work to take on life. He was *my* Hogan.

Woodrow and Gus

A photo of my great-niece Sarah, a gifted horsewoman--she is lovely, like her Mom--set me to reminiscing about the miniseries *Lonesome Dove, and* what a grand job the production company, Motown, did of making television literate for the nights, so many years ago, when it was broadcast. I will never forgive the cable provider, however, which dropped the signal the last half-hour of the last episode during that first broadcast of Larry McMurtry's wonderful novel.

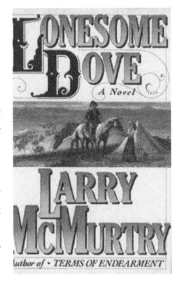

The scene that still stands out happens in a little frontier town. A cavalry scout is viciously beating former Texas Ranger Woodrow Call's illegitimate son, Newt, with his quirt. Woodrow--Tommy Lee Jones--sees the commotion from the end of the street, understands instantly what is happening, and leaps into the saddle to rescue Newt.

Gus, Woodrow's longtime friend and fellow former Ranger, follows. Gus has to lasso Woodrow to keep him from killing the cavalry scout because, among other insults visited on the unfortunate man, Woodrow has softened up a smithy's anvil with the scout's skull. When he's reasonably calm, Woodrow announces this to a gathering of stunned townspeople: "I hate rudeness in a man. I won't tolerate it." It's a lovely, albeit violent, moment.

But what's even lovelier is the ride Woodrow makes to rescue Newt. Jones is a polo player in real life and in an instant, he vaults into the saddle, gets the horse's head turned around and is off down the street. That ride--that furious gallop--is seamless. There is absolutely no movement on Jones's part; it's as if he'd been welded to his mount and the two are, as the Aztecs thought of Cortez's cavalry, one being. I have never seen a more beautiful moment of horsemanship.

When I taught at Mission Prep in San Luis Obispo, our senior English teacher, Mary Isaaksen-Bright, assigned *Lonesome Dove* and I was a little taken aback. No Bennet sisters, no tormented Russian boarders, no *Pequod!* Then I, Mr. Smartypants, read McMurtry's book and realized that Isaak's choice was perfect.

McMurtry is in love with our language and in his hands. English can be malleable and plastic, more like paint or music than prose. It's easy for a writer in that place to get clever and precious, where you can see he's showing off. You don't get that sense with McMurtry. Instead you get the feel for the language as it must have really sounded on the frontier.

That is why I am so impressed with Charles Portis's novel *True Grit*--the two excellent films adapted from that novel didn't need all that much adapting: The films' contraction-free dialogue and Mattie Ross's narrative are lifted word-for-word from Portis. What Portis did in writing that book--I think the best picaresque Western novel since Robert Lewis Taylor's *The Travels of Jaimie McPheeters*--is to strap his readers securely into a time machine and transport them backward. There we are, in the midst of spectators with wicker baskets of fried chicken wrapped in picnic linen, waiting impatiently for condemned men to swing from the gallows in Fort Smith, Arkansas. It is remarkable writing.

McMurtry's *Dove* is the same. Even the names that he gives his characters show an imagination alive with the wonderful sounds and combinations of sounds that can make a book come alive. For example:

- Jake Spoon
- Lippy Jones
- Deets
- Blue Duck
- Mox-Mox the Man Burner
- Dish Bogget
- Pea Eye
- Peach Johnson
- July (pronounced, as my Dad did, JOO-ly) Johnson

Of course, the most memorable character of all is Gus, and Robert Duvall was perfect in the television role. Duvall always has, in almost any situation, a faintly bemused look on his face, which I think meant that Augustus McRae was listening to a symphony nobody else could hear.

He's a perfect foil for the Puritan Woodrow and is never afraid to needle his partner and best friend. Under the joshing, Gus is a Romantic, in the best sense of the word. He protects the weak. His relationship with Laurie the prostitute is touching. Laurie is in shock after a vicious gang rape and beating. Gus doesn't do what other action heroes would do--immediately track down the savage men who did this and air-condition them with his revolver. He instead becomes like a father to Laurie, stays with her, feeds her, and gives her time and space to begin to recover.

Similarly, Gus is utterly loyal to his friends but he will not hesitate to hang one, like Jake Spoon, who's crossed the line from honor to barbarity. He's loyal in another way, as well. You discover that there has always been only one woman in the world for him, Clara, and he'd lost her a long time ago. When he finds her again, she's become a rancher's wife. It's missing Clara that accounts for the melancholy that Gus's bemusement hides so well. It is easy to admire a man so strong and, at the same time, so vulnerable.

318

Grace Under Pressure: Pfc. Arthur Carlson

The Old Guard, the 3rd U.S. Infantry regiment, is responsible for state funerals. The horse chosen to follow President Kennedy's caisson on the weekend after November 22 was named Black Jack, after General of the Armies John J. Pershing.

Black Jack was a beautiful animal, jet-black, a Morgan/Quarter horse cross, and he had a difficult personality. He had never been broken to saddle, hence his role in the president's funeral as the riderless horse with the spurred boots reversed in their stirrups.

If Black Jack liked anybody, it was Private First Class Arthur Carlson, chosen to be his handler that day. Carlson, who had all of six months' training handling horses since being assigned to the Old Guard, was apprehensive. He said later he knew that if he messed up, he'd be walking guard duty at a radar station in Greenland within a week. Black Jack, however, had never given Carlson trouble.

On the Sunday after the assassination, the caisson was carrying Kennedy's coffin to the Capitol to lie in state. Carlson, trailing the coffin, was leading the horse through a tunnel when a large metal gate collapsed. The echoes of its impact unnerved Black Jack. He would be agitated for the next two days, perhaps the most important days in the sixteen-year-old horse's life.

They were no less important to Pfc. Carlson. He was only three years older than Black Jack.

A restless Black Jack and Pfc. Carlson stand by as the president's coffin is carried out of the Capitol. U.S. Army Photo.

The horse's agitation was visible on live television. In both the procession to the Capitol and the final procession to Arlington on the day of the funeral, Black Jack fought Carlson every step of the way. The horse tossed his head up and down, snorted, pranced, turned nearly sideways as if to dare Carlson to let him go and even tried crossing in front of the young soldier. Carlson was forbidden by protocol from speaking to the horse to try to calm him. All he could do was to maintain an iron grip on the bridle and try to keep his balance. Then, as the two waited for the funeral cortege to begin after the funeral mass at the Cathedral of St. Matthew the Apostle, Black Jack stomped on Carlson's foot. The soldier at first thought some of his toes were broken, but he showed no reaction. The shoe was ruined. Through all of this, Carlson kept control of his charge. The young man was magnificent.

The ironic result of the television coverage of those days was that millions of Americans fell in love with Black Jack. He got fan letters. A Washington D.C. matron somehow discovered that Black Jack had a sweet tooth—for butter brickle cake, no less--and baked him one every year on his birthday. Visitors flocked to the Old Guard stables at Fort Myer, Virginia, to see the famous horse. It was then that his fellow soldiers discovered something extraordinary about the animal. Some visitors could not only approach him, but the horse allowed them to stroke his neck and muzzle. Their touch seemed to calm him. He even nuzzled his visitors gently in return.

Black Jack, as it turned out, loved children.

Elvis: The Searcher

A two-part HBO documentary on Elvis, *The Searcher,* was absorbing, and it helped that two musicians, the late Tom Petty and Bruce Springsteen, were among the commentators, because they seemed to understand Elvis so well. The documentary was also, of course, heart-breaking, because Elvis never exactly found what he was searching for.

The program made you wonder, still, about some of Elvis' mysteries that may never be fully understood: About the dead twin, the family's early poverty, the almost Jesuitical sense of mission he felt to overcome his family's seeming failure and to heal their heartbreak. And you wonder about his mother. It wasn't that he was a mother's boy, according to the documentary. It was instead that the son and the mother were extensions of each other. They were, in some ways, the same person. He never recovered from her death.

"Jailhouse Rock." Wikimedia/MGM.

She died just before he went into the Army, which was a pivotal and in many ways tragic break in his career. He lost his mother and he lost contact with that first vital wave of rock 'n' roll, which surged and subsided while he was overseas. He also discovered, in Germany, the uppers that would keep him awake on overnight duty.

He really wanted to be a movie star, but he hated the stupid movies, too, three a year at one point, each with meaningless "Elvis" soundtracks. Significantly, the one possible exception to stupid Elvis musicals was *King Creole*, when so many of the supporting musicians were African-Americans. His delight in performing the music for this film is transparent.

Later, he did Vegas and the insane, exhausting tours out of a damnable sense of duty to his manager, Colonel Tom Parker. This, along with the singer's increasing dependence on prescription drugs, were the forces that helped to destroy him.

But the rich and hopeful first half of the documentary portrays a young man alive to every sound coming from every black blues club on Beale Street in Memphis, alive to every stylish walk he saw there "A'hm gonna USE that!" he told a friend. (I can't vouch for that *Forrest Gump* scene.) Elvis was alive, most of all, to Gospel, and he understood also the Scots-Irish ethic that permeates Southern culture and country music. That tradition, in his time, was kept carefully and jealously at the Grand Old Opry. The emerging young star *horrified* the Opry; it was the Louisiana Hayride that spread the Gospel of Elvis instead.

When he first went into Sun Records he took everything he'd absorbed growing up and created, in a studio no bigger than a custodian's closet, *Elvis*. Sam Phillips knew instantly that he had found in this young man a turning point in music history--and then was generous enough to let him go to RCA Records because he realized Sun just wasn't big enough for Elvis's talent.

Elvis knew that he was like no one else, either. In the documentary, Bruce Springsteen spoke movingly about Elvis's early recording sessions and about his own, about how the epiphany that visited both of them. Both realized just how powerful their talents were, and the realization humbled and terrified them.

My Neurotic Hero: Horatio Hornblower

Terence Morgan as Lt. Gerard and Gregory Peck as Hornblower in the 1952 film. Wikimedia Commons.

My first adult reading had to have been the trilogy of Horatio Hornblower novels my father had bought some time during World War II, possibly when he was stationed in London. He liked the books so much that they may have inspired him to take the steam train down to Portsmouth to see Admiral Nelson's HMS *Victory*. One of the souvenirs he brought home with him, besides several bottles of Cointreau, was a little tin box of hard candy, its lid embossed with the image of the great ship on which Nelson--Hornblower's real-life inspiration, just as Hornblower would inspire *Star Trek's* Captain Kirk--had died in 1805. My mother kept the box for years to store bobbins of her brightly-colored sewing-machine thread.

Hornblower, like Nelson, was a Royal Navy officer during the Napoleonic Wars, and he became so popular the his creator, C.S. Forester, could not get rid of him, just as L. Frank Baum could not get rid of Dorothy nor Conan Doyle kill off Sherlock Holmes. Forester would eventually write nearly twenty in the series that followed the hero from his days as a green (This is meant quite literally. See below.) midshipman, with feet the size of shovels, to his last posting as an admiral in the West Indies, and in the process, his novels would spawn a little trailing fleet of fictional acolytes: Nicholas Ramage, Richard Bolitho and, of course, Jack Aubrey, the creation of Patrick O'Brian, a writer--like spy novelist John LeCarré--who has, through the force of his prose, leaped the gap between popular fiction and literature.

If Hornblower's leap didn't quite make it, blame his big feet. But that was what immediately lovable about Forester's character: He was imperfect, a little cranky, relentlessly critical of himself, and modern. In the first few pages of the first novel in series, we learn he is disgusted because he, a frigate captain in his thirties, is beginning to develop a pot belly. He is irritable, too, given to shouting "God damn your eyes!" at his coxswains and servants.

Like his real-life inspiration, Lord Nelson, he starts each voyage confined to his cabin, where he is violently and spectacularly seasick. He sits a horse, elbows akimbo, buttocks and saddle at war with each other, with no more grace than Ichabod Crane did. He is trapped in an unhappy marriage with the frumpy Maria. Had they lipstick in Napoleonic Europe, Maria's would have been very red, liberally and inaccurately applied, and since she was constantly weeping at her husband's departures, her mascara would've run like printer's ink.

Fortunately for Hornblower, Forester kills Maria off by the third novel, replacing her with the far more elegant Lady Barbara, sensitive to and soothing of her husband's many moods. She is, I think, a fictional counterpart to the sensitive and soothing Clementine Churchill, who deserved a Victoria Cross for not only putting up with Winston, but for her courageous persistence in loving him. Hornblower's men love him, too--a phenomenon he can't quite understand, which is charming in itself--because he inspires them and he is, in his prickly way, devoted to them, despite their tendency, in battle, to be skewered by splinters or reduced to jelly by enemy cannonballs bouncing their way along the main deck. ("Jelly" is a favorite of Forester's, since it was in such short supply, I suppose, in wartime England)

Not that this moodiness of Hornblower's was ill-earned: As a very young officer, his first prize ship—a "prize" was a captured enemy vessel that meant money for a crew, and Hornblower was given command of this one—was a French coaster hauling a cargo of rice. What Hornblower and his prize crew didn't realize was that the little ship was holed below the waterline. So sea-water rushed into the hold and the rice did the usual thing that rice does when it gets flustered and wet: It expanded, tearing young Hornblower's little command into pieces, the ship's planks exploding like gunshots, before he and his crew had to be rescued.

Hornblower has a history of leaks. In a later novel, *Hornblower and the Atropos,* as a junior post-captain, he's given the honor of commanding Lord Nelson's funeral barge. Balanced on the barge is the massive coffin that contains the tiny admiral and, in mid-Thames, it begins to spring leaks. Hornblower manages to bring the barge safely to its destination, St. Paul's, for Nelson's funeral, but not before suffering what has to be the most epic panic attack in English-language fiction.

Even his fighting ships betray him. His first ship of the line, an early 19th century equivalent to a battleship, *Sutherland,* is Dutch-built and so is shallow-drafted. She's meant to protect a coastline on which Hans Brinker occasionally skates, and so she sails with all the grace of pig iron. The French sink *Sutherland,* good news for Hornblower, but capture him and Mr. William Bush, his stolid and mildly dim First Lieutenant, which is not so good. Hornblower will eventually escape and go on to command, as a commodore, a little fleet of ships in the Baltic, including a bastardization of naval architecture called a bomb-ketch, which is essentially a floating mortar and so graceless as to make *Sutherland* look like a clipper ship.

Forester wrote so many Hornblower novels and wrote them so well that one of my favorites was not a novel and was not written by him at all. A gentleman named C. Northcote Parkinson, thanks to his discovery of the mythical Hornblower Family Papers, wrote a biography, *The Life and Times of Horatio Hornblower,* as if his subject was not mythical at all. It is enchanting.

The best part reveals another facet of Hornblower's character that redeems his crankiness and his seeming ill-luck: He is a man of immense courage, given to incredible moments of premeditated audacity. That daring is complemented by his moral center, part of what makes him so critical of himself, and that's clear from the first moment we meet him, as a midshipman. A little later, as an immensely junior lieutenant, he is assigned to the luckless ship of the line *Renown,* whose captain, Sawyer, is mean-spirited, vengeful, and flagrantly paranoid. He makes Bligh or Queeg look liked Billie Burke's Glenda the Good in 1939's *Wizard of Oz.*

Before Sawyer can foul up a mission against the Spanish by court-martialing his officers on trumped-up charges of mutiny, he mysteriously tumbles down a hatch, fractures his skull, and so command passes to a far more capable man, First Lieutenant Buckland. Buckland will then lead the *Renowns* to a daring victory (the shore party is commanded by Bush) over the perfidious Spanish, who, in Hornblower's world, are just as perfidious as they'd been in 1588, Good Queen Bess's time.

At a much later time, 1970, it is Parkinson, thanks to the Hornblower Papers, who reveals the ultimate and shocking truth. Sawyer was in part right: There *was* a mutiny, but it was, according to C. Northcote Parkinson, a mutiny of one, on the part of the lowly Fifth Lieutenant, Horatio Hornblower. While *Renown's* coterie of officers fretted about what to do about their mad captain— they were seized with paralysis with the enemy virtually within sight—it was Hornblower who shoved Sawyer down the open hatchway. It was, ironically, an action motivated by Hornblower's unfailing devotion to his duty, and it was the mad Captain Sawyer who was preventing *Renown* from doing hers.

Missing Muhammad Ali

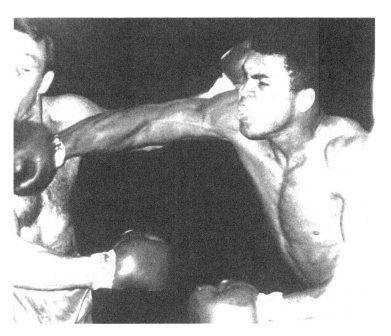

Ali vs. Brian London, August 1966. Action Images.

I used to teach my students how to write an argumentative essay by using the boxer Joe Frazier as an example. Lead with the weakest part of your argument, or even acknowledge the strength of the argument of the other side, I told them, then *counterpunch*: The concluding paragraphs should support your thesis and demonstrate your veracity. Recalling Frazier, of course, immediately makes me think of Muhammad Ali.

Frazier, Ali's nemesis—one in a series-- was what was called a Philadelphia Counterpuncher: He'd take a punch and at his opponent's moment of imbalance, he'd retaliate. He was a savage boxer. Opponents said that Frazier hit so hard that they thought they were going to die. He hit so hard that the disbelief on Ali's face when Frazier knocked him down in their first fight is indelible. Frazier hit him just as hard in the rematch, the "Thrilla in Manila"— he said afterward that he'd landed punches that would've knocked down the wall of a house—but Ali took them, kept talking to him, kept making delicate little circular gestures to Frazier with one glove, goading him to come in closer.

Ali's left jab was his most famous and most electric weapon, but what finally put Frazier away was a staccato series of rights, the last one quick as a cobra strike; it traveled only a little more than eighteen inches and it left Frazier on the canvas in the fetal position. Death would travel more slowly than Ali's right, but the fight was so brutal that, in some ways, this was the night that both men began to die.

* * *

From *The Telegraph* (UK), from an interview with Ali's business manager, Gene Kilroy:

I remember a lady came by our camp in Zaire and said her son was sick.

"Ali said: 'We'll go visit him.' She took us to a leper colony. The staff would put the food down and walk away. Ali was soon lying down with the lepers, hugging them. I took about 10 showers when we got back. Ali just said: 'Don't worry about it, God's looking out for us.'"

* * *

330

At a press conference at the Waldorf-Astoria before leaving for the 1974 Zaire fight against George Foreman, the "Rumble in the Jungle," Ali recited a poem about his training:

I've wrestled with alligators,
I've tussled with a whale.
I done handcuffed lightning
And thrown thunder in jail.
You know I'm bad.
Just last week, I murdered a rock,
Injured a stone, hospitalized a brick.
I'm so mean, I make medicine sick.

* * *

The novelist Norman Mailer, going into the Zaire fight, said that Muhammad Ali was afraid. Foreman had destroyed Frazier, destroyed Ken Norton—two fighters who had beaten Ali--in two bouts that had lasted two rounds each. Mailer implied that the volume of Muhammad's poetry was in direct proportion to the intensity of his fear.

But Ali had watched films of those fights, and when Foreman had knocked those men down, he'd meekly and quickly retired to his corner, breathing heavily. He didn't have the stamina it would take to escape the trap Ali was laying for him in a fight he intended to be a marathon. And so, round after round, Foreman pounded a crumpled Ali, gloves up, forearms locked at the elbows, in merciless showers of blows that would have hospitalized most men. Ali whispered to him, from the ropes, after one particularly jarring punch, "That the best you got, George?"

In the end, Mailer probably was right. Ali, the victor over an opponent he'd exhausted, *was* afraid of George Foreman. That is why he was so remarkable. George Foreman grew to love Muhammad Ali. That is why he is the greatest

* * *

331

My late brother-in-law, Tim O'Hara, took my nephew Ryan, then a little boy, to meet Ali at a Los Angeles-area sports-card show and signing. Ali signed a pair of boxing gloves for them, and took a moment to look at Ryan and remark on something I'm not sure Ryan had ever much liked. "I love your curly hair," The Champ said softly.

* * *

An incident in Famine Ireland is told vividly in Thomas Gallagher's book *Paddy's Lament.* An English clergyman and his companion climbed into their carriage to leave a stricken town. A thirteen-year-old girl, expressionless, her clothing in tatters and so exposing ribs like an accordion's bellows, her clavicle and shoulder joint with their contours visible just below her skin, began to run after the carriage. When the horses picked up speed, so did she. The clergyman, distressed, kept looking out the carriage window. The girl and her long, bony legs were keeping pace with them. She did so for two miles. The clergyman could finally take no more, ordered the driver to stop, and gave the girl money. She took the money, expressionless and silent, and turned her back on them to walk home.

In the film *When We Were Kings,* African children, in the same way, ran after Ali's car. They weren't expressionless. Their faces were radiant with joy. They weren't silent. They sang for Ali when his car stopped for them, a call-and-response song so beautiful that it makes you shiver to hear it. What the clergyman gave the little girl would have kept her alive, but only for a short time. What Ali gave these children would feed them all their lives.

Hal Moore and the Battle of Ia Drang, 1965

Lt. Gen. Hal Moore at West Point, 2010.
Wikimedia Commons courtesy
AHodges7.

I thought it important to place the story of a warrior close to the story of a warrior who was also a conscientious objector. I admire both men.

When I taught U.S. History, we spent a day every year studying the 1965 Battle of Ia Drang. Lt. Gen. Hal Moore has just died, at 95, and he was the commander of the 7th Cavalry troops who fought in that battle, a turning point in the Vietnam War. Moore was, to put it mildly, a "quality human being." His men came close to being overwhelmed by two regiments of North Vietnamese Army regulars. One company was virtually annihilated, like their predecessors, Custer's 7th Cavalry. But Moore and his men--he was, to his boots, both commander and father--- hung on, with Moore calling air and artillery strikes virtually on his own position, and so they defeated superb North Vietnamese troops.

Sadly, we drew the wrong conclusion from that victory. We were assured, I think, that air mobility and firepower would defeat the NVA in a standup fight, which was absolutely right. But the lesson the North Vietnamese learned was to never fight Americans that way again.

To help my students better understand the Vietnam War, we took a second look at our Revolutionary War, which we'd studied at the beginning of the school year. We had the same disadvantages the British did: Long lines of supply, a war that grew increasingly expensive and one that gradually lost the support of politicians and citizens. The Vietnamese understood their country—both its terrain and its people—were fighting for their independence, so they had a clear cause (Ho Chi Minh's Declaration of Independence borrowed heavily from Jefferson), had invaluable foreign support and, after Ia Drang, they turned to hit-and-run tactics. The one time they departed from what they'd learned at Ia Drang came during the Tet Offensive, and that was, for them, a military disaster. If it was a psychological victory for the Vietnamese, which it was, that was out of their hands. That part of Tet—the profound disillusionment of the American people—was a natural consequence of a trail of lies from their own government that went back to Dienbienphu.

The fact remains that Moore and his men were unbelievably brave, and a good part of that bravery came from Moore's steady leadership, positive and encouraging—and clear, because each of his boots understood him and his orders throughout the battle.

One of his men, a British immigrant, Rick Rescorla, would go on, in civilian life, to become a civilian security consultant. After the Lockerbie Pan Am bombing, Rescorla urged his bosses, Morgan Stanley, to move out of the World Trade Center, which he sensed was an inviting terrorist target. Morgan Stanley agreed with him, but their lease ran until 2006.

So Rick Rescorla died in the South Tower on 9/11. His life, and death, marked two low points in American history, two failures in foreign policy that were mitigated, in both Vietnam and in the Twin Towers, by individual heroism and personal sacrifice.

That's Rescorla's photograph on the cover of Joe Galloway's gripping account of the battle, co-written with Moore. The paradox of discovering such admirable people in the midst of such unspeakable violence is something that bewilders me. The book, which makes these men approachable and human, is a vivid account of survival which still seems, so many years later, to be almost superhuman.

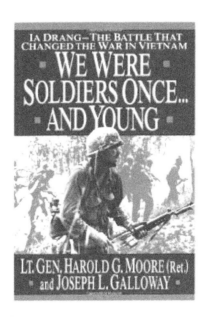

Scrooge and Redemption

Every year, we come back to *A Christmas Carol,* in all its film variations, from Alistair Sim's archetype to the Muppets, and the story seems to mean as much now as it did when it was first published at Christmas in 1843.

Dickens' novella was an instant sensation. It was beautifully timed: The Prince Consort, Albert, was bringing German Christmas traditions to England and transforming it into the holiday, down to gloriously lit Christmas trees, that Americans recognize today. I can still remember the German words to "A Christmas Tree" from Branch Elementary School:

Du grunst nicht nur zur Sommerzeit,
Nein, auch im Winter, wenn es schneit.
O Tannenbaum, O Tannenbaum
Wie treu sind deine Blatter!

And for that I have to thank Albert, doomed to perpetual marblehood by his neurotic widow. But even Victoria read her Dickens. (And her Harriet Beecher Stowe: *Uncle Tom's Cabin* made the Queen weep.)

And the rest of England was moved, as well, by literature, thanks to Dickens. Since his novels were serialized in newspapers, the Queen's subjects were as addicted to them as modern Americans are to *Game of Thrones* or to the next *Star Wars* release.

A Christmas Carol was every bit as much about the nature of evil, especially when it's deliberately chosen, as it was about Christmas. What saved Scrooge from the evil path he'd chosen was the chance at redemption, a theme constant in Dickens' works, from Pip to Sidney Carton.

One way that evil manifested itself in Dickens' England was, surprisingly, in the Industrial Revolution's impact on the environment. Already the white moths that lived had lived for so long on birch trees in the Midlands and in London's suburbs were disappearing because the birch bark was no longer white: It was soot-gray, stained by the smoke from coal-fired factories, even from Bob Cratchit's office stove. The white moths became fodder for hungry birds and, as the devoutly Christian Darwin realized, nature selected the grayish mutations who were less conspicuous.

Other victims were human beings. Child labor, like little Copperfield, Dickens's equivalent in the bootblack factory, was commonplace and so were the debtors' prisons where Dickens' father, thinly disguised as the feckless and delightful Micawber, spent time. Meanwhile, Parliament's Sadler Commission gathered the testimony of children who had watched numbly as their friends' arms were crushed in the maws of power looms and of mothers whose lives were so fragile that they were never quite sure of just how old they were.

`Are there no prisons?' asked Scrooge.

`Plenty of prisons,' said the gentleman, laying down the pen again.

`The Treadmill and the Poor Law are in full vigour, then?' said Scrooge.

`Both very busy, sir.'

`Oh! I was afraid, from what you said at first, that something had occurred to stop them in their useful course,' said Scrooge. `I'm very glad to hear it.'

Prisoners walked the twenty-one wooden steps of the treadmill, which sometimes ground corn, but that purpose was secondary to its real aim, which was to break men—and women-- down. They were forbidden to talk. They rested every 864 steps, except for prisoners who appeared to be lagging. They were taken off the treadmill and flogged.

Child labor would persist in the West well into the twentieth century. Lewis Hine photographed this eleven-year-old mill girl in 1908 North Carolina. Children were prized as bobbin-changers on power looms like this one because they were small and nimble. It was dangerous work. Library of Congress.

Unlike those prisoners, or the poor, Scrooge is uncommonly and inscrutably lucky. (He doesn't much deserve it, does he?) Dickens offers him salvation through a series of haunts. First he is greeted by what he dismisses as an "indigestible bit of beef" that turns out instead to be his former partner, Marley.

"But you were always a good man of business, Jacob,' faltered Scrooge, who now began to apply this to himself.

"Business!' cried the Ghost, wringing its hands again. "Mankind was my business; charity, mercy, forbearance, and benevolence, were, all, my business. The deals of my trade were but a drop of water in the comprehensive ocean of my business!"

Scrooge's onetime boss, Fezziwig, whom he encountered again through the Ghost of Christmas Past, understood this. But it was the business of Victorian capitalists like Jacob Marley to magnify profit at the expense of humanity.

Factory owners were helped in this by an influx of humanity to the cities. They were evicted country folk whose land had been enclosed. Their numbers, ironically, were only increased by a surge in population. That, in turn, was made possible by the increase an increase in food supply, thanks to the progressive farmers--Thomas Hardy's squires, like Mr. Boldwood-- who had done the enclosing. So there was an infinite number of prospective industrial workers and a finite number of industrial jobs. Early in the story, Scrooge suggests a possible solution:

`If they would rather die,' said Scrooge, `they had better do it, and decrease the surplus population.'"

In this passage, Dickens is mocking the economics--then called "the dismal science"--of Thomas Malthus, who argued that while the food supply increased arithmetically, the population increased geometrically, so starvation was a necessary and inevitable corrective. So, argued David Ricardo, Malthus's acolyte, were low wages: Since there were always more workers than there were jobs, wages, obedient to the laws of supply and demand, would always be depressed. It was a law of nature, the capitalist could say, and the capitalist could do nothing—*nothing*-- to violate a law of nature.

The Ghost of Christmas Present introduced Scrooge to reality:

"This boy is Ignorance. This girl is Want. Beware them both, and all of their degree, but most of all beware this boy, for on his brow I see that written which is Doom, unless the writing be erased.

"Have they no refuge or resource?" cried Scrooge. 'Are there no prisons? 'said the Spirit, turning on him for the last time with his own words. 'Are there no workhouses?'"

Scrooge's one positive quality was that he was teachable. In this passage, he's beginning to demonstrate anguish—and even shame. Not all wealthy men are teachable. Some are incapable of shame. But for Scrooge, this painful moment smoothed his path, along with the fearful, silent Ghost of Christmas Future, to redemption.

At Christmas we celebrate the hope that we, like Scrooge, will find redemption. Many of us--perhaps almost all of us?--hunger for a force powerful enough to recognize, understand, and then burn away our shame. Beneath that is our core, the person who is our truest self. In guiding Scrooge to that wonderful moment, waking on Christmas morning, when he finds himself redeemed, Dickens ennobled all of us.

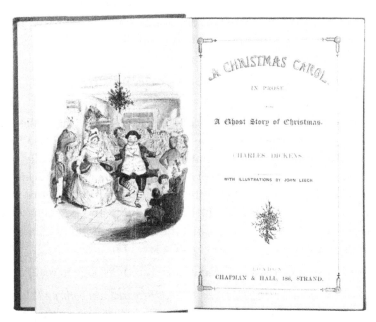

Fezziwig's ball and title page from the original 1843 edition of A Christmas Carol. *Wikimedia Commons.*

Epilogue: November 2013

I've been thinking about the assassination of President Kennedy a lot the past week, since we're marking the event's fiftieth anniversary. He was important to my family, with part of its heritage Irish, and my parents responded, too, to a young man who was the first president from their generation. The remembering, then, has made for me a very emotional, and sometimes tearful, week.

Mrs. Kennedy and the president in Venezuela, 1961. The Kennedy Library.

But I'm an academic, too, and so I know every detail down to the commas of the seamy stuff in Kennedy's life. His father was predatory and amoral: He lobotomized one of his daughters and, when another daughter would have a 16-year-old classmate spend the night, he would lift the covers and climb into bed with her.

His mother was emotionally distant: She used her faith to draw curtains around herself and live in a world lit by stained glass and made safe by priests. She never forgave Kathleen, the incandescent "Kick," because she'd married a Protestant and, when he was killed in combat, she fell in love with another.

Mother and daughter had not reconciled in 1948, when Kick was killed in a plane crash.

Joe, the anointed son, fated to be the first Irish Catholic American President, blew himself up over Suffolk in 1944 during an experimental mission in a radio-controlled bomber packed with explosives. He was trying to steal the glory back from his younger brother, the *PT-109* hero. Joe was an arrogant bully.

I remember the name of the young woman—it was Mary Jo Kopechne–who drowned in Teddy's car.

I know all that. I know how doom stalked this family, and it did so largely because they'd earned it. I know all of that, too. I know that John F. Kennedy was a terribly flawed man. I miss, however, what he *meant* to us.

Kennedy greets Peace Corps volunteers at the White House. National Archives.

Kennedy's short time with us was transformative. One example: Among young people, there was a renaissance of our folk music that coincided with his presidency. It was as if we had rediscovered in music our national identity.

343

It was a heritage that we'd somehow forgotten; it was joyful yet also impatient—patience has never suited Americans—with injustice. Our history, in songs about John Henry's hammer, the Underground Railroad's Drinking Gourd, Dust Bowl Oklahoma or the Shenandoah River, was living again.

It wasn't a coincidence that so many Americans not that much older (and some, like President Carter's mother, much, *much* older) than I was joined the Peace Corps. Other young people were volunteering to register black voters. Three of them, during the Freedom Summer after Kennedy's death, were buried in a shallow grave in an earthen dam in Nashoba County, Mississippi.

In a vivid contrast to such crude brutality, this White House introduced every American then alive to cellist Pablo Casals. While pundits justifiably mocked the President's enthusiasm for James Bond novels, Kennedy's passion for Byron was far more enduring and it was Robert Frost who became the co-star at the Inaugural.

August 1914: Belgian troops, with dogs towing their machine guns, go into action. Imperial War Museums

Had Kennedy not been reading Barbara Tuchman's superb account of the summer Europe collapsed into the First World War—*The Guns of August*—

there is a good chance none of us would be alive today. Kennedy had picked up the book during the autumn of the Cuban Missile Crisis. He quickly understood that the blunders Tuchman so skillfully described represented lessons in leadership that he needed to heed.

We didn't know that, of course, in October 1962. I haven't forgotten how palpable the fear of the time was. My father came home empty-handed from Williams Brothers Market on Grand Avenue—today's Donna's Interiors--because the shelves had been stripped bare by our equally terrified neighbors.

But it also seemed, in Kennedy's time, that most Latin Americans and even larger numbers of Europeans *liked* us. The imperious Charles de Gaulle, the President of France, had a crush on Mrs. Kennedy, who spoke effortless French, as transparent as eighth-grade boy's. Her Spanish was more cautious, but Mexicans erupted in cheers when she spoke to them in their language in June 1962. The President's triumphant visit to what was then still one of the poorest nations in Europe—Ireland—finally secured the bond made by the Irish Brigade, scythed in neat rows in front of the stone wall at Fredericksburg.

Feb. 20, 1962: John Glenn climbs into his space capsule at the start of the mission that would prove so frightening. Courtesy NASA.

345

My job, at age ten, in Kennedy's presidency was more prosaic and didn't involve trips abroad. It was my obligation, I decided, to shuffle out to the living room at 4 a.m. in my pajamas, wrapped in a blanket, no matter how cold the night before had been, every time a Mercury astronaut was to begin his mission. (Half the time the launches were scrubbed and so I would fall asleep in class that day.) When it appeared the heat shield on *Friendship 7* had become dislodged and there was a real chance that John Glenn's re-entry would incinerate him, I prayed and so was deeply touched the reply: Parachutes suddenly appeared on the flickery television screen above the little bell-shaped capsule as it swung gently in its descent to the sea.

The young astronauts symbolized American vitality. The young president had been, for most of his life, a semi-invalid, a resemblance that connects his life to Franklin Roosevelt's. In both men, physical frailty was their greatest gift, because it spared them their assigned destinies as spoiled rich boys who would lead lives of little consequence.

FDR mastered his polio by imprisoning his withered legs in steel braces and building a massive upper body that he learned to throw forward in order to force his legs to follow. On December 8, 1941, the president lurched toward the House lectern to ask for a declaration of war. It was a terrifying moment because his balance was never secure. He refused to fall, and that refusal was a remarkable metaphor for the nation he was leading into the struggle to preserve democracy.

Kennedy fought his illnesses in waves—Addison's' Disease, or the bad back that radiated the kind of pain Inquisitors dream of. An accumulation of infirmities dogged him all his life. He was sometimes so sick that one brother mused that if a mosquito ever bit Jack, the mosquito would die.

Like FDR, Kennedy masked his vulnerability with lies--and with a skillfully managed diet of images that either projected athleticism, in touch football, sailing, golf (sparingly, because he didn't want to Americans to connect him with Ike's golf addiction), or that showcased the beauty of his wife and his children.

His gifts were cerebral rather than physical. Unlike FDR, he possessed a first-rate intellect and with it, a sense of intellectual detachment and the ability to compartmentalize his emotions. The latter would poison his marriage, but, in 1962, it was these traits that saved civilization from nuclear destruction.

346

Many hated Kennedy. Some of that came from the memory of his father's bizarre stint as our ambassador to England, when Joe Sr. had unwisely pronounced England finished and urged détente with Nazi Germany. Some of it came from the family's arrogance, its seeming entitlement, its assumption that they were aristocrats—"lace curtain Irish," to borrow the old pejorative.

But a more visceral and widespread hatred was directed toward Kennedy's Catholicism, the same bigotry, so deeply rooted in the Old Confederacy and the Mountain West, that had poisoned Al Smith's 1928 run for the presidency. That was only a year after jubilant French Catholics had mobbed Lindbergh at Le Bourget to make him one of their own. But this kind of hatred is not only poisonous, it's nearly indestructible. The administration was warned, in fact, in the fall of 1963 that Dallas harbored cells of intense hatred for Kennedy.

Kennedy in Fort Worth on the morning of November 22, 1963. His emotional impact is reflected in the faces of the crowd. National Archives.

But what happened in November 22 Dallas was even more shocking because of the good will that had greeted the president. The film images,

347

assembled by *National* Geographic producers and televised last week, were revelatory. You could sense the energy the president was absorbing from the Texans who came out in such numbers to cheer for him. I had never realized how enthusiastic those crowds were. There was a warmth and a kind of celebratory communion in them that stunned the apprehensive Kennedy advance people and his Secret Service detail.

The last words he heard came when Gov. Connally's wife, Nellie, beaming and proud, turned to him in the limousine and said, "You can't say that Dallas doesn't love you, Mr. President."

"No, you certainly can't," he replied. Those were the last words he spoke.

The Connallys and the Kennedys in the Dallas motorcade. Courtesy Victor Hugo King.

Friday had begun with rain in Fort Worth. By the time Air Force One touched down at Love Field in Dallas, it was Kennedy Weather, bright, crisp, autumnal sunshine. The beauty of the day was quickly obscured by blurred images, snatches of rumor, the eloquent televised pause of newscaster Walter Cronkite in a moment of grief not even he could master. It seems, sometimes, like Dallas was the last bright day we have ever had, and our time and our nation have ever since been stalked by shadows.

I don't remember shadows like those before Dallas, but I was very young. What I'm beginning to believe now is that most important and salient point of November 22, 1963, wasn't that we loved the Kennedys, though, in my house, we truly did.

What was far more important was that we loved being Americans, and it was that self-regard and self-confidence that seemed to die, too, with such explosive violence in Dealey Plaza.

Children greet an American transport plane as it prepares to land during the Berlin Airlift. U.S. Air Force.

What we lost in Dallas wasn't the kind of jingoism that comes so easily to some 21st Century politicians; it wasn't arrogance. It was our faith in ourselves—the faith that Lincoln had articulated so well with his "few brief remarks" at Gettysburg, almost exactly 100 years before Kennedy's death. We may have lost it, but that doesn't mean it's gone completely. It's ironic, but I've seen flickers of that faith most often in my travels abroad with Arroyo Grande High School students.

I will never forget the sunburst over Derrynane Bay during our stop for lunch on the Ring of Kerry. In the little restaurant was a little sign, carefully lettered, that read "Happy Fourth of July to our American friends."

We were visiting Reims Cathedral when a Frenchwoman insisted on giving us a personal tour precisely *because* we were Americans, and it was American money, from the Rockefeller Foundation, that was painstakingly restoring shell damage to the Cathedral from 1916.

GIs chat with a little Dorset girl, nicknamed "Freckles," who would become one of their most loyal friends during their time in 1944 England. Imperial War Museums.

Once a Bavarian woman approached Mr. Kamin, our German teacher, and his students near Munich and thanked him and them for the kindness World War II GI's had shown her when she was a little girl. There were tears in her eyes. Of course, many of the young Americans she remembered with such emotion had died before Mr. Kamin's students were born.

Young Americans, including young men like those soldiers, may be the best evidence we have of the faith we've had in ourselves—the faith that we will ultimately do the right thing. In my experience, there are few images more evocative of this than visits to places like the American cemeteries in the Ardennes, at Colleville-sur-Mer above Omaha Beach and in the Punch Bowl on Oahu. Those visits never made me want to wave flags or blow trumpets.

I always think instead of men who were once wavering toddlers, who took their first steps to a little smattering of applause from their parents. They waited expectantly and sleeplessly on Christmas Eves stalked by the Great Depression. When they did sleep, it would be with a dog close by. I think of boys whose hands shook when they tried to pin the corsage on the dress of their prom date. And then they aren't boys anymore: They're young men fresh out of Basic whose last moments in America, maybe a few free moments in San Diego or Philadelphia, were marked by ribald laughter and 3.2 beer or poker, by any distraction that would somehow increase the distance between themselves and the troopships waiting to take them into the crucible.

So I never think of patriotism at places like Colleville-sur-Mer. I think of baby shoes and I think of mothers.

Or I think of somehow pulling off a preposterous temporal fraud.

Somehow I would get a chance to teach the boys I know only from their tombstones the history of their country. Perhaps I could help them to understand what they would never have the time to understand: In their lives, no matter how short, there was a light so powerful that it would destroy the greatest darkness the world had ever known.

The young men I would like to teach have been dead a long, long time, and so has the president who emerged from their generation. But I am so grateful that I am old enough to have recognized their light—*our* light—last week. I was watching the news and saw an aircraft carrier group and a Navy hospital ship headed at flank speed for the Philippines, devastated by a massive typhoon.

John F. Kennedy understood that the most fundamental American value is generosity, and so the ships in that television image reminded me of the president whose life so influenced my own. It reminded me that I live in a country I love so much that my love is greatest in the anger I feel when it is clearly in the wrong, warmest when my fingers touch cold marble in Normandy, brightest in the flame that marks the grave where my childhood, too, is buried.

Kennedy's grave, Arlington. Tim Evanson photo.

About the Author

Jim Gregory was raised in the Upper Arroyo Grande Valley, where his education began in the two-room Branch School. He graduated from the University of Missouri and earned his teaching credential at Cal Poly.

He taught history, literature and the social sciences for thirty years at Mission Prep in San Luis Obispo and at his alma mater, Arroyo Grande High School. He was named the Lucia Mar Teacher of the Year in 2010.

Since retiring in 2015, he's written four books intended to link local history with events in American history: *World War II Arroyo Grande*, *Patriot Graves: Discovering a California Town's Civil War Heritage; San Luis Obispo County Outlaws: Desperados, Vigilantes and Bootleggers* and *Central Coast Aviators in World War II*. Both *Patriot Graves* and *Outlaws* have won national recognition, with the latter winning first place in Western history in the 2017 National Indie Excellence Awards, a competition for independent and small-press publishers.

Gregory lives in Arroyo Grande with his wife, Elizabeth, a teacher at St. Joseph High School, his sons John and Thomas, two Irish setters and one Basset hound.

Made in the USA
Monee, IL
14 January 2022

88980803R00215